AN OUTBACK LIFE

AN
OUTBACK
Mary Groves # LIFE

ARENA
ALLEN&UNWIN

WARNING
Please be aware that this book contains names and images of
Aboriginal people who may now be deceased.

First published in 2011

Arena Books, an imprint of
Allen & Unwin
Sydney, Melbourne, Auckland, London

83 Alexander Street
Crows Nest NSW 2065
Australia
Phone: (61 2) 8425 0100
Fax: (61 2) 9906 2218
Email: info@allenandunwin.com
Web: www.allenandunwin.com

Cataloguing-in-Publication details are available
from the National Library of Australia
www.trove.nla.gov.au

ISBN 978 1 74237 705 6

Set in 12.5/16 pt Sabon by Midland Typesetters, Australia
Printed and bound in China by Hang Tai Printing Company Limited

20 19 18 17 16 15 14 13 12 11

Dedication

This book is dedicated to the memory of my amazing mother, Eileen Mary Elkins (nee Breen), who had faith in me completing this task; and to the support and endurance of my wonderful family who made this story possible. Thank you also to my sister Kate for her encouragement, and my cousins Ellen, Marian and Doreen who shone the light when I lost my way.

Contents

Author's note

I have not used real names in these stories and the terminology I use is that of the 1960s and 1970s. I apologise for any remarks that may seem sexist or racist; they are not intended to be derogatory, but were the terms used by black and white people in the Territory in my time there. I have also endeavoured not to expose any Aboriginal tribal secrets to which I have been privy.

Distances and directions and the monetary system have changed over the years since the introduction of the metric system, but I have kept these as close as possible to their periods.

Introduction

Foreboding overwhelmed me as the Cessna 310 continued to circle us again and again. What on earth was going on? Then a loud explosion shook the homestead. A rush of icy adrenaline coursed through my veins and I froze for a moment before dropping the phone and rushing through the back door into the garden to investigate.

My Aboriginal house girl Katie, clutching my baby, ran under the palms across the yard towards me, wide-eyed with panic.

'That plane, missus, him been pinish up longa dam!'

I will never forget those words. 'That plane's finished up in the dam!'

Cold with shock, I looked towards the dam, only 300 metres from the back of the homestead. I could see billows of black smoke. I had no idea what to do next, but I started to run.

Thirteen was a number that haunted our family and it was happening again on 13 March 1975, in the middle of the monsoon season, almost three months after the notorious Cyclone Tracy had devastated Darwin, some 260 kilometres by air to the north of us.

My husband Joe and I were managing Fitzroy, a cattle station west of Katherine in the Northern Territory. The property was 1001 square miles and consisted of rugged red escarpments and valleys of grazing areas that ran to the mighty but hostile Victoria River.

A group of agronomists and wealthy Americans, senior officials representing the Rockefellers' Standard Oil Company, had arrived to do feasibility studies. They were looking at the prospect of growing sugar cane on Fitzroy, and in fact in the whole Angalarri basin that ran through to Kununurra in Western Australia. This cane would be used for sugar, ethanol and a new concept in hardwood building material. They were planning to utilise the water from the massive Ord River scheme at Kununurra. This ground-breaking venture would open up a whole new and exciting facet in the stagnant Territory economy.

Alan Chase, an ambitious American entrepreneur and part owner of Fitzroy Station, was behind the project. Alan had also been instrumental in attempts to grow rice in the Humpty Doo area in the Top End in the 1950s. The attempts had failed because of wild-geese invasions, but he nevertheless remained determined to break the age-old curse on Territory enterprise. I had received an excited call from him in America saying, 'Mary, make that place look like a million dollars, I've got some big investors coming to visit.'

How I was supposed to prepare for important visitors on our limited budget I had no idea, but I set about scrubbing, painting and rearranging bedrooms, finishing on the morning of their expected arrival by covering the bathroom walls with a bamboo print contact paper in an attempt to camouflage the gaping cracks in the fibro walls.

The group landed on the muddy airstrip just in time for lunch, and our quiet off-season operation immediately went into overdrive with introductions, suitcases, cool drinks, endless telephone calls, lunch, sightseeing and afternoon tea (or 'smoko', as we called it). Eventually the congestion eased with several visitors departing that afternoon, leaving four fellows to work on the station with us for ten days.

Many times in the past, we had dragged our beds out onto the front lawn when the heat in the house made sleeping impossible. I worried about the visitors bunking together in the only two rooms available in the hot fibro homestead.

'Do you think you'll handle the heat okay?' I asked as I showed them to their accommodation.

'Sure, we've been in hotter places than this,' they assured me.

They were a great bunch of blokes: Dick was young, blond and good-looking in his early thirties, and Ralph and Glen were both comfortable, well-travelled middle-aged men. And then there was Walter. At thirty-eight, he was a confident, tall, dark-haired, handsome man with a high intelligent forehead, and I was immediately attracted to the twinkle in his eyes. When we first met he had grasped my hand firmly for that extra second, and it was obvious that the attraction was mutual.

'Pleased to meet you, Mary,' he'd said, 'but what's a good-looking girl like you doing hidden away in a place like this?'

Hmmm. I reckon that unfamiliar compliment and the little bottle of Wicked Wahine perfume that he had brought me from Hawaii won my heart immediately. I figured then that a little harmless flirtation never hurt anyone – not anyone with brains, anyway. As always, my typically Australian, ruggedly handsome husband made it glaringly obvious that he was the boss rooster in our hen house, but still I hoped that Walter's gift-giving would set a good example.

I saw very little of Joe as the days flew by, catching up only at mealtimes and to sleep. These were exciting times and he was enjoying the new challenges. There were sugar cane tests planted in the backyard, and maps lay everywhere supporting the endless in-depth discussions and phone calls. The Yanks had all fitted in comfortably with the pace of station life and were more seasoned than we had imagined. They not only managed to sleep in the heat but they lined up for the shower like everyone else. They too were soon hanging out for the daily bread bake, seduced by the aromas from my busy kitchen. Like everyone else, they relished the mounds of home-baked cakes and desserts, the limited fresh vegetables, and the endless meals of beef, cooked in every way imaginable to avoid monotony. They also welcomed the occasional silver barramundi or black bream that some lucky fisherman was usually able to snare.

All too soon the group was preparing for their departure back to America.

On the evening of 10 March we threw an impromptu going-away party. The children – Paula, eleven, Joey, eight and Stephen, six – had designed a little concert as a present for their new American friends, at which they sang and recited their classic Aussie poetry. Although Mary-Lyn was only a toddler, she was still a very cute part of the chorus.

That evening during dinner, the children tried valiantly to teach Walter the famous Banjo Paterson poem, *The Man from Ironbark*, but although he found the poem intriguing, he also found its colloquialisms almost impossible to grasp. When the kids were finally in bed, Dick, the younger American, pulled out his guitar and, with a few too many rums as accompaniment, we all sang and caroused until the wee hours.

After an early breakfast, while Walter prepared to leave with his decidedly hung-over team, he had us all in hysterics with his recital of *The Man from Ironbark*. He was determined to get it right, but we rolled about laughing as he tried to replicate an Aussie rendition in his broad American accent.

Joe left with Glen and Ralph in our flash Ford Fastback to do some reconnaissance on the neighbouring stations for a couple of days, while Dick and Walter hired another plane to fly to Kununurra for further negotiations. Being the wet season, the staff were on leave, so I was left with the children and the Aborigines, and, apart from some particularly heavy rainfall, life on the station quietened down and soon returned to normal.

On the thirteenth, I woke feeling lethargic and with a constant pain in my kidney area. It persisted all morning, so just after lunch on that hot, sleepy afternoon I decided to grab a nap. The chores were done and I took a peek to check that the children were still playing outside under the ever-watchful eye of my trusted help, Katie. The kids always found some way to occupy themselves, normally playing under the fruit trees with their toy Matchbox earthmoving equipment. They would build miniature roads and bridges in the red dust or the mud around the roots of the lemon trees, or they would play with the green frogs, lizards or the baby crocodiles they sometimes kept in the huge, empty water tank that was sunk into the ground just out the back. Mary-Lyn was playing happily with Katie on the lawn, so I retired to my bedroom.

I had no sooner settled when I heard the unexpected drone of a small plane approaching. I assumed that it was the Salvation Army's flying padre, who was famous for turning up unannounced, but just that morning I had laid out two big white crosses as 'closure' signs on the airstrip because it was too wet and boggy to use, so I assumed he would not attempt to land.

'Go away,' I growled. My head was throbbing, I had a temperature and I certainly wasn't in the mood for visitors. But I listened, concerned, as the plane began to circle unusually low over the homestead.

As the airstrip was a couple of kilometres away, it was customary to circle once or twice to signal an impending landing and a required pick-up, but this plane kept circling.

I stayed inside, fearing that if I signalled back that the pilot would attempt a landing that could end in disaster. I now knew, by the size of the plane, that it was not the flying padre. The plane continued to circle too low, flying alarmingly close to the homestead. I was becoming increasingly worried now.

Then the phone rang.

'Struth, give us a break,' I grumbled, running up the passage to the office to answer the call.

The radiotelephone system operated with heavy wire stretched between two huge aerials for reception. They stood outside, towering above the sprawling homestead. To book your calls you could sit for hours with your finger ready to push a red lit button, trying to beat your neighbour to it when the line became available. It was almost as difficult to receive calls, but we had all learned to master the technique to some degree out of sheer desperation.

The young agronomist who had played the guitar at our party was on the phone.

'Hi, Mary, it's Dick,' he said, sounding slightly frustrated. 'I'm ringing from Katherine. I just wanted to let you know that some of the group are flying over from Kununurra to Fitzroy today. I've been trying to get through to you for hours but this darn phone service is atrocious.'

Now at least I had a rough idea of who was on the plane that was acting so erratically. My stomach churned with fear as I prayed that Joe was not on board.

As the plane approached again the roar of the engines was deafening. Above the din I yelled, 'Okay, Dick, thanks for letting me know.'

No sooner had I spoken when . . . BANG! The handpiece slipped from my fingers and I ran outside to investigate. There I intercepted Katie. 'Katie,' I yelled, 'you gotta find all them kids belonga me and keep him all safe now. You hear?' Then I ran barefoot over the rough ground towards the smoke. I would have to do whatever it took to help the plane's occupants – and as there were no blokes around, I would have to do it alone.

'Oh God,' I prayed, 'please don't let Joe be on that plane.'

I was alarmed to pass my eight-year-old son Joey bolting back from the crash site. Dressed only in his little red shorts, his face was white with fear as he ran through the rough undergrowth back to the homestead and away from whatever horror he had just seen. With neither of us stopping, I yelled over my shoulder, 'Keep going to Katie, Joey, and don't move from the homestead.'

I arrived at the dam in minutes to a sight that was absolutely terrifying and beyond my comprehension. In the middle of this small waterhole sat the twin-engine aeroplane, fully ablaze.

Scrambling across the hardened mud, I waded into the water, desperately trying to find a path through the burning fuel to the plane, but it was soon painfully obvious that I could do nothing.

I searched for a sign of life from the plane. I yelled for someone to answer me. There was nothing. I yelled for God to help me and to help them, but there was no reply. The plane continued to burn fiercely while the registration UHSDE on its tail stood untouched, like a gravestone in the muddy, chest-deep water. Nothing but the roaring flames moved, and the only sound was the whooshing of the inferno. It was an eerie sensation to listen so hard for a voice, a cry, a scream, but hearing only the flames and the silence.

As the flames gradually died down, the silence became deafening. I still had no idea who was trapped in this fireball, or how many, or if my husband was on board.

After what seemed an eternity, I turned my back on the smouldering wreckage and walked slowly back to the homestead with only the sloshing of my wet, muddy jeans and the thud of the homestead's diesel generator breaking the quiet of the bush.

Katie had the children gathered in the office when I returned. It was obvious that they were trying to comprehend what had just dropped out of the blue and turned our ordinary day upside down. I had no time to explain; I had to find their father.

I picked up the phone to try to track Joe's whereabouts through the Timber Creek police station, but the line seemed dead. I went outside and was dismayed to find that the telephone aerials were draped across the front yard. On further inspection, it was obvious that the plane had flown into the aerial tower. It had brought down the lines, cutting them and leaving us with little chance of outside contact. The explosion I had heard earlier was the plane's propellers flinging deadly shrapnel through the roof. It had sprayed across the side of the homestead that faced where the steel aerial now stood, pathetically bent and twisted.

The lights on the telephone handpiece were still working, so I prayed that our reception and transmission were not totally ruined. Anxiously, I sat with my finger on the button, waiting, hoping, that someone elsewhere ran out of conversation and would let me on the line. I waited for half an hour but my attempts were fruitless.

'Paula, do you think you can sit here and do this while I look for your dad?' I asked finally. 'You have to be really quick. When the red light goes out, push this button. Just ask to be put through to the Timber Creek police station urgently, that it is a matter of life and death, and don't take any nonsense from them. You will have to be tough, love,' I said, and kissed her on the forehead.

I turned to Katie. 'Katie, you stay here now and look after Paula till I get back. You savvy?'

'Yes, missus,' she replied.

The two boys were subdued as I loaded them and Mary-Lyn into the only vehicle on the station, the D6000 cattle truck, and then, praying that it had enough fuel, I went looking for help.

The red truck pounded along the deserted road towards Timber Creek. Nothing made sense. 'Why the crazy flying?' I wondered. And the words that kept going through my head were, 'Stupid bastards! Those stupid bastards!'

After about half an hour of hectic driving, I met Joe returning home from a neighbouring property with Glen and Ralph. I wanted to cry with relief, but I couldn't. Pulling to a halt in the middle of the Victoria Highway, I jumped out of the truck and realised I was still muddy and barefoot. As they walked towards me, smiling, all I could say in response to their surprised queries was: 'Those stupid bastards! Those stupid bastards! They are all dead in the dam.'

'What's wrong, hon?' Joe asked. 'What are you talking about?'

Their faces paled when they realised what I was telling them.

Joe immediately sent the two Americans back to Timber Creek in our car to alert Constable Terry Milleara, the area's police officer, and with Joe now driving the truck, I clasped the children to me as we returned to the station in silence. It felt surreal. Joe didn't talk and I couldn't cry. There didn't seem to be much point.

By the grace of God, little Paula had found a weak telephone signal and had finally managed to contact Terry, almost half an hour after we had left, so he was soon on his way. Eventually, later that afternoon, I was able to contact the telephone exchange supervisor in Katherine, and soon we were receiving priority on the badly damaged service. I kept busy making phone calls in the office until sunset. By then, I had ensured that the remaining Americans had been connected to their loved ones, trying to soften the blow, before the news broke back in the States of the fate of these high-ranking executives.

As darkness fell, I was still at my post, unaware that I was in shock. Then Ralph, the older American, came into the office and put a gentle hand on my shoulder. 'Hey, Mary, it's time you knocked off, girl,' he said sadly. 'You've done all you can do. Here, get this into you.'

I was not a drinker, but I downed that Scotch straight and went into meltdown. I sat at the desk and, with Ralph's support, my tears finally flowed. I cried particularly for our new friend Walter, who, I now knew, was among the five charred bodies still smouldering in the dam.

Nothing could be done to retrieve the bodies until the wreckage and the water cooled down, so the charred remains sat in the dam all night in a light, drizzling rain. As Joe slept that evening, I lay awake beside him for hours, swamped in sadness, reliving the day's horrible events.

The sun rose next morning to a beautiful day that seemed oblivious to the remains that still sat in the wreckage. The staff kept the crows away from them with rifle shots until the forensic pathologist arrived at about 11 a.m. It seemed like an eternity, but finally the remains were retrieved, put into body bags and sent off to Katherine. All we had left to remind us of Walter was a pair of his shoes that he had left at the homestead. They stood hauntingly empty now, and they seemed so symbolic that I eventually sent them home to his family in America.

Joe took the other three Americans back to the cyclone-twisted city of Darwin for a few days' rest prior to their return to the States. I stayed at the station with the children to oversee the comings and goings of the aviation invest-igators and the pumping out of the dam to enable them to collect the wreckage and any evidence that may have become hidden in the mud.

This awkward investigation lasted for days while the aviation officials came, stayed and went. Then, finally, apart from the inquest, it was all over.

As time went by, we heard nothing from the station owners regarding the disaster; we were obviously the least of their problems. Nor did we hear anything more about the sugar cane scheme. It all soon petered out, and life on Fitzroy once again returned to normal, except that the dam contin-ued to haunt me.

Early one afternoon, after everything had settled, I sat on the lawn watching little Mary-Lyn play and pon-dered the enormity of it all. Katie plopped herself down cross-legged beside me and, with a big happy grin, said, '*Kudjiri*, might be time we go longa river and catch him big barramundi, ay?'

Katie called me *kudjiri* (boss missus) only when she wanted to make me feel good and, as fishing was her solution to most problems, I gladly accepted.

It was a memorably beautiful, lazy afternoon as we walked to our special spot on the big river. It was flowing fast and brown after the recent rains but we headed for the quieter inlets. Everything seemed awash with blue, green and deep golden shadows as we settled along the bank and began to unroll and bait our hand lines.

Katie and I had never discussed the crash. There didn't seem much point dwelling on it, and death was a leery subject for Aborigines to talk about. Each new day in the bush brought its own set of survival circumstances and we had learned to just keep on keeping on. So, as we sat waiting for the fish to strike, we discussed the world in general.

'Missus, this bush country here, him belonga me fella. What that country like belonga you fella when you been piccaninny?'

This unexpected question caught me unawares. How could I begin to explain the differences between my very 'proper' childhood in Victoria and her wild bush country existence? As I grappled for the words to best describe to Katie those distant Melbourne days, I began to realise how much I had forgotten, how much of my past and of me I had simply turned my back on and how much I had really changed.

Our life stories could not be more different, but here we both sat at the water's edge, similar only in gender but intrinsically connected by time and place on this wild river in Australia's isolated Top End.

The three older kids were fishing further upstream and, nearby, little Mary-Lyn squealed with delight as she sat and fiddled in the jar with the brown grasshoppers that we had caught for bait.

And so, while the fish were biting over the following weeks, we dodged the storms and managed to go each afternoon to that same spot where, with Katie's gentle prompting, the story contained in this book began to unfold.

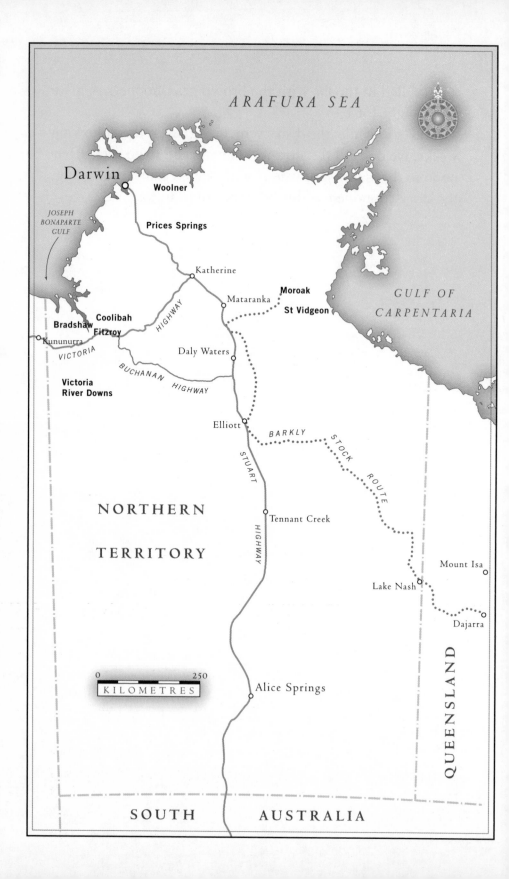

ARAFURA SEA

Darwin
Woolner

JOSEPH
BONAPARTE
GULF

Prices Springs

GULF OF
CARPENTARIA

Katherine

Mataranka

Moroak
St Vidgeon

Coolibah
Bradshaw Fitzroy
Kununurra

VICTORIA

Daly Waters

HIGHWAY

BUCHANAN HIGHWAY

Victoria
River Downs

Elliott

BARKLY

STOCK

ROUTE

STUART

NORTHERN

TERRITORY

HIGHWAY

Tennant Creek

Mount Isa

Lake Nash

Dajarra

0   250

KILOMETRES

Alice Springs

QUEENSLAND

SOUTH   AUSTRALIA

1

Melbourne memories

As a child in Melbourne, with its cold winters and unpredictable summers, I had read many romantic stories of Queensland and dreamed of marrying a Queensland station owner. I dreamed of a homestead on a hillside beside a river that ran to the sea – a hillside from which I could see forever. Little did I realise at the time just how prophetic my dreams were.

My father, who had spent many years in the army, was a strict disciplinarian, and he ran our large family according to military and religious principles. My mother was beset by constant struggles, including chronic asthma and twelve pregnancies. Yet without the perseverance of this courageous woman, I would never have experienced this wonderful outback life. It was my mother who made the astounding decision, at the age of forty-five, to uproot most of our family from Melbourne and move to the isolation of Australia's Top End.

This was an era when women would not dream of going out without hat and stockings. When well-dressed commuters travelled from the suburbs on the green and yellow trams that screeched to a halt outside our little white weatherboard home at the army barracks on Sturt Street in South Melbourne. On their route, they'd pass the many factories, Wirth's Circus and the Trocadero Dance Palais, then cross the Princes Bridge over the Yarra River to Flinders Street station, and on through that bustling grey and green city.

As I remember Melbourne, a lifetime away now, I recall the poppy garden. The garden was my mother's pride and, in the heart of that grey concrete jungle, it was truly a joy to behold.

When the spring sun shone warmly on our paved backyard, the garden would come to life with the humming of bees, harmonising with a background of rowdy whistling canaries, whose breeding cages hung on walls in every possible position. I loved nothing better than to see the scraggy, baby heads emerge from the nests, but on this day the poppies were far too alluring. Knowing Mum's garden was taboo, I played around its rocky edges with the monkey-faced pansies, making the snapdragons roar, until, finally overcome by the euphoria of spring, I lay on my back on the cool pavement. A beautiful yellow butterfly gently landed on my knee and I counted the dragonflies that flitted to and fro. Mostly, I was entranced by a poppy that leaned lazily above me on its hairy green stem, its vivid apricot petals contrasting against the deep blue sky. 'How far does that sky go?' I wondered.

Born in 1944, as the Second World War neared its end, I came fifth in this middle-class Catholic family of seven boys and four girls. Apparently I was Mum's only difficult delivery: I had to be pulled with forceps, kicking and screaming, but this early display of dogged tenacity would prove to be a valuable commodity in the years ahead.

I was four when we moved to the army barracks on the corner of Sturt and Miles streets, across the road from the military repatriation centre where injured soldiers would go to have their limbs replaced. Surrounded by factories, this area was a beehive of activity throughout the day, but deserted and lonely after knock-off time.

One evening when I was about ten, my parents decided to go to the movies, leaving the six younger children in the care of my two older teenage brothers, Terry and Jimmy. It was before the advent of television, so comic books were distributed among us for entertainment. Dire consequences were threatened for bad behaviour, but, as the evening rolled on, it developed into the usual free-for-all between the two babysitters. As the four youngest slept, the radio blared in the background while the boys wrestled like bull terriers on the floor. Barbara, two years older than me, toyed with her long blonde plaits as she sat sucking her thumb, her nose stuck in a comic book, while the boys thumped against the underside of the large dinner table with enough force to make the sauce bottle roll onto the floor. I decided that this would be a great time to slip out unnoticed to try out my dad's big black pushbike.

I was fascinated by my father's bike. I would polish its silver headlight and trimmings, studying the dynamo minutely. Quite often I had clambered aboard the bike as it leaned against the weatherboards and mused at how one leg or the other was always too short to reach both pedals at once. Now, finally, the opportunity was here for a test run.

A cool grey dusk was settling as I anxiously peeped out along Miles Street. There was not a soul to be seen, so, hoping not to attract my brothers' attention, I quietly slid open the big garage roller-door.

The door squeaked loudly as I gently slid it closed again, and then I was free! Awkwardly, I lumbered the bike against the fence to mount up. I found that if I was careful and rolled from side to side, I could pedal quite easily. Totally engrossed in what I was doing, I clumsily made it to the end of Miles Street with the wind of exhilaration in my hair, but on turning the corner at the army stables, along where Kings Way now runs, my elation evaporated. I heard a male voice behind me and visions of my father's angry face flashed through my head. I froze, thinking that I had been sprung, and stopped immediately, precariously balancing the big bike as it threatened to crash onto the road. Glancing over my shoulder, I was horrified to see a total stranger standing in the twilight, a big man in a dark, flapping overcoat!

He moved slowly towards me, mumbling a request for strange street directions, and as he continued his sly approach he asked, 'Where do you live, little girl?'

My fear went into overdrive. Somehow scrambling aboard the bike, I fled. At the next corner, I turned the front wheel so hard that it ran completely right-angled to the back one, but I managed to balance, then pumped the pedals furiously to the next corner, where my friend Billy's family lived at the opposite end of the army barracks to us. These were our closest neighbours.

As I neared this corner I felt safer because a tram was slowing to a stop outside their door. But to my alarm, it stopped for a minute and then, ghostlike, it quietly lurched off and was gone.

Still the footsteps pounded the pavement behind me. My heart sank when I saw there were no lights on in Billy's home. Without stopping, I pedalled on down Sturt Street. In my innocence, I had no idea what might happen if I was caught, but I knew I didn't want to find out.

I swung back into Miles Street and, coasting down the length of the fence, I crashed to a halt. With strength born of fear, I rolled the garage door open just far enough to drag Dad's precious bike inside. Rolling it shut again, I slipped the lock and sat frozen with terror in the half-light as stealthy footsteps padded by, coins jingling in my pursuer's pockets as he ran.

As the shock subsided I regained my breath and ran to the safety of the house.

'Terry! Jimmy! Please lock up the house,' I begged. 'A bad man was chasing me.'

But they completely ignored me, and Barbara wasn't interested, so I figured that it was safer not to mention it again. I was fully aware of Dad's big leather strap and the punishment I would be dealt for my escapade. So the incident was filed away in the annals of time and nothing was mentioned about it to my parents for almost forty years.

Looking back, I realise that I always had a rebellious streak. One Saturday afternoon, my mother realised that I had not been to my weekly confession. This was the family ritual, so, at seven years of age, I was sent scurrying to the church to confess my sins.

Usually, we children were not permitted outside the front gate alone, so to go all the way to the church on my own was an amazing assignment. As I made my way through the now-quiet factory area, I considered my quandary: I didn't have a sin to confess – what was I to do?

As the afternoon began to fade, I peered from behind a large elm at the old grey chapel with its austere facade. It seemed completely deserted. My heart pounded with nervous excitement as I plucked up the courage to dart across the street. I entered the sombre building and crossed myself with holy water at the door.

The late afternoon sun illuminated the stained-glass windows, throwing soft shadows onto the empty rows of polished wooden pews that filled the church. A candle flickered upon the white-clad altar, where vases of white, orange-tongued lilies stood to attention. The faint aroma of incense and wax lingered in the air as I proceeded to the confessional box that stood off to the left. As the door squeaked closed behind me, I kneeled in the shadowy silence of the timber cubicle, frantically trying to remember some sin from the past week.

'Oh, well,' I thought, 'I'll just have to make something up.'

A quiet voice came from behind the darkened screen, asking, 'Have you come to confess your sins, my child?'

I recited in my best grown-up voice, 'Bless me, Father, for I have sinned.'

'What are your sins, my child?' was the screen's reply.

Searching for something I considered sinful, my cheeks flushed when I realised I was about to lie to a priest. Would I burn in hell?

'I looked at myself in the mirror with no clothes on, Father, and these are my sins,' I blurted.

There was stony silence from behind the screen. When the voice spoke at last, it was to deliver what I considered the extreme penance of ten Hail Marys, double what I had expected. Mortified at having picked such an apparently wicked sin, I left the box and genuflected to the altar, made the sign of the cross, and kneeled in a pew to commence my penance.

But if God had made me with no clothes on, how could it be so bad to look at myself that way? Indignantly, after saying five of the ten prayers for the lie that I had told, I refused to continue. That was probably the day I began to think for myself, having obviously reached the age of reason. It was a turning point in my life. Almost of its own accord, this innocent rebellion would blossom over the years into a barrage of questions about religion and philosophy. I didn't know it then, but, boy, did I get some interesting answers along the way!

I stood on the steps of the church in the dusk, pulled my purple angora jacket tightly around me, and excitedly commenced the long journey back home. Along the deserted streets I ran, through the playground at Park Street and on past the stony-faced factories in the sprinkling rain, dodging around the old lady who wandered the streets with a bucket to pick up manure from the cart horses for her garden. I ran all the way to the safety of the six-foot green gate of my home, arriving just as an empty tram rattled by on its way to the city.

It was almost dark when the gate clanged shut behind me. It was now quite cold and a light drizzle continued to fall. Home, with its dinner smells and familiar voices, never felt cosier.

That simple weatherboard house always felt cosy. I loved the way the sun streamed through the windows on a summer's day and the way Mum's knees looked when she kneeled with her dress rolled up to scrub the wooden floorboards almost daily. Eileen, my mother, was a beautiful woman of Irish and English heritage, whose vivid blue eyes contrasted strikingly with her thick, almost black, shoulder-length hair.

Life was simpler then. Sunday was a day of rest, devoted to church and family. No shops! It was fun to go driving to the beach or to the Botanical Gardens, rolling down the green lawns or searching for the blue wrens that hid in the hydrangeas. This was before the invention of indicator lights and Dad would make his hand signals from the car when turning or stopping. When he broke his right arm, Mum would reach over and signal for him. On colder evenings we would arrive home after our day out to have a dinner of lunch leftovers. Then, with the radio playing, we would congregate around a roaring wood fire. I often watched the day's adventures fly up the chimney in the flames through tired eyes as I drifted off to sleep.

New babies, one after another, became a normal event at our house and the baby bottles and flannelette nappies always held a strange appeal, unlike my father's constant ranting and raving throughout the ensuing turmoil. This was something we took for granted; it was just the way things were.

Dad's rank in the army was warrant officer class one. Standing six feet four, he cut an imposing figure in the military parades in his uniform, and with his black moustache I thought him very handsome.

As I got older, I was often kept home during my mother's confinements as cook, nurse and laundry maid, to launder the mounds of military uniforms that Dad required. So as not to attract his wrath, his uniforms had to be impeccable. This was considered woman's work and I guess the early domestic training never went astray.

I certainly had to earn Dad's favour, but I didn't mind so much, particularly when he took me along when he conducted the military band at the hall in St Kilda. Sometimes he took me to Puckapunyal and the military rifle range to watch the shooting competitions, never realising how much of a role guns would play in my future.

We always lived in army barracks. Although Dad worked away from home a lot, he never saw overseas action, but insisted that someone had to train the men who did. I guess that became his life. On his better days, he would wake us with the sound of the military reveille played on an imaginary bugle. After a few drinks with his army friends, Dad was not averse to marching his children up and down the living room while barking orders: 'About turn!', 'At ease!' or, 'Attention!' until Mum insisted that her exhausted babies be allowed to lay down their imaginary rifles and go to bed. Every now and then, he would thrill us with a recital of 'Old Man River' in his wonderful baritone. These occasions and our family beach picnics were some of the few happy times I spent with my father; mostly he was an unapproachable, extremely moody man, prone to bouts of violence, and we lived in constant fear of those occasions.

2

Changing times

I was twelve when my father left the army in 1956, after twenty-two years of service. Finally, we left army life behind and my parents bought a two-storey, red-brick delicatessen with large display windows. It was on the corner of Pickles and Lyell streets, South Melbourne, and they both worked it, together with Barbara and me whenever possible. We were not far from the beach and we had lots of neighbours. Although we didn't socialise, it was a big change from the isolation of the army barracks.

The world around us was changing quickly too. The cart horses that had delivered ice, bread, firewood and milk gradually disappeared from the streets as the car took precedence. Another noticeable development was the increased number of migrants filling the suburbs. With the influx of Italians, cappuccino cafes were gradually introduced, while novelty dim-sims could be bought from the enterprising, pig-tailed Chinaman who set up his steaming cart on the city's footpath. But the basic culinary delights from the family kitchen were what really held post-war families together. It was always a large family gathering at mealtime at our house and the smell of the Sunday roast of lamb or beef with fresh vegetables, gravy and Yorkshire pudding and fresh scones still lingers.

Soon television arrived, to the dread of those who warned that life would never be the same – and it wasn't. We pressed our noses up against the store windows in the city in wonder to watch the black and white images of Betty Cuthbert and the 1956 Olympics flicker across the screen. Music was changing too, as Elvis Presley and rock 'n' roll music arrived on our shores. I danced to 'Blue Suede Shoes' and 'Jailhouse Rock' at a couple of 'home before twelve' teen parties, and enjoyed them immensely, but I felt unusually drawn to all things country. I preferred listening to Smoky Dawson's country music sessions while I dreamed of living in Queensland.

I had another dream for my future too: nursing. Mum was often unwell with asthma or pregnancies and I was frequently kept home from school to care for her. I felt a responsibility and really wanted to become a nurse to help her. After having come sixth out of a class of forty in my Year 8 exams, I wanted to start nursing immediately, but, although I did well in my last year, my father never considered me a particularly good prospect for further education. I was therefore selected to work in the shop, to free up Barbara to follow her nursing career. Barbara was a beautiful girl with blue eyes and long blonde hair, but apart from my blue eyes, there was nothing outstanding about my looks. We children were all fed the same, but I was obviously genetically predisposed to weight-gain. With my troublesome, short, straight, mousey blonde hair, I was what Mum referred to as 'pleasantly plump', but what my father would jokingly refer to as his 'five-by-five' (five feet tall by five feet wide). So, naturally, all this left me with the impression that I was certainly not the pick of his crop.

But despite the putdowns, my enthusiasm was undiminished. Obviously I had not learned from the Sturt Street bike incident because, just on dusk one evening, I took Mum's new bike for a ride. Mum was in hospital again after a miscarriage and my father was busy in the shop. The temptation was too great, so, abandoning the mound of ironing, I took off around the block. It was lovely to mingle with the locals out enjoying that beautiful summer evening, but my heart sank when I returned to find the back gate locked. I was in big trouble! My worst fears were realised when I was confronted by my enraged father wielding an electrical cord. There was nothing much I could do or say to defend myself as my legs were flayed repeatedly, leaving nine huge red welts. An unforgettable experience, to say the least, but although I gave up joyriding on pushbikes, he never broke my spirit.

Mum never found out about most of the beatings we took from my father and we knew better than to worry her with our troubles. She had enough on her plate.

Luckily, she had Dad's mother, Mary, to lean on. She was the family matriarch and Mum's constant support. A tall, refined and handsome lady, Mary was born in India of Spanish and British military heritage, on 5 June 1883, in Fort St George, Madras. Her parents, William and Bridget, still carrying ugly memories of the 1857–8 Indian uprising, chose to emigrate to Australia at the end of his active service in the British army. When Mary was ten months old, they embarked on a lengthy and torturous sea voyage. She told me that it took them a gruelling nine months, on four different ships, before they finally arrived in Australia.

When Grandma required a gallstone operation, followed by six weeks in bed to recover, I was sent to nurse her.

I stayed for a fortnight in her single-fronted, brick cottage on a corner of Rae Street in North Fitzroy, while she convalesced. A passage led from the little front porch to two small, dimly lit bedrooms, through the snug living room and then to a kitchen with a cosy wood fire, where we cooked and ate. The bathroom and 'dunny' were out in the little cobbled backyard where a few vegies and her rhubarb grew.

Stumbling into puberty, I had begun to notice that boys were actually quite different, and the boy across the cobbled lane fascinated me. He was the son of the dear Italian woman who brought us chicken soup, bolognaise and all that rich, nourishing foreign food that, because of her illness, Grandma could not eat. Maria sometimes invited me across the lane to the warmth of her tiny Italian kitchen. She made me feel like part of her family, patiently instructing me in the art of preparing their unusual cuisine. This included the rich tomato sauce that, after hours of preparation, was part of the fantastic bolognaise that ended up in the bin at Grandma's. As Maria spoke no English, I couldn't explain that because of Grandma's illness the food would only be wasted. Maria was horrified, and so was I, the day she lifted the rubbish-bin lid at Grandma's to expose the wasted offerings.

Although Italians were becoming part of the landscape, they still experienced the usual suspicions and rebuffs reserved for migrants, but I loved Maria and her family. She was a forty-something, typically plump, homely Italian woman who was distinguished by an egg-sized hollow on her forehead above her left temple, the origin of which eluded me.

Maria's son, Tony, on the other hand, was a good-looking, dark-eyed boy of fifteen, and there was an air of innocent attraction between us. We secretly arranged a rendezvous very early one morning that summer at the beach near my home. The crystal-clear water showed rippling sand beneath us as we swam. Then we strolled shyly hand in hand for miles along the shore, soaking up the sunshine and leaving the first footsteps in the untouched morning shoreline. But soon after that first clandestine meeting, my whole life turned topsy-turvy. Suddenly we were leaving town. I never saw Tony again, but my memories of him and his wonderful family have added a warm Mediterranean influence to my often-chilly recollections of Melbourne.

Just at that crucial time for me, our lives took a huge twist when Mum's doctor told her that if she wanted to live, she needed to get as far from Melbourne's weather as she could.

Dad loved Melbourne but, after having looked death in the face too often, Mum finally had her way and replied to an advertisement for a store and post office in a place called Mataranka in the Northern Territory. This really was about as far away from Melbourne as we could go.

My baby brother Stephen was only a few months old when Mum flew to the Territory to check out this opportunity. Having made this huge decision to buy, she returned home excited about our future prospects and in no time we were packing for our family of ten to head north.

Our heads were spinning with the excitement of it all. It happened so quickly that the fever of packing had developed a life of its own, but soon we were sobered by the thought of those we would leave behind. Most of all, it was going to be sad to leave Grandma and my older brothers, who by then were getting on with their own lives.

Terry, my eldest brother, was a tall, handsome young man whose dark hair and blue eyes owed a lot to our mother's Irish heritage. Eight years older than me, he was a quiet achiever, succeeding at one academic challenge after the other. He did a stint in Antarctica and had a mountain named after him there. He was interested in space science and technology, which, in the early 1960s, had not developed in Australia, so, sadly, he moved his family to the United States. He went on to become a renowned research physicist and, in 1979, he received the Harold Brown award, the US Air Force's highest honour for research and development, for his work on the over-the-horizon (OTH) radar. This radar can view targets beyond the horizon, 'seeing', as it were, around the earth's curvature.

Jimmy, on the other hand, was the image of our father, slim, good-looking, and with the same dark, foreign complexion that, because of racial taunts, Dad had grown to hate. Because Jimmy was a reminder of Dad's own unhappy youth, Dad made his life hell. In Dad's eyes he could do nothing right, for which Jim never forgave him. He was even forbidden to practise his clarinet in the house. I would often hold my school music book for him to practise from whenever Dad was not around. Jim left home at sixteen, which led to a turbulent youth and confrontations with the law. But, against all the odds, he became a competent engineer and a very successful musician.

My third brother, Dennis, was run over in the schoolyard on his eighth birthday. Dennis was born with blue eyes, snow-white hair and a most angelic personality. He was usually the peacemaker in our childish squabbles. On that awful day, he was let out of class for an errand, but was run over and killed while trying to save a stray dog from the wheels of the milk truck. His untimely death broke my parents' hearts. I was only four, but still remember the cloak of sadness that fell over our home at the time.

These were the brothers that we left behind us in Melbourne to begin our new life on the last frontier. This parting is ingrained in my memory as if it happened only yesterday.

This was my family: unique, and yet not that different from so many other Australian families of the day.

3

Goodbye civilisation

It took our family convoy ten days, in two cars, to travel well over 2000 miles from our corner store in South Melbourne to our general store at Mataranka in the Top End of Australia in 1959.

We had loaded camping gear and anything else that we could squeeze into the old grey Vauxhall Victa sedan, the trailer and the snappy new yellow Hillman Minx station wagon that Mum drove. There were eight excited children, from sixteen years right down to eight months. The oldest three – Barbara, myself and Kate – travelled with my father while little sister Frances and my four little brothers, Mark, Peter, Gregory and baby Stephen, travelled with Mum.

Our trip to Mataranka was an adventure. I loved the tiny country towns we passed through along the way, with their little wooden churches surrounded by pepper and willow trees. We camped in those churchyards. On one occasion I found a huge blue-tongue lizard trapped in an old fruit tin and, as a team, we nervously extricated it from its prison. This was my first experience with real wildlife. It would certainly get much bigger, better and more exciting as we went along.

Somewhere soon after Adelaide, the roads turned into narrow, corrugated tracks of powdery red bulldust. To this day I have no idea why this dust is referred to as 'bulldust', but often it was so deep that we would bog easily. At other times, the vehicles vibrated and skidded like we were driving over a corrugated tin roof. The potholes were sometimes deep enough to cause broken axles or other serious damage, but after several flat tyres and blowouts, Mum and Dad managed to get us safely through to Port Augusta at the top of the Spencer Gulf, where we stayed in a caravan park for a day or so waiting for the train connection.

From Port Augusta we loaded our cars and took a long train ride to Marree in the north of South Australia. Among the passengers was a group of young stockmen who had been drinking and were in quite a boisterous mood, so Mum and Dad were kept busy shepherding their daughters out of the way of these rowdy ringers. This was our first introduction to Aussie cattlemen.

'Jesus, you silly bastard, what the bloody hell are you talkin' about?' the larger of the four men yelled at his mates, above the rattle of the train.

That was enough to cause my mother to erupt and, like a bantam hen, she fluffed up her feathers and flew into these big, strapping – and, I might add, not bad-looking – young fellows.

'I'll not have you use that language in front of my family,' she admonished, while Dad stood sheepishly by, looking totally embarrassed. I was amazed by her courage, and so too were the young fellows, who respectfully toned down their conversation for the rest of the journey. But imperceptibly, things were changing. As the train rattled on north through that hot, dry, treeless wasteland, I'm sure my parents must have had second thoughts.

After several hours we alighted at Marree. There we boarded the original Ghan train, on which we had sleeper cabins, for the rest of the two-and-a-half-day journey. I would gaze for hours from the windows, mesmerised, as the seemingly endless gibber plains of the Simpson slid by. I scanned the horizons and saw the occasional big red kangaroo that seemed to vaporise into the shimmering heat haze, but otherwise nothing out there appeared to move.

We made a welcome stop at Oodnadatta and at other tiny townships that supported the railway sidings and the huge cattle stations of the surrounding areas. We had never seen black people before. I was a little scared, but fascinated, when I saw the Aborigines along the tracks waving to us in welcome as we pulled into the sidings.

It was fun to eat in the train's diner, balancing our soup as we rocked and rolled along the bumpy tracks. In those days, no music or movies were provided, but people occupied themselves reading, socialising or playing cards in the lounge carriage.

On the second morning, I lurched down the corridors of the train headed for the canteen. I stopped between carriages where a young woman was standing alone watching the ground below her sweep past. She reminded me of a movie star who was about to take that fatal leap and I could see by her shaking shoulders that she was weeping. Concerned, I tapped her on the shoulder and above the commotion of the rattling wheels, said, 'Hello, why are you crying?'

Startled, she turned to me with puffy, red eyes and replied, 'Because I'm unhappy, of course, so just go away.'

'Are you sure I can't help?' I persisted.

'Why should you care?' she said sarcastically.

'You know, you could easily fall from there,' I pointed out.

Her manner softened and she began to cry again, with pain or loneliness distorting her somewhat ordinary features.

'Listen,' she sobbed when she saw I wasn't leaving, 'I am hungry and pregnant and nobody wants me. You know only bad girls get pregnant. You're only a kid – there's nothing you can do.'

'Well, I could give you my money,' I said hesitantly. 'And my mum has eleven kids, so maybe she'd be able to tell you what to do.'

Fumbling in my pockets, I pulled out my twelve pennies of pocket money and offered it all to her. At last a shy smile lit up her sad face.

I turned to help an old lady as she battled through the carriage doors, and when I turned back the mother-to-be and my twelve pennies were gone. I never did ask her name and I never saw her again, so I could only assume that she had bolted off to the canteen to buy some food. I hoped the girl hadn't fallen or jumped; there was no sign of her along the tracks. So I shrugged my shoulders and returned to our carriage without my anticipated chocolate bar, rather bemused and confused and promising myself that I would never wind up in her condition – though in truth, as a good Catholic girl, I had practically no idea how she got that way in the first place.

My mother was aghast when I told her that I had offered her services to a strange, pregnant girl I had just met and also that I had given her my pocket money. I had thought it was the good Christian thing to do, but was I in for a surprise!

'Mary, you are so naive,' Mum cried in exasperation. She was convinced that her fourteen-year-old had been conned and explained patiently, 'Mary, there is no more pocket money where that came from, and we need every penny we have for the long journey ahead.'

Finally, our train rattled over the Todd River and into Alice Springs. We had reached the Northern Territory.

Now there were stark, white, shady ghost gums lining dry red creek beds, which were a backdrop to activity, colour and character that was totally new to me. Along the Todd River there were coils of smoke rising from several campfires, around which Aborigines sat. Large white cockatoos and flocks of pink and grey galahs squawked and flew up into the gums. Children in ragged clothes played in the morning sun, and they waved to the train as we passed. Skinny camp dogs slept on the hot sand. The flat landscape now bulged into red, rocky outcrops and hills that seemed to surround and protect the railhead of this sleepy township affectionately called 'Alice'.

We were beginning to weary but a bit of shopping and exploring in Alice freshened us up. There seemed to be few women about and, although sparsely populated by our standards, the township felt friendly with an old-world charm about it. Bow-legged stockmen in moleskins and boots sauntered about the pubs, stores and stock agents, while Europeans, Aborigines, Chinese and Afghans mingled freely.

Our vehicles had travelled on the same train and, after several hours, they were retrieved and repacked. That same day we continued north along the Stuart Highway towards our destination.

During the war the military had built a road between Alice and Darwin, but by now this road was in terrible disrepair. It was a narrow strip of rough, potholed bitumen shouldered with red bulldust. It would disappear completely into bulldust for many miles at a time. Sometimes it was little better than no road at all.

We expected to be at our destination in two days, after another fifteen hours driving at our top speed of sixty miles an hour. This was considered fast driving then, but care was essential, as the roads were littered with the carcasses of a variety of hapless marsupials and white-faced cattle constantly wandered onto the unfenced highway.

There were no motels and certainly no comforts along the way as Mum battled with her babies and her asthma on that journey. We camped and bathed at boreholes along the track. After unpacking each night, we young-sters slept in the cars, while Dad and Mum and the baby slept on their mattress in the trailer. Meals were usually bread, jam and tinned tucker, warmed on our little kerosene stove by the side of the road. Here the red dirt permeated and stained everything it touched, including our skin and hair.

The desert gave way to rough, hilly scrub. By now we were experiencing plagues of flies that constantly crawled into our eyes and mouth as we ate and caused eye infec-tions if we were stung. There was no air-conditioning and no car radio, and in the intolerable heat I tried to sleep the hours away, crammed into the Vauxhall's back seat among the supplies. I reckon that the fumes of the petrol we carried, mixed with the smell of the leather seats, dulled the senses and helped to relieve the monotony of those miles. As we drove, that incessant haze of powdery bulldust seeped through every opening. Finally, we would set up camp in the late afternoon and the children were let run wild before bed.

Then we'd wake to the smell of the new dawn. It was an exhilarating experience to wake at Bonnie Springs well and see the wild brumbies watering at the cattle trough.

That somehow compensated for what we had endured on the journey and definitely buoyed our spirits.

Mum's driving experience was limited. To make matters worse, she had little sense of direction. Despite the lack of signposts this shouldn't have been a problem because the Stuart Highway offered only two choices, north or south. But after setting off from one camping spot about 300 miles short of Mataranka, Dad drove for half an hour before we noticed that Mum was not behind us. Nearly two hours later, we finally caught up to her, headed south again. Granted, with so much distraction, it was difficult to remember which side of that monotonous roadside we had pulled into the night before, but I wondered then whether Mum was having second thoughts about our daring adventure and was making a run for it.

That painful day seemed to go on forever. It felt like we would never reach our destination as we drove and drove through the boring flat scrub into the glaring afternoon sun.

There was not a lot of conversation after ten monotonous days of 'I spy', constant travel and camping. But our very tired and dusty convoy, with its eight children at varying stages of endurance, was thrilled when we finally approached Mataranka around nine that evening.

It was a clear and starry night. We were on the outskirts of town, no more than a kilometre from our destination, when a huge brown horse suddenly appeared from nowhere and reared like some monster in the headlights. Dad swerved, but we still struck it, coming to a sickening, grinding halt with the heavy trailer askew. It's strange how he remained so calm in a situation like that. No sense in blowing a fuse when the damage was already done, I guess.

It happened so quickly that I don't think he even had time to swear, but he did mutter a few expletives when he saw the damage to his favourite car.

The horse limped off into the bush, apparently not badly hurt, but we were left sitting on this lonely highway, within cooee of our destination, wondering what to do next.

Dad decided to unhook the trailer and to slowly drive the last half-mile into town. And so, after our epic journey, with water pouring from the crumpled radiator and still shaking from that frightening experience, we limped up to our new home at Mataranka.

4

Well past the Rubicon

'Welcome, welcome, come right in,' cried two matronly ladies in unison as they appeared out of the shadowy innards of this strange building.

Introducing themselves as Poss and Jess, they ushered us into what seemed to me to be a scarcely furnished tin shed that I never dreamed could possibly be our new home. They seemed very old to me then, but they were probably only in their sixties. They had taken up residence in this ex-military shed after the army exodus from the town, but were now intent on moving back to a more comfortable existence in Darwin.

After Dad explained the predicament with the Vauxhall, they decided we must have hit one of their old horses, so they took torches and went back to search for it to ensure it wasn't injured. Meanwhile, we kids hungrily devoured a supper of tea and boiled fruitcake that they had prepared for us. We were tired but glad at least to be at the journey's end and at the start of our new life. We were well past the Rubicon. There was definitely no turning back now.

My acute senses were on high alert and I looked around in amazement as the soft yellow light of the kerosene lamps played across the bare eaves. Finally, I realised that this spartan corrugated-iron shed was actually going to be the family's home and business.

I was disappointed. This was not the solid bricks-and-mortar that I was used to. Bare angle-iron supports covered with corrugated-iron sheeting sat on the cold cement floor. The old furnishings were minimal. There were no coverings on the floors, but a thin coat of green paint was wearing away in the living area. Rooms were separated by corrugated-iron walls, and curtains rather than doors hung in doorways. Faded cotton curtains also hung over the flyscreens that served as windows. Two naked light-bulbs flickered threateningly in the kitchen and living room, while the pungent smell of the old kerosene lamps and refrigerator permeated the warm, clammy night air. This was a strange and unattractive place indeed, certainly an anticlimax to our journey; but it was definitely more appealing than camping again along that hard, dusty highway. That night, we slept soundly on our camp bedding laid on the old army stretchers that we had inherited with the shed.

When the sun rose the next morning, our new life began to unfold. The pub was the only other business in town. Jess and Poss stayed there until the handover was completed. During that time they showed us how to operate the telephone exchange, which consisted of a switchboard with plug-in connections on many cords. There was an L-shaped counter in the store, on which a professional-looking set of scales and weights sat. Behind that sat some display shelves, and the small counter off to the right served as the post office and the switchboard. The public telephone stood outside, to the left of the entrance. To say this was an open-plan design would be an understatement. It was nothing like the modern delicatessen we had left behind us in Melbourne.

The smoky old kerosene refrigerator was the bane of our lives. It kept the 'lolly water' (soft drink) cool for the travellers. Drinks for the 'blacks' were kept underneath the refrigerator. Poss told us that this was their customers' preference because in their natural environment they were unused to cold food or drinks. There was no other refrigeration, but there was a Coolgardie safe, a large double-lined box packed with charcoal and covered with hessian. It had a tray for water that siphoned into the hessian through which the air flowed to keep our food cool. This system serviced the house, the store and the cafe. Eggs were powdered or oiled to keep them longer. Powdered milk and oily, often rancid butter came preserved in tins.

As I looked about the property that morning, it was obvious that most of the structure and the limited fit-out was ex-army. And in stark contrast to Mum's garden rockery in Melbourne, army tank-tracks bordered the limited lawns, separating them from the all-pervading red bulldust that led onto the Stuart Highway at the front of the store. Here a token coconut tree stood and a couple of poinciana and white cedar trees gave a little welcome shade. A few pink phlox grew along the front veranda that was covered in Dutchman's pipe vines. Discarded military junk, old car bodies, batteries and the like lay rusting in the dump at the rear of the store. Behind that was the Aborigines' camp, consisting of a tin shed, swags rolled out on wire stretchers and a cooking fire under some trees.

After spending that first day unpacking and settling in, we prepared a frugal dinner and went to bed for a well-earned sleep, only to be awakened in the wee hours by a terrible commotion. We all ran to investigate the noise and found the kitchen crowded with cattle, large and small. Flabbergasted and fearful, we stood and watched them raiding the flour drums and anything else that was not bolted down.

'What do we do, Jim?' Mum asked.

'I haven't got a clue,' he replied.

The hops that were set in bottles to make the bread the next day were slopped together with broken eggs, flour and dry milk powder that covered the floor. The old white cow eyed Dad with indignant disdain as he brandished the broomstick at her. When he got one animal moving, another beast would simply fill its sloppy hoofprints. Our limited supplies were in a total mess, and the cattle were having a ball! Poss and Jess had forgotten to tell us that the store came with a small herd. They had hand-reared Sunshine, the cow who was now bringing back her calves and any other strays she found along the way, to raid the premises. Dad finally called Arthur, our new gardener, from the camp, and he quietly herded the cattle away. We left the mess until the next morning to clean up. There was nothing we could do but see the funny side of it and start all over again.

When I was younger, I'd read many comic books about the war. It had seemed a lifetime away then, but I was a soldier's daughter, and now, only fourteen years after the war's end, my new environment seemed strangely familiar. Being a large, strategic military base, Mataranka had accommodated thousands of army personnel during the war but had since reverted to a blink-and-you-miss-it roadside township about six hours' drive south of Darwin, and it was still coming to terms with the military exodus. The family was a welcome addition to the township, doubling its population and, with three teenage daughters, we created quite a lot of interest in the male-dominated Top End.

To me, life had become a series of amazing adventures, some more exciting than others. As my father liked to say, 'For you, Mary, life is just a bowl of cherries,' and so it seemed. Everything was a novelty.

The toilet, in an outhouse way out the back, was a four-gallon-drum affair that needed to be carted away regularly. The shower facility was part of the corrugated-iron shed attached to the main house and, if you were lucky, there was hot water from a system that we affectionately called a 'donkey'. This was a fuel drum set up on the water line under which a fire was lit each morning.

Laundry was now done by hand, rubbing the clothes on a corrugated scrub board and using bar soap that we sometimes made ourselves. Following that, the clothes were boiled in the wood-fired copper that stood just outside the lean-to laundry in the backyard. The ironing that followed was done with heavy black Mrs Potts irons that were heated on top of the wood stove in the kitchen. They were so heavy and clumsy that we upgraded quite rapidly to the more modern kerosene irons, but they smoked and caught fire.

Early in the piece, hurricane and pressurised kerosene lamps were the order of the day and the rickety generator sometimes gave light and pumped water. When we cranked this old motor over, the large drive belt for the pump would slip. The trick was to spread treacle on it to give it grip. Petrol was pumped by hand for the customers. It was not unusual for travellers to pull up at the petrol bowsers and demand fuel at any time of the day or night, and, however rude they seemed, we were trained that the customer was always right.

I don't remember my father's temper being as bad as it had been in Melbourne, and peace reigned for a while under these unfamiliar and trying conditions. But these conditions were all constant reminders of the civilised existence we had left behind in Melbourne, which Dad never let us forget, constantly admonishing Mum with, 'What in God's name are we doing here in this godforsaken country at the arse end of Australia?'

Mum tried to teach my younger siblings by correspondence at the store, without sucess. So, as a determined ex-school teacher, she applied to the South Australian government, which administered the Northern Territory, to establish a schoolhouse in one of the railway fettler's cottages. She built up the student numbers required for this approval by selecting suitable Aboriginal youngsters from the neighbouring stations. It was a mammoth task, as these children were used to total freedom and, after being kept awake by the corroborees most nights, the pupils would invariably arrive at school sleepy and dishevelled. Quite often Mum had to drive out to Mataranka Station to fetch these children for class. This, of course, doubled Mum's workload, but it was how the first school at Mataranka became a reality, in the railway cottage at the far end of town.

As well as being the school teacher, Mum was the registered postmistress. Dad ran the general store and saw to the maintenance. Between us, all aspects of the business operated smoothly enough and, with our help, Mum managed to juggle her work, her asthma and her family with remarkable aplomb. She was driven by some inner force to retain her class and dignity as she continually battled for survival in that environment. Diarrhoea and sandy blight, that painful eye infection caused by flies, were constant challenges. Mum never complained, but I remember her crying in agony with that dreaded eye disease as she was taken to the nearest doctor, over sixty miles away in Katherine. I often wonder now where she got the strength to push on when the whole family went down, one after the other, with the dreaded Asian flu. This deadly outbreak killed more than one million people worldwide but, with our limited communications, I am not sure that my parents were aware of its severity. It caused raging temperatures, flu symptoms, vomiting and scouring, and most of my siblings caught this potentially fatal disease. I don't recall ever being so unwell. We crawled around through the heat of the day looking for anywhere that was cool enough to die in comfort. I believe that Mum had looked death in the eye so often that she could only live in hope.

5

Our initiation

We youngsters felt privileged to have a full-blood
Aborigine, Charlie Marang, working intermittently as our
gardener when he wasn't off on tribal business. He had
had his front teeth removed, which he said was typical
of didgeridoo players. He told me that along with other
budding young musicians, he had been trained by elders to
play the didgeridoo for hours, with the end of their instru-
ments held underwater to strengthen their lungs. Charlie
always had a twinkle in his eye. He had travelled around
a lot more than most Aborigines and had a more sophisticated view of the world. He was an acclaimed musician and
had played at many major public events and eisteddfods in
Darwin. Charlie was a slight man, but I doubt I will ever
hear anyone play the didgeridoo the way he did. His lean,
muscular body would flex and spasm and become part of
the instrument, as he pumped and expanded those rhythms.
Seated in the dust, with his didgeridoo placed against the
tin shed for acoustic effect, he would mesmerise us with
the growling, rumbling and howling of his instrument as it

brought to life any tune we requested. It was early 1960 and he hadn't heard much rock 'n' roll, but he could still do an awesome rendition of 'Jailhouse Rock' on his didgeridoo.

Didgeridoos were fashioned from hollowed tree branches, then had a smaller mouthpiece embedded with the black wax that came from the nest of the sugarbag flies. We would hunt these little black flies to their nests in the tree hollows and, with the help of the blacks, would cut them down to raid the rich, dark-brown honey as a special sweet treat. It tasted somewhat like a mixture of honey and molasses, and was delicious.

My father often discussed war events with Charlie, who could recall the Japanese bombing attacks on Mataranka. Charlie also claimed military experience, so when Dad asked him what his rank was, Charlie replied, 'All them myall (wild) blackfella been steal him sugar and flour, boss, so boss soldier been give it me hat, an' shirt, an' rifle, an' him been tell me, "Charlie you gotta watch him that store."'

'So they fitted you out with uniform and rifle to keep the wild blacks out of the rations. What happened then?' Dad asked.

'Well, I been marching up an' down, boss, looking after them stores, but that Japanese plane him been fly over an' been drop him bomb, boss. Bang, bang, bang.'

'What did you do then, Charlie?'

'I been reckon bugger that store, boss. I been drop him that gun, and I been look up and talk, "Good Lord, Jesus Christ, you gotta be lookin' after this ol' Charlie Marang," and I been runnin' sixty-sixty longa bush.'

With that, we all burst out laughing at the vision of Charlie ditching his chances of heroics and running at top speed to hide in the scrub – which, of course, was what any sensible man would do.

When asked if any soldiers were killed during these air attacks at Mataranka, Charlie replied, 'Only off him big truck, boss. All these fellas been loaded longa big truck and him been turning corner and hit him tree. This truck, him been roll over and fifteen men all been get 'im killed.'

'Kill' was a term the blacks used for hitting rather than dying, so there was always a bit of confusion as to whether Charlie meant dead or injured. Alarmed, Dad exclaimed, 'Really! Fifteen men dead, Charlie?' but he was quickly reassured.

'Oh, no, boss, nobody been dead, him just been get kill 'im longa arm and leg and some fella longa head. No one been get kill 'im dead!'

And that was the way of it with Charlie. He was a laugh a minute and I think he knew it. But I reckon he also had a few laughs at our expense, as he patiently educated us in the use of pidgin English.

Charlie was also responsible for teaching us to ride horses, after a fashion, and taught us to throw boomerangs and spears with woomeras. However, my lessons came to an abrupt halt when I put a shovel-nosed spear through a new, corrugated-iron shower recess that Dad had just erected in the paddock beside the store for our weary, travelling customers.

As my father stormed across the paddock towards us, there was a sharp intake of breath from Charlie, who muttered to me, 'Only Jesus gotta help you now, missy,' and when I turned around he had miraculously disappeared, leaving me to face the roar.

'What the bloody hell is going on over there?'

My heart sank and I reckoned I was dead for sure. I suppose Dad had a right to be furious and, as he pointed out, it was just as well the shower recess was not occupied at the time!

Thinking back, Charlie always seemed to have a hand in any mischief we got up to. There was the time I asked him to catch Jerry, the huge bay horse that we had run into on our arrival. Charlie probably thought I could ride as he put on Jerry's bridle, and so did I. It would be bareback, but I figured all I had to do was get on top and the rest would happen automatically. Wrong, wrong, wrong! As Kate, Mark and Frances stood watching for our parents, I had a handful of mane and a foot over his back when Jerry began to spin until, like a rag doll, I was flung into the dust and the victorious Jerry galloped off into the distance. Dusted and bruised, once again I had to face my father's tongue-lashing.

'Who the bloody hell has got the time to be running you all the way to Katherine hospital?' he roared unsympathetically. But the dressing-down certainly helped to distract my attention from the pain I was silently enduring. Luckily, no bones were broken and the trip to hospital wasn't required.

It was also Charlie who helped us catch the huge swamp goannas for a fellow who had offered to pay us ten shillings each for them. My brother Mark and I could see ourselves becoming very rich. We held these creatures in a wooden box, waiting on the return of the collector. When he never turned up, Dad insisted we let the hapless creatures go. We simply tipped over the box and was dragging one out by the tail when Charlie warned, 'You fella better watch out, them buggers gotta run up first thing close by, and you two fella close by.'

Terrified, I was left hanging onto the huge goanna's tail while Kate and Mark held it down with garden rakes. Here we were, holding that three-foot lizard, too petrified to let him go – but I swear I could hear Charlie laughing as he wandered away, leaving us to work out our own solution. All we could do, after an interminable time, was count to three, let go and split in different directions, while the old goanna slowly lumbered away, just happy to be free.

Three other Aborigines also worked for us: Arto and Marla, a young married couple with a baby, and Marta, who was Marla's mum. Their English was not good, so pidgin became our natural way of communicating. They were a fine-looking, healthy and happy family who became as attached to us as we were to them. Social groups would often gather at their camp behind our store. These men and women proudly displayed patterned chest and shoulder scars that fascinated me. As Marla explained, these were tribal scars, received in ceremonies. The skin was cut and ashes rubbed in the wounds. They would then heal as shiny black initiation scars, indicating a true adult Aborigine.

We girls were often invited to the women's special corroborees. Sometimes, in ceremonies to get a man, the girls would sing the same words repetitively, and dance until the feathers dropped from their scanty costumes. I still remember the words of the corroboree song 'To get-'im your fella' – and beware! I am not beyond using them for my own purposes should the need arise!

Our parents seldom socialised and, isolated from children our own age, we had no normal social adolescence. This introduction to Aboriginal culture certainly added richness to our otherwise boring lives. Surprisingly, our parents trusted our staff implicitly, and we sometimes went horse riding or fishing and hunting with them. They taught us their bush skills and took us looking for bush tucker. Among other things, they taught me that if I saw ants eating berries or fruit, then it would undoubtedly be safe for me to eat. I loved to go on little walkabouts, walking in single file through the swamps, picking bush bananas and hunting goannas from their holes. We would invariably end up at some shady billabong, cooking our catch on the campfire that smoked lazily nearby. No comparison to Maria's kitchen in Melbourne but we would nonetheless wander home weary and well fed.

These were happy, innocent days and I consider myself very privileged that the women told me the stories that made up the bush lore of their area. They told me about the headless white woman in the long white dress who haunts the banks of Warlock Ponds, not far from Old Elsey Cemetery. That area was made famous by the stories of Jeannie Gunn in her book, *We of the Never-Never*.

Our little post office in the corner of the store was the hub of communication for the whole district. To get the mail through was of paramount importance as it was the only form of outside contact for many isolated communities. We also had to be totally dedicated to the manual exchange, which we manned continuously, and we handled all telephone and telegram communications with its slow, laborious plug-in system.

Early one morning I answered an urgent call from Mrs Smith, the owner of the Mataranka Hot Springs guest-house, some twenty miles away.

'Hello, Mataranka, what number, please?'

'Mary, put me through to Darwin hospital urgently. I've got big problems out here.'

'Can we help?'

'No, I just need to find out if old Roy, my gardener, is dead. We sent him up to Darwin hospital with pneumonia over a week ago. I just need to check on his condition to shut old Violet up before she kills herself.'

'What's wrong?'

'Well, I woke up this morning at daybreak to a hell of a commotion in the backyard and I found old Violet performing a "sorry".'

'A what?' I asked.

'Oh, that's when the blacks wound or inflict pain on themselves to mourn their dead. She thinks Roy's dead, so she's been sitting on the woodheap banging herself on the head with an axe all night, and she's in a right old bloody mess. She just keeps wailing, "Ol' Roy, him been finish up alonga Darwin hospital, missus."'

'I told her, "Rubbish! I didn't get any message that the old fella's dead." But she insists, "Yes, missus, him been properly finish up." So I need to know urgently if he's okay.'

Mrs Smith talked like a tough bush woman, but I could hear the concern and the panic creeping into her voice.

Nothing had come through the post office and Violet had absolutely no other outside connection, but the Aborigines were able to communicate through their powers of telepathy on a much more efficient level than we could on our clumsy manual exchange. Compared to Violet's apparent instant telepathy, it took over two hours and many telephone calls to finally confirm that the old man had in fact died the night before.

This telepathy appeared to be sustained through constant, uncontaminated contact with the earth's energy, and it was a common occurrence among the Aborigines that I knew. I gradually became aware that these seemingly uneducated people were privy to an ancient wisdom gleaned from the earth itself.

6

Mataranka – home of the snake

The blacks told me that Mataranka is an Aboriginal word meaning 'home of the snake'. We were constantly removing snakes from the store and our living quarters. Huge king browns seemed to think that we were invading their territory and would regularly take up residence. At least once a week there was a snake alarm. They usually measured anything up to ten feet long and most were poisonous. Eventually, I developed an uncanny knack of tracking them down when they hid around the property – then it was usually a savage fight for survival and occupancy of the house.

We were startled early one Easter Sunday morning by a loud commotion in the house.

'Mum, Dad, quick, there's a huge snake in the kids' room,' my brother Mark yelled.

Bleary-eyed, we sprang into action.

'Quick, Jim,' Mum screamed, horrified. 'This thing is after the baby.'

She tried, but was unable to enter the little bedroom without confronting the snake, its huge coils blocking the entrance that led into the open breezeway adjoining the living room. In the dim light, she could barely see the front half of the snake, so to confirm that they were unharmed, she called anxiously through the screened window on the breezeway to wake my two little brothers, Peter and Greg. The boys were then only four and six years old and they woke excited, expecting to find Easter eggs. Instead, they were terrified by the intruder.

'Mum, Mum, there's a really big snake in here and it's heading for Stevie,' Pete cried in a plaintive little voice.

Little Gregory added, 'Mummy, its head is really, really big!'

'Don't be scared now,' she soothed them. 'Stay in bed, under the covers, both of you.' Then, trying to ease the tension with a joke, she added, 'It's after your Easter eggs, but we'll soon have him out of there, boys.'

Mark grabbed the shovel while Dad, still in his pyjamas, went to grab the twisted-wire whip that we kept specifically for this purpose. But neither of these weapons looked equal to tackling the twelve feet of dull brown coils, as thick as a man's arm.

'What is it? Is it poisonous?' Dad yelled over his shoulder.

'Dunno, but it's too bloody big for a shovel, it's got to be a python,' Mark answered, trying to see the snake's head.

He straightened his glasses and sized up the situation as the snake slithered cautiously towards the cot, its scales sounding like rustling leaves on the cement floor. The baby slept in a meat-safe cot which was enclosed in flywire to keep out mosquitoes and other creepy-crawlies, but the hatch on it was now slightly ajar and my baby brother was clearly looking like a tasty morsel to this marauding reptile. The python's tongue flicked continually, sensing the little warm body in the cot. Realising that the wire and the shovel would be useless, Dad shouted, 'Quick, Mary, get the rifle and some ammo from the office.'

Within minutes I was back. I slid a bullet into the breech of the .22, and handed it to Dad. He was rattled now, as he had no way of getting between the snake and the kids, and he felt it was too dangerous to shoot in that enclosed area. Then Mark lashed out, hitting the coils hard with the shovel, and the snake was distracted from its prey. It swung backwards through the door, mouth open, hissing angrily at the intrusion. It reared as if to strike, slithering and twisting, and then it was all over as Dad shot it between the eyes. This was an Easter surprise that nobody had expected.

There were rare taipans and other species, but the browns seemed to reign supreme. When the dry-season fires burned through the spear grass each year, a large number of snakes would lie carpeting the highway, having been burned out of their cool-weather hibernation. They were so groggy that I was able to walk among them without challenge.

In those days it was considered that the best snake was a dead snake, and around the home I guess it was, but it was almost forty years before anyone I knew was bitten. To me, this proves that although many snakes are poisonous, they are relatively harmless if left alone in their own environment.

In the late dry season, around October, the wild willy-willies would roar through town without warning, heralding the annual rains and scattering anything in their path. They were like mini dust tornadoes and my brothers would break up the smaller ones by running into their centres. Soon, the monsoon rains would pelt down on the old tin shed for weeks on end, until the mould almost began growing over us in our sleep – if we could sleep at all, that was, given the deafening cacophony of frog song that the torrential rains encouraged.

I loved the wet season, but after months of incessant rain, even I began to wish it away. Everything smelled musty and washed clothes were seldom dried. By April, when the wet season usually came to an end, you could set your watch by the huge knock-'em-down storms that blew through town each afternoon. As the old-timers said, these winds were strong enough to blow a blue dog off its chain. They were called 'knock-'em-downs' because they were fast and furious and would flatten the eight-foot-high spear grass that by then covered the land.

Radio reception was never good, but it was worse through the wet. We youngsters would sit with ears glued to the radio listening to *Party Time Saturday Night* through the scratchy static reception from Darwin. Most of our spare time was spent reading, writing and dreaming of other places. Our days were mostly long and arduous, but we eventually came to terms with the unfamiliar conditions. The perishables would arrive on Sunday by refrigerated truck, if we were lucky. Usually, the local stations collected them immediately, along with the drums of flour, sugar, fuel, mixed groceries and their mail.

Bread-baking was a regular chore. It took hours of setting hops or yeast, mixing, kneading, proving and baking, until the huge golden-brown loaves emerged from the wood-fired oven. These would be devoured within the day. Any bread that did go stale was quickly used for a delicious English bread pudding. This was made by soaking the bread in milk, wringing it out, adding syrup, mixed fruit and spices, eggs if you had them, and dollops of butter, then baking until golden. Yum!

I worked for hours, scrubbing and washing the laundry by hand. My only company was Matteti, the banned feral cat whose kittens I had secreted in the army dump behind the house.

Being a teenager, my body worked automatically while my mind wandered. As I carted water in a bucket for the boiler, I imagined that I resembled the biblical Rebecca at the Well, so, to break the monotony, one sunny day I acted out this scenario. I chose to use the huge earthenware jugs I found lying on the old army dump. Merrily filling the copper boiler with water from the jugs, I loaded the baby's nappies and stoked up the fire. I remembered vividly my mother and grandmother sitting for hours in Melbourne, hemming those flannelette napkins for baby Stephen. But when I thrust the stick into the boiling copper to retrieve them, I found them practically dissolved. All that remained were the hems that had taken so long to complete. I was mystified! Horrified! What a predicament! Finally we worked out that the large jugs I had used to imitate Rebecca were, in fact, battery-acid bottles left over from the war. Now we had a baby with no nappies and no store for miles. Consequently, baby Stephen's last nappies were fashioned from flour bags and he still laughs about how the 'self-raising' flour bags have caused an ongoing problem for him, as most fellows would understand.

Sometimes it was cool enough in the dry season to wear a jacket, but mostly the weather was extremely hot, so my parents decided to dig a swimming pool in the yard beside the cafe, using shovels. This put us all in high spirits, and the spade brigade, including Mum and Dad, was on high octane until we got to about ten feet in length by five feet deep. Then the novelty wore off and the procedure came to a sudden halt. I am not sure what the reason was, but our swimming pool was filled with rocks and became a grease pit for the run-off from the kitchen. However, when a pit had to be dug for the installation of the underground fuel tank for the new electric bowsers at the front of the shop, willing helpers were conspicuously scarce and a labourer had to be employed to do that digging.

By sixteen, I was running the cafe and the truckies used to drive all the way from Alice Springs to have a meal at Mary's. No instant takeaway then but sizzling mixed grills with steak and kidney pie, or huge roast meals with vegetables and freshly baked bread. I prided myself on having a meal on the table from scratch within fifteen minutes. Lord knows how hard it was to keep up supplies, because sometimes they came through only once a fortnight, providing there were no floods or breakdowns.

And then there was the pig! Often the blacks would arrive with what finally turned out to be quite a menagerie of orphaned animals, but Penny the pig was the most memorable. She was red and black and of feral stock. I knew nothing about pigs but I soon learned, and as the months passed she grew out of control. She was reared with our dog Skipper the retriever, and barked like him, claiming equal rights to the property and family.

'Mary, keep that bloody pig out of the cafe,' was almost a theme song. If I was to keep the pig, I was warned, I had to lock her up, but this was a joke to her and she simply nosed her way out of every enclosure we erected. As she grew she learned to graze independently, and if my parents weren't watching closely, she slept beside my bed.

In the evenings my family kneeled to pray together around the open-plan living room. We were into the third set of prayers one evening when Penny came grunting into the house. I prayed a little harder for her sake, hoping that she would keep going, but to my alarm, she let out a squeal of delight, nudging a few of the kids who tried hard to pretend that she was not there. Then she came directly to me, plonking her large plump body heavily across the back of my legs, pinning me to the floor in my long night-dress. Expelling a few satisfied grunts, she proceeded to settle in for the prayer session.

In vain, we tried to maintain our solemnity, but Mark began to chuckle followed by uncontrollable outbreaks throughout the room as Penny punctuated our prayers with her loud grunting. When Dad and Mum also started to cry with laughter I realised with relief that Penny would live a little longer.

Almost human, she was becoming a novelty for the tourists in the cafe. By now she was nearly as big as I was and would invariably materialise under their tables immediately the food arrived, demanding her share. Penny finally wore out her welcome when she scattered the pub's clientele, so my parents gave her to the policeman in exchange for half a goat. We kids watched in horror as they dragged Penny away. We heard her squealing, 'Help me! Help me!' as plain as day.

Because we had only flyscreens for windows in the kitchen, the wild cats would raid the cooking fat or dripping tin late at night. Dad usually shot them but, busy in the office one evening, he yelled, 'Mary, there's a bloody cat in the kitchen. Get the gun and shoot it.'

He knew that I loved cats, but I had angered him during the day when he found my kittens hidden in the army dump. I knew that underpinning this order was a reprimand and I was in no position to defy him. He had taught me to shoot well and was proud of my uncanny accuracy at target practice. Having to kill that cat distressed me no end; it was a clean head shot but I felt terrible as the ugly grey moggy's nerves twitched and died away. After making sure it was dead, I hoisted it by the tail and walked across the highway to dispose of its limp body. Then an amazing thing happened. Ten minutes after it was shot, the cat was hanging dead in my grip when Skipper, the dog, ran up beside us. Suddenly I felt the cat's powerful energy run up my arm and every hair on its body stood on end. Too scared to move, I stood on the highway in the moonlight as the cat's tail hairs exploded back to life in my hand. This was a natural response for a wild cat encountering a dog, but not when the cat was definitely dead!

Not long after that experience, the dog belonging to the publican sat outside our store and howled mournfully all night. Usually the only time it ever came near the store was to fight Skipper, but this night it had a message and the lonely howling was incessant. 'There's blood on the moon tonight,' Dad warned when the dog refused to be chased away. Sure enough, the next day we learned that the dog's owner had died the night before, far away, in Darwin. How did her dog know?

These things were just spooky to me then, but they fascinated me rather than frightened me. As a teenager, I had little comprehension of the physical, let alone such extraordinary metaphysical occurrences, but time would change all that.

7

An out-of-body experience

George Conway was a stockman who lived with his Aboriginal partner, Ami, in a camp at Warlock Ponds near Old Elsey Cemetery, and we soon became friends with this unusual couple. He would have been good-looking once, but now in his seventies he was weather-beaten and sandpaper-dry from age and smoking. He wore his Akubra pulled low on his forehead and his milky eyes peered through round-rimmed glasses. He was never clean-shaven, a cigarette usually dangled from the corner of his mouth and his old bandy legs were always encased in moleskin trousers, protected by leggings worn over his riding boots and spurs. Ami, on the other hand, was grey-haired, in her late fifties, and always dressed neatly in the bright coloured floral frocks that we sold through the store, though she never wore shoes. A stunner in her day, she was now matronly with pendulous breasts and hair tied back in a yellowed grey bun.

Although a thorough gentleman, George was as tough as greenhide and he liked a drink or three. One long, hot day, after being on the booze in the pub for too long, he passed out on the railway tracks on the way back to his camp. We were devastated when we were told that the once-a-week train from Larrimah to Darwin had come through and scuttled him. Luckily, he had almost rolled clear, and just a few fingers on his right hand were mangled. That night, we kids watched fascinated as he sat nonchalantly in the back of an old ute ready to go to hospital, while others fussed around him trying to make him comfortable. There were no painkillers available but all he really wanted was cigarettes, and we watched aghast as the almost severed, bloodied fingers dangled down his gnarly old hand when he inhaled. But George survived that ordeal remarkably well and was soon back in his camp and mustering again.

I was about sixteen when Barbara arrived home for the day from Darwin, where she had been nursing. Mum and Dad took advantage of this opportunity and we were left in charge of the store while they drove to Katherine for mass.

It wasn't long before a couple of young fellows that Barbara knew from Darwin arrived and the usual rule for youngsters was applied: While the cat's away, the mice will play.

Conveniently, George's stock camp rode into town that afternoon and unsaddled in the bush across the road. When George sauntered into the store Barbara pounced. 'Hey, George, do you reckon we could borrow some horses for a ride, seeing as you're in town for a bit?'

George was a man of simple means and few words. Like most men in the Territory his vocabulary was limited to necessity. I don't think we ever had a conversation. Usually, we would ask the questions and he would answer in gruff monosyllables. 'Sure, kids,' he said, 'just watch out. Off up the pub now. I'll get 'em about five o'clock. Me boys will saddle 'em up for you. Seeya later.'

Barbara's friends didn't excite me at all and I felt uncomfortable about the plans; still, I wanted to be a good sport. We had borrowed the horses before but nobody had ever asked if we could ride properly. I guess that was taken for granted. Anyway, most old bushies reckon that the best way to learn is by your mistakes.

There was a grey, a piebald, and two bay horses. I drew the bay with three white feet and a snip on his muzzle. Being stock-camp horses, they were lean, patient, long-haired brumbies that were used to working as a team; when one ran, they all ran. It was really hot that afternoon as we galloped through the dry scrub and the spear grass, jumping trees and generally going wild, as young people do.

After a while the horses were hot and lathered and so was I. We weren't wearing any hats, so I was probably sunstruck. Feeling decidedly weak and wobbly, I called out, 'Barb, I've had it. I don't feel good. Let's go home.'

But Barbara and the boys ignored my protestations and started off again. Alarmingly, my horse cantered after them, so grabbing hold, I hung on and prayed. 'Oh God, no! Not again!'

I must have blacked out as I galloped, because I suddenly realised that there were no reins in my hands. I began to crawl out over the cantering horse's mane to retrieve them and, of course, I soon slipped and was hanging under his neck. It was impossible to hold on, and I hit the ground heavily. It felt like dozens of hooves pounded down upon me; then silence. It seemed like the world had stopped breathing.

In the silence that followed, I felt myself evaporate and, as a separate entity, was fully aware of looking down on my tangled body from high above as it lay crumpled on the ground. This detachment felt like a natural progression as my consciousness was drawn upwards, and like steam from a kettle I went. There was no pain, no emotion or concern for the body as it lay like a discarded overcoat. But, at the same time, an acute responsibility for that 'coat' on the ground held me like an anchor.

'Are you going to get up?' a stern voice repeatedly and impatiently asked the 'coat' on the ground. 'Are you going to get up?'

It may have been Barbara's words, though it seemed like my own inner consciousness, or perhaps the voice of some higher power, but I do know the real 'me' was not down there on the ground and I had no intention of responding. But happily, my spirit obviously wasn't ready to continue the upwards journey, and the alternative wasn't an attractive option, either. Obviously, I felt content to stay put for a while.

After what must have been an hour it seemed as if someone had flicked a switch and turned on the movie again. I regained awareness and was surprised to find myself riding the grey horse some kilometres away from the site of the accident.

It was now late afternoon and as I slumped along in the saddle, I heard myself ask, 'What happened?'

Barbara's reply was less than sympathetic as she rode in sullen silence beside me. 'Don't ask me that again or else . . .' she growled.

How they had managed to get me aboard another horse and riding I will never know. I felt no pain, but I was shaking badly. I was extremely weak and felt disoriented as we rode another mile or so to the nearby Mataranka Station, where the manager's wife checked me over to make sure that I was okay. She gave me a headache tablet and then, somehow, I rode that horse all the way home. I don't remember getting there; I only know that I was an extremely unwell young lady when my parents returned home later that evening.

'Hey, Mary, you stay in bed and I'll tell Mum you got the flu, all right?' Barbara was still cranky with me for being so inconsiderate and ruining her visit, but I was in no condition to care.

Apparently, when Mum popped her head in to check on me, I was fast asleep. As luck would have it, Bishop O'Loughlin from Darwin had arrived with my parents and was staying for dinner. This was such a big event that my absence was barely noticed.

I slept heavily that night and was pretty groggy for the next few days, but I soon got well. The subject was never discussed and soon became a thing of the past, but I never forgot that experience. Although I didn't realise it at the time, this was my first out-of-body experience. Throughout life, I am constantly reminded of how lucky I was to have actually experienced the separation of my spirit energy from my body. This separation gave me a profound understanding of what is referred to as the body and the soul. I didn't understand it then. It was just one of those weird experiences that you didn't talk to anybody about.

By now, my fascination with the natural world and Aboriginal spirituality seemed second nature to me with my lessons continuing through Ami, but sadly, because of my youth, I took it all for granted. Although the little I did absorb proved invaluable, I regret now that I didn't listen more.

As for George, he had enjoyed a long, tough and colourful life but he didn't live long after his run-in with the train. He returned to his camp with Ami to start work again, only to succumb to cancer. As a tribute to him, he was buried at Old Elsey Cemetery and was to have been the last person to be buried there. It was a sad day when I stood beside Ami as they buried her beloved George among those historical graves and the ghosts of the Never-Never.

8

Joe

It was early June 1961 in that tiny Top End town of
Mataranka and I was the impressionable, almost-
seventeen-year-old buxom blonde serving behind the
counter in the general store.

He seemed to materialise from nowhere and stood in
the doorway of the old tin shed, silhouetted by the day's
afterglow.

Joe Groves was a horse-breaker, drover and a rodeo
rider, the likes of which I had innocently worshipped
as a little girl. Some weeks before, he had arrived from
Queensland and was breaking in horses several miles
away at Mataranka Station. He was soon joined by his
younger brother, Ray, who was equally handsome. We saw
few eligible young men at Mataranka – and my parents
certainly didn't consider Joe eligible!

I would anticipate Joe's visits whenever he came to town
but usually had to be content to catch occasional glimpses
of him as he came and went. Joe and Ray would come to
the store to see us, but instead they would be confronted

by my father, who would chase us girls out the back. He would tend to their needs and, frustrated, the boys would toss their ice-creams into the bushes as they left.

Dressed in his ringer's outfit, Joe looked much younger than his thirty-three years. He always wore the customary high-heeled riding boots with American Levi's jeans and body-hugging R.M. Williams shirts that showed off his fit, muscular body. He had a way of pushing his Akubra back to sit at a jaunty angle, which would drop a rag of blond curls onto his forehead, adding a little softness to his otherwise rugged appearance. But on one particular evening he was dressed like I had never seen him before. He was wearing a neat white nylon shirt opened casually at the neck to expose just enough chest hair. His usually tousled locks were slicked back, but still fell with that careless coil onto his forehead that accentuated his penetrating blue eyes. He had a strong nose with a bump on the bridge and gently flared nostrils with yummy lips and a square jaw. He was as fit as a Mallee bull and drop-dead gorgeous! I had served him in the store several times before without losing my composure, but that evening Joe's masculine good looks almost caused my eyes to hang from their sockets. I could hardly breathe. Talk about chemistry! 'Oh God, don't let him notice,' I thought. But how could he not notice? It felt like a slow-motion movie as I studied all these details, but in fact it was an instantaneous appraisal done in the time it took my heart to resume its regular rhythm. 'Breathe, girl, breathe!' I said to myself.

'G'day,' was all he said.

My heart started to beat again, although somewhat erratically, as I regained my composure. This was Saturday night and I wondered if it were possible that Joe was actually planning to invite me out. I knew I would not be permitted to go, but at least an invitation would show he was interested.

Shyly, I returned his smile and walked towards the counter, trying not to stare, but I did notice then how the nylon shirt accentuated his muscular shoulders and tapered neatly into the trim waist of his fashionable, black-belted terylene trousers. To this day I will never forget my amazement when, on further inspection, I realised that this almost impeccable vision ran down to a pair of totally bare feet!

'Any mail?' he asked.

The post office was closed, but I reluctantly handed him a perfumed letter that was obviously from his girlfriend down south.

Because I operated the telephone exchange and sent the telegrams, I knew Joe had this girlfriend who he sometimes called and who was costing him plenty, financially and emotionally. Happy to see he wasn't in a hurry to open her letter, I began to prattle on about anything that I thought would interest him.

'Read any of these?' he asked, rifling through the paperback novels on the counter.

I blushed a little then, hoping he hadn't guessed that these were the secret source of my sex education.

'Oh no,' I fibbed, 'they're new books. We're not allowed to read them.'

He seemed lonely. He didn't want much. The few items that he asked for, I deliberately made hard to find; anything to keep him there. Mum and Dad were still out the back so we chatted for a while, with me throwing in a few very obvious suggestions about what everyone elsewhere would be doing on this Saturday night. Somehow my hints seemed to fall on deaf ears. I assumed he thought I was just a kid, but I was old enough to know that this hunk had broken more hearts than he had horses. When he walked from the store that evening, I envied the lucky lady that he had dressed for. At seventeen, I didn't know and cared even less about his age, or his past. I may not have been his first woman, but I certainly had visions of being his last.

Surprisingly, Joe made a rare visit to the cafe one afternoon several months later to show me his rodeo albums, as he had promised to do on that first evening. By then we were on comfortable talking terms and he casually mentioned that he had met an old mate up at the pub and was considering doing a long droving job for him. My heart sank. Joe must have noticed my disappointment, but he promised to fill me in on all the details when he returned. Little did he know that my romantic mind was in overdrive, wondering how I could run away from home and go droving with him!

Over time, and with a bit of help from Joe, I gradually began to piece together how this extraordinary droving trip developed.

The pub was usually the main meeting place and business centre in outback towns, and what better excuse could a man find to be there than business? Joe told me how he had run into Ken Hall, a well-known stock and station agent from Dalgety's, at the pub by chance. He had previously worked for Ken as a drover in Queensland.

After several carefully timed ales and the usual small talk, Ken asked Joe if he was interested in taking some stock into Queensland.

'Forget it, Ken, the last thing I want is a droving job,' Joe had laughed.

Apparently, they entertained the bar that evening with yarns of feats of endurance and derring-do, and shared quite a few bottles of rum. Joe said that when he woke up next morning, he ran his head under the cold tap in the old corrugated-iron bathhouse, stared into his bloodshot eyes in the little cracked mirror that hung above the sink, and tried to remember what had transpired. 'Sneaky suspicion you've put your foot in it, old man,' he thought.

Stepping outside, he squinted in the bright morning sunlight and saw Ken gingerly emerging from a hotel room. The penny dropped and Joe remembered that the night before he had in fact sealed his fate for the next six months. He had earned himself a plant of thirty horses complete with packs and saddles, and a job to walk more than 1000 mixed feral scrub cattle over 900 miles to the Dajarra railhead in Queensland.

Both men avoided the word 'breakfast' and drank a strong black coffee together in the morning sun in the beer garden. They confirmed the arrangements that they had discussed the night before and, with heads throbbing, they shook hands and parted company. Joe immediately set out to drive the two hours over rough dirt roads to Moroak Station to meet the owner of the cattle.

Old Les MacFarlane was a big man and was a typical, hard-drinking Territory character. Mrs Mac had offered a smoko of black tea and boiled fruitcake, then quietly disappeared into the store. Joe felt his head would split when one of Mac's four boys ran by squealing as he played with the Aboriginal kids outside the storeroom.

Noticing how ragged Joe looked, Mac teased, 'Here, Joe, have a hair of the dog that bit ya.'

Pouring a huge slug of OP rum from the bottle that sat on the kitchen table in the homestead, he splashed a touch of water into it from a water bottle that hung in the breezeway. Ignoring his refusals, he slapped the enamel mug into Joe's trembling hand. With Mac's encouragement and one big breath Joe downed half the potent brew before they headed up to the airstrip paddock to inspect the cattle.

En route, Mac admitted to Joe that the stock were pretty rough, but suggested that, with a bit of clever handling, he was smart enough get them to Dajarra without too much trouble.

'There's no market for them locally, but Queensland is offering good money for cattle. If I can just get them there, I'll get these bloody banks off me back. Ken tells me you're the man for the job, so what do you say? Do you reckon you can handle it?'

'Reckon that depends,' Joe replied tentatively.

Arriving at the paddock, Joe baulked at the poor condition of the stock. It would take more than a stiff rum to have him find these stock acceptable under any circumstances. They were of all ages, mixed sex and some were quite obviously in calf. All in all, this group was a drover's worst nightmare.

'You've got to be bloody joking, mate,' Joe said incredulously. 'How the hell do you expect me to get these scrubbers through to Queensland in their condition?'

He figured that it was some sort of practical joke until Mac jovially reminded him, with a serious undertone, that he had shaken hands to seal the deal the night before. So, as a man of his word, Joe had no choice but to give it his best shot. As it turned out, this would be the last of the major droving trips to leave the Top End before the cattle trains took over completely.

Joe spent the following weeks preparing to leave, and I could only admire him from a distance as he came and went. But one afternoon he popped into the cafe for a visit and to pick up his albums. Our connection then was still platonic – well, mostly. Cooling water trickled through the thick vines that surrounded the cafe veranda as we sat leafing through his rodeo pictures and talking about his planned trip but, as I had expected, it wasn't long before Mum appeared and demanded, 'And what do you two think you're up to?'

With a cheeky grin that took us both by surprise, Joe replied, 'I'm just asking your daughter to marry me.'

That was about as close as I would ever get to a proposal from Joe.

'Oh, yes, her and how many others?' was Mum's stern reply.

'Well, you too, if you'll have me,' he teased, without missing a beat.

That left Mum stumped for words, and she retreated. I think she needed to have a bit of a giggle in private, but still this was the last time I had alone with Joe for a very long time.

Joe, Ray and the whole Moroak stock camp commenced shoeing horses and sorting packs, saddles and gear in preparation for the long haul into Queensland. They were planning to live for months in isolation with only the comforts of their swags. Swags consisted of a sheet of canvas with several blankets and all personal clothing stuffed into the pouch sewn into the canvas to form a pillow. All private belongings are contained in the swags which were rolled thinly and thrown over pack saddles along with the huge bags of flour and sugar. Flour bags would be first rolled in water to create a hard outer crust to repel the weevils. Large saddle bags would be tightly packed with stores and hung on special hooks, with metal water canteens, billycans and camp ovens. All these essentials were strapped aboard the pack horses. The men would carry their own tin quart pots with handles and lids. These pots could be used for boiling tea or to collect drinking water from boreholes along the way, and, like their hats, were always considered a particularly personal item.

The boys came into the store occasionally for rations, tobacco and new equipment for the journey, but all too soon they were gone, leaving me and my dreams of running away to join them as a cook behind. Just as well, for as it turned out I was the last thing Joe needed to contend with on that long, arduous journey.

On 18 April 1962, the weather was reasonably cool. The monsoon season had just passed, but already the dust was rising as the long train of almost 1000 scrub cattle and thirty horses slowly moved off Moroak. They were cheered on by old Mac and his family, along with all the residents from the blacks' camp, who had assembled along the track to see the drovers off. Joe, as boss drover, rode in the lead. His brother Ray and four other stockmen fanned out and took their places around the herd, while Billy the cook followed behind with the horses and pack saddles.

The dust settled behind them as they headed for their first staging camp, several weeks' slow walk away, at Warlock Ponds near Old Elsey Cemetery.

To expedite their departure, Joe had borrowed the men from Moroak Station for the first leg of the trip while he waited on the stock agent to secure their replacements. Some days after reaching Warlock Ponds, they were met by the agent with two young Aboriginal men in their early twenties. At least six men were required for such a trip, but Banjo and Rankin were the only men the agent could find who were interested in working on this long walk into Queensland.

After making plans to meet again along the way, the agent departed with the promise to bring more ringers before they went through Elliott, the halfway point between Darwin and Alice Springs, sometime in the following month.

'Good luck, Joe,' he said.

Joe replied, 'I need more than luck, mate, I need men. Make sure you bring me the men and the mail before I reach Elliott.'

Ray had originally planned to accompany his brother all the way to Dajarra, but to Joe's dismay he had since been offered a job that suited his family situation better; one that he couldn't refuse. So the following day, Ray and the Moroak boys took their leave from Warlock, leaving Joe alone with his two new stockmen. Cam White, the local stock inspector, signed the permits and waybills and immediately Joe started moving the cattle quietly down the old telegraph line to Number 7 Bore near Elliott. The stock had to be inspected there again and dipped for ticks before they were moved off down the much-fabled Barkly stock route on that epic journey into Queensland.

Although I secretly planned to run away and join him given half the chance, I guess I really didn't expect to see Joe again. While all this went on I made the most of my days at Mataranka and waited impatiently for my life to unfold.

9

Bucking the system

Our days at Mataranka consisted of routine schooling, church, meals, constant work and very little socialising, so we all looked forward to the annual races. People would descend upon the tiny town in droves. The carnival atmosphere was contagious and the town would explode into life. The outlying stations would bring in their grass-fed stockhorses to race and the bookies would take bets on them, and the two-up game was always a great drawcard. A rodeo and gymkhana would follow on the Sunday, and it would be a wonderful mingling of people from all walks of life. For such a special occasion, we would sell huge red king crabs that were bigger than dinner plates. These were a luxury for the inebriated, bow-legged ringers, who would usually stand at the counter and crack them open to devour them on the spot. The mess was something we endured and I still associate the smell of crab with the Mataranka races.

Barbara returned home on one such occasion, and we three older sisters, now fifteen, sixteen and eighteen years old, made our debut, after a fashion, at the Race Ball. This was the first time we had been presented socially as young ladies. I dressed in a slim-fitting, white lace brocade frock with matching white high heels that I had sacrificed my total savings on; I was paid only a couple of pounds a week and the dress and shoes had cost me around seventy. I had found this outfit in a southern mail order catalogue. A few girls my own age had come down from Katherine with their beaus and they wore the modern rock 'n' roll outfits of that era. Although I probably looked overdressed, I felt quite sexy in a Marilyn Monroe kind of way; like a princeless Cinderella.

There were probably a hundred people at the dance, which commenced after the races in the pub gardens underneath the beautiful poinciana trees. The music was supplied via the pub's jukebox. Then, after the pub closed, the dance continued down at the Mataranka Station homestead.

Even under the ever-watchful eyes of our parents, we girls really had a ball. We were high on music and dance and just the fact that we were actually stepping out of the doldrums. I'm sure my parents felt they were throwing their daughters to the wolves. There were a few lads our own age down from Katherine and some station managers and ringers enjoying the evening, but although Dad was meant to be introducing his daughters to society, he was very particular about who we danced with. As insurance, he would ask a larger lady to dance, only to rudely use her as a battering ram, clumsily colliding with any fellow seen dancing too close to us. Dancing on a three-penny piece, he called it. No, nothing less than a successful scholar or doctor would do for his daughters.

Crocodile hunting was legal then and there were several groups of wild young men from the south who would venture out to those huge, isolated rivers to shoot or trap these reptiles for a living. We never heard of a crocodile attack and even with this constant hunting, their numbers never dwindled. These fellows earned excellent money for crocodile leather in the south. At one time they arrived back at Mataranka from their holidays, driving an expensive Rolls-Royce, wearing battered cowboy hats, shorts, singlets and, of course, no shoes. Mum and Dad were still not impressed by their success, so naturally we good Catholic girls were automatically shepherded away from these scruffy fellows, and probably just as well too.

Dad remained the military-styled disciplinarian who ruled his brood with an iron hand, which we constantly tried to avoid. Heaven help us if we were ever in the way of one of his tirades. But eventually this particular worm turned.

As a child, I had injured my hand by running it through the washing-machine wringers. Consequently, I developed a habit of holding it in a limp-wristed manner which drove my father to distraction. I was doing this while I cooked for customers over the hot wood stove one Saturday afternoon.

While no one else in the family was allowed to swear, my father wasn't bound by the same rules. That particular day, he marched into the kitchen roaring, 'What the fuck have I told you about standing like that?' and, lashing out with his huge boot, he kicked me solidly between the legs.

The pain shot through my body and I saw red. I had finally had enough. I turned, looked him in the eye defiantly, and tipped the pan of food upside down on top of the stove. I told him to feed his own damned customers and I walked out.

I kept walking for hours that afternoon, lost, way out the back of Mataranka, following the dusty army roads that seemed to go nowhere, until I finally circled the town and arrived back at an old deserted fettler's cottage on its outskirts. I was hot, dry and hungry but at least there was water there. I had nowhere else to go, but I was determined that I wasn't going home. When the family, searching for me, pulled up outside in the car, I disappeared underneath the house and sat holding my breath.

'Have a good look, son,' my father called to Mark.

'She's not in here,' Mark yelled in reply, after a cursory glance around the house, and they left.

It was almost dark when the policeman, old Denny Connigan, turned up with his black tracker and his dogs, so I decided to turn myself in. We didn't talk as Denny drove me home that evening. He had a fair idea what was going on, but it was domestic, so he asked no questions and we kids were trained to maintain the family's privacy.

I kept out of my father's way as best I could that evening, but he was livid, drinking and yelling about how he had searched for me in the heat until his tongue was swollen, but it fell on deaf ears because, just quietly, I was glad.

Mum would never argue with my father. She would never give him that satisfaction. She seemed to be able to handle him most of the time with what he called her 'silent act'. My mother was his rock. In his own way he loved her to distraction but she could shatter him with her usual reply to his constant nagging for a response: 'Jim, you may wear me down physically, but you will never get inside my head.'

We were used to his outbursts, but one evening I was horrified to find my mother hiding from him in the shed in the backyard. It brought memories flooding back of another night when, as a little girl, I had found my mother in the same situation in the cold laundry in our backyard in Sturt Street. I never saw evidence that my father ever hit my mother, but there were times when she was plainly terrified of him and I hated him for that. I couldn't help her and I could see no solution. All I could think to say to her was, 'But, Mum, you married him!'

She didn't need to be reminded. She looked at me with lonely, sad eyes as if I were chastising her and replied in her usual stoic way, 'I know that, Mary. I'm not complaining.'

And she never did. She was purely the mother and never the friend or confidante, so she never shared her feelings with us, always keeping us in our place. She seemed locked in an invisible capsule for survival and nobody could get to her. As an isolated, submissive Catholic wife, she had no one to confide in apart from the priest. However, she was determined to successfully complete what she had started, whatever the cost, and the personal cost of marrying this Catholic military man was enormous. He should probably have been treated for some personality disorder, but in those days that was never an option, so we could do nothing but lie low and wait for these 'turns' to blow over.

Confess your sins each Saturday and start all over again. This was an easy option for Catholics like my father, but no amount of church or confessions could excuse my father's behaviour, which changed little over the years. To give him his due, there was no government support then, and having to educate and provide for the eleven children that he and my mother produced was a mountain to climb in any man's language. Although they were no longer support-ing their first three sons, they had needed to become very resourceful to provide for eight children in this unfamiliar no-man's-land.

All work and no play definitely made for a pretty monoto-nous life. Apart from a few singalongs with guitar-strumming cowboys in the cafe, there was no entertainment in town, but there were some good times to be had if you made your own fun. To watch movies, we had to drive an hour to Katherine, so my parents bought a sixteen-millimetre projector and ran black and white movies for the locals.

Larrimah was the closest little town, forty-seven miles south. It was about the same size as Mataranka and was at the end of the railway line from Darwin. June was the pub-keeper's daughter from Larrimah, and she would sometimes come to the movies. She was a beautiful young woman, just a few years older than I was, and she used to swan into the store with her beaus, looking for all the world like a stray movie starlet. She wore nylon stockings with straight seams and high-heeled shoes with swirling taffeta skirts, and she would leave me fantasising about one day being just as sophisticated and worldly as she appeared to be. I really envied her freedom.

I was the family comedienne, but although life for me may have seemed *just a bowl of cherries*, I was bursting at the seams to shed my childhood. I felt trapped and my mind continued to wander to the goings-on I imagined in the outside world. I had my whole life ahead of me but I felt like a prisoner. To my frustration, my father contin-ued to thwart my every romantic endeavour. At one stage, he chopped my hair short and my fringe off to ensure I looked unattractive to any potential beau. But, like any normal teenager, I still saw it as my prerogative to buck the system.

In a desperate bid to have my despair recognised, I got hold of some sleeping pills. Then, one afternoon, just like in the movies, I lay on my bed in a dramatically attractive position for my fashionable swan song. Warily, I took a small handful of the pills, only to wake hours later posi-tively refreshed, but feeling awfully foolish and dejected that nobody had noticed my possible demise. Obviously, if I had really planned to die, I would have taken the whole bottle, with terrible consequences, but this pathetic cry for attention was rather comical. I could hardly complain to anyone about my failure to attract the attention I was seeking by my dangerous and foolish shenanigans so, with a shrug, I abandoned the idea.

I spent most of any spare time I had with the Jerry the horse and Blackie, my poddy foal. Blackie was probably six months old and had no mother when I spotted him alone in the bush, and I yarded him with the help of my brother Mark. At thirteen, Mark was adept at most of the handyman chores required for survival around Mataranka. We spent hours running Blackie through the bush on foot, eventually trapping him just on dusk in the Mataranka stockyards. Then we led and pushed the reluctant foal the several miles home. Finally I had Blackie, a horse of my own, and he soon became friendly with Jerry.

Early one afternoon, several months later, my father was roaring again. 'What the bloody hell are those horses doing at that trough? You know we're low on water.'

Why he had not cut the water to the trough was beyond me. As I began to walk over to chase the horses, he appeared with the .22 rifle, which he began to load.

'I'll teach the bastards to stay away from here,' he growled. I thought perhaps he would fire into the air. It never entered my head that he would actually shoot our horses until I heard that sickening thwack.

As Jerry reared and limped away I turned on my father, standing with the rifle in his hands. 'You bastard!' I swore.

He looked at me like a guilty little boy and tried to explain that he'd only meant to hit Jerry's rump, not his gut. I ran off after Jerry, who by now was lying by the railway tracks to die a slow, agonising death. It was heart-breaking to watch as Blackie, now a young stallion, tried valiantly to make Jerry get to his feet. But Jerry died that night. To make matters worse, when we went to burn the carcass the next day, we found that Jerry had been butchered by a local family for meat. There was no apology or consolation from my father and the subject never arose again, but I was devastated.

Totally fed up, I hitched a ride out of town on one of the delivery trucks. There was only one road through Mataranka, so everyone knew everybody else's movements, and it wasn't long before my father was hot on my trail. He was alerted by the truckies themselves, who were concerned for my welfare.

Because most of the truckies and bus drivers were our friends, I was relatively safe during my escapades, but I understood years later the worry I must have caused my poor parents.

10

Incorrigible adolescence

While I was struggling to shed the shackles of family, Joe was battling the elements on his epic journey across the harsh, dry, unforgiving country between Mataranka and Dajarra in Queensland.

With 250 miles of the Birdum stock route and its gnarled Bullwaddy thickets behind them, Joe and the two men still had the worst to go. The rest of the drove would take them along the arid Barkly stock route, across the Queensland border and into Dajarra. The stock would be watered at the government bores set up at intervals specifically for droving. By 1962, because there was so little droving activity, these bores were usually in disrepair; water was a blessing and never a promise.

It was always going to be a long, slow journey, as the animals had to be inspected and dipped for ticks several times before crossing the Queensland border. This involved holding them up for several days in the government yards and with a stock inspector present, plunging each animal into a trough of tick poison. It was Joe's intention to move the stock as slowly as possible, feeding them along the way on whatever they could forage. In this way he anticipated that they would be in much better condition for sale at the other end of the journey.

He had already chosen the cattle that would lead the herd. Behind them, each animal then selected its own position to travel in the group, a position which they would invariably hold for the entire trip. This positioning made it much easier for the boss drover to notice if any cattle had been lost during the previous night's watch.

Each man knew his own job and there would be very little conversation along the way, as the three were kept busy tending to the work of six men.

Usually there was a designated horse tailer and cook. This rider would be in charge of the spare horses and pack saddles with the precious supplies and would push them ahead to a designated spot to set up camp and prepare meals. But in this instance, because they were so short-handed, the horses were trailed along behind the cattle.

Joe prepared the food. The staple diet consisted of potatoes and onions, salt beef, damper with syrup and black tea with plenty of sugar for the boys. He did any cooking on the days that the stock were held up to graze. Dampers were baked in camp ovens in the ground and Johnny cakes (a flour and water mix) cooked on the coals. It was rare that their own animals were slaughtered for beef; the only meat they could carry was dry salted.

They had no vehicles or communications, so as Joe moved further inland our updates on their progress from stock inspectors and passing travellers ceased and he was soon out of sight and out of my young mind.

Back at Mataranka the sun still rose and set and the seasons changed, but not much else did. Nothing out of the ordinary happened. Barbara had not settled into nursing in Darwin, so she returned home for good. The business had increased and she was helping out in the shop. By then, Mum had handed the school over to teachers supplied by the government.

A big event for us was the day a box arrived from Myers in Melbourne containing three new cotton frocks for Mum's forty-ninth birthday. We sold bright cotton floral dresses in the shop, but special clothing had to be ordered through catalogues and this was an exciting occasion indeed. We girls threw a party for her that weekend, and I styled her beautiful, dark brown hair into the coiled beehive fashion of the day. She looked spectacular. I made and decorated a special cake and between us all we had put together some snacks while my father managed the refreshments. Denny, the policeman, and his wife were invited, along with a couple of the local station managers and their wives, and soon the party was in full swing. It was wonderful to see Mum so light-hearted.

Over the next few months, Mum had a few emergency trips to Katherine hospital as her asthma began to progressively worsen, along with Dad's disposition.

Suddenly, it seemed Mum became aware of how my father had been treating us, and she decided it was time to act. The move was sudden and left our heads spinning. She gave us a choice: we could go with her or stay. Leaving Barbara and Mark with Dad in the store, she packed up and headed back to Melbourne. This was almost three years after we had moved north. With her other six children loaded into her little station wagon, Mum set off on that huge trip as the sole driver. She drove the entire journey, back along that red, dusty highway, across the desert through Oodnadatta. We stopped only to camp with friends at Tennant Creek, Alice Springs, Port Augusta and Adelaide. Finally, after a week, we arrived at Grandma's home in North Fitzroy. Mum had finally taken a stand. We were free at last.

There was no government support then and no relatives, except Grandma in her tiny cottage, interested in accommodating such a large family. My brother Jimmy, who by now was financially secure, was prepared to set Mum up in a general store and look after her, but after a constant barrage of pleading phone calls from my father she decided that the best place for her was back in the Northern Territory with him and her family. Dad flew down and Mum turned the little Hillman around and they drove all the way back to Mataranka with the little ones, but not before she ensured that Kate, Frances and I were going to be all right.

I had a good voice and, if I could not be a nurse, I wanted to become a singer. I certainly didn't have my father's approval, but Mum had decided to give me this chance to follow my dreams on my own steam. She was not able to support me, but called in a favour and secured a job for me as a receptionist at Superior Dairies, the ice-cream factory in Port Melbourne. She left me in a boarding house for young ladies run by the Mercy nuns near the Albert Park Lake. At the same time she left Kate and Frances at a boarding school at Kilmore in country Victoria, where she herself had been schooled as a young girl. I guess she thought that the nuns would keep her girls in line and safe.

This desperate attempt to give us a second chance at civilisation had happened all too quickly. As I kissed my mother goodbye, I felt I was being deserted. I was left in this cold, wet city with a new trench coat and five pounds in cash to my name. At least I was free, to some extent, but living in Melbourne had certainly lost any appeal for me. I missed the Northern Territory and the familiarity of my hometown. The other boarders had friends and family and seemed to get on with their lives undeterred, but I felt like a misfit. I soon found myself broke and miserable. By the time I had paid my rent there was little left over from my wages and, without support, I had no idea and no hope of ever pursuing a career in singing or anything else.

I shared my room with Kathleen whenever she was in town. She was part Aboriginal but had her Irish father's colouring. I suspect that the nuns had carefully selected her as my roommate, and it turned out to be a good choice. We got along really well and spent hours together chatting and making the ruffled petticoats that were worn in that era. The explosion of rock 'n' roll was now running like adrenaline through the veins of most of my generation and I was no exception. The nuns were often driven to despair by the racket of our impromptu dance sessions. I loved to rock 'n' roll.

An activity I didn't love so much was smoking, but it was fashionable, so I did it, even under threat of expulsion by the nuns.

'Look out,' Kathleen whispered as the soft white fingers of Sister Rosemary quietly pushed open our bedroom door one evening.

'Who's smoking in here?' snapped the nun as she made a beeline for my bed.

'No one, Sister,' we chorused.

Lying with my knees up, in desperation, I had quickly jammed the lit cigarette, filter first, into my belly button, pulling the sheet up to my chin. As she approached me, I told her that I was naked and I dared her to pull down the sheet. Instead she snatched the cigarette packet hidden beside my bed and strode out of the room just as the burning cigarette began to protrude through the large brown circle that it had burned on the sheet. I was pretty worried as I bundled the evidence amongst the laundry the next morning, but at least I was safe for another day. I was a free spirit and the nuns complained to my parents that I was incorrigible. I would not knuckle down to their discipline.

Meanwhile, at work, a mysterious and fascinating invention called a photocopier had materialised, and I had horrified the management by photocopying a five-pound note, just to try it out. I wondered why nobody else had thought of it before.

'Why is everyone so amazed?' I wondered, not realising that it was illegal.

It wasn't long before I received a letter from management explaining that they were overstaffed and, sadly, because I was the last to start, I would therefore be the first to leave. So, only three months after I'd arrived in town, Dad, who was alerted by the nuns that I had lost my job, turned up unannounced to collect me and take me back to Mataranka.

11

The Barkly or bust

Joe and his men had pushed on for months through drought conditions and then blinding storms, when man and beast could only turn their backs into the rain and wind. In the midst of a storm, lightning would sometimes transfer from the horns of one beast to the next, simultaneously lighting up the whole herd with sheet electricity. There were no campfires or swags unrolled on those evenings.

Their lips and hands were cracked and bleeding from the wind and weather. The cold at night was unbearable, and often dry cow dung was used for fires because of the shortage of trees.

The cattle had to be watched twenty-four hours a day, so sleep was limited. With so few stockmen, they would take turns at a few hours' shut-eye on their swags on the hard ground, sometimes too tired even to unroll them. Sleep-deprived and edgy, they would sometimes flop exhausted to sleep, then find themselves running for horse or tree cover as they woke in terror to the dreaded drumming vibration of rushing cattle, either real or imaginary. It took very little to cause these wild cattle to rush (or stampede), and there is almost nothing more frightening than the rumble of a thousand sets of hooves, while the ground trembles beneath you in the dark.

More often than not, after many a hard, hot day, they would arrive to camp at bore sites with the 1000-plus thirsty animals, only to find the bores broken down and no water available. They would have no alternative but to push on in the hope that water would eventually be found.

There were times when the thirsty stock had to be watered in tiny, muddy waterholes. It is difficult to convince a thirsty beast to wait its turn, so before the cattle could smell the water, the herd was divided into smaller groups. Usually, one man would stand in the middle of the waterhole to spook the cattle and stop them rushing and muddying that precious water, while the other men tried to hold the rest of the mob back. On occasions, to avoid perishing from thirst themselves, the men had to strain muddy water through their hats to drink. If that wasn't enough to cause dysentery, then the foul water from some of the bores was enough to cause them to ride along for days with their pants undone in preparation for a quick dismount.

As they moved slowly towards Dajarra, all they dreamed of was a drink of fresh water. But still, the miles crept by, day after day after long, weary day, on towards the edge of the much-fabled and mysterious Min Min light country. Joe could only hope that Rankin and Banjo were not familiar with this legend, because they would surely flee and abandon the drove.

There is no scientific explanation for the Min Min phenomenon, but the Aborigines say that these mysterious balls of light are ancient ethereal mothers looking for their babies. These spooky, unidentifiable balls of light appear to stalk or to lead travellers, luring them for miles across gullies and through fences, only to disappear as mysteriously as they came, defying any logical or scientific explanation.

Joe's only outside contacts for those months droving were the occasional stock inspectors and the owners of several properties that he passed through along the way. At those times he would replenish his supplies and pick up any news available. At every opportunity he would send telegrams to Ken demanding more stockmen, but to no avail.

After three months and 700 miles, the herd was dipped again at Lake Nash, near the Queensland border, still almost 200 miles from their destination. Only then did the agent finally arrive from Cloncurry with two of the promised stockmen.

'What took you so bloody long?' Joe growled, but his frustration fell on deaf ears.

The agent beamed as he shook Joe's hand. 'We knew you could do it!'

'No bloody choice!' Joe replied.

Off in the distance the cattle looked fairly calm as they grazed on the reserve. A thin haze of cigarette smoke rose in the morning sun where Banjo and Rankin sat on their horses with their whips hung over their shoulders.

'One more day and the boys would have been out of tobacco. Then there would have been real trouble,' Joe warned.

Unloading the stores Ken had delivered, he turned and greeted the two new fellows with a handshake and they retrieved their swags and saddles from the tray-back.

Joe offered the new men billy tea and told them to hook their swags on board the packs, then saddle up.

'We're moving out of here straight after lunch,' he said. 'Shouldn't take us more than a fortnight to hit Dajarra, I reckon.'

Bruce and Alan were in their thirties. When they shook hands with Joe, he said he had a gut feeling that they were going to be trouble – their hands were soft and their handshakes were weak – but Joe was in no position to be choosy. He figured that anything was better than nothing at the time.

Things went well enough until the cold midnight shift several days later. Joe had just rolled out his swag by the dying campfire after a long shift watching the herd when he noticed that Banjo and Rankin were riding back into camp while the others still slept.

'Who the hell's supposed to be watching the cattle and fixing this bloody fire?' he demanded.

'I'm buggered,' came the sullen reply from under the canvas.

'So who's not?' Joe roared. 'Get off your bloody back and give those blokes a break.'

'Get stuffed,' was the muffled reply.

With that, Joe exploded. He grabbed the camp shovel and dumped a load of embers from the fire onto Alan's swag.

'This'll get you up, you lazy bastard.'

And sure enough it did. Alan flew out of the swag, kicking at the coals and frantically shaking the smouldering ashes from his swag. Not surprisingly, a hot-headed altercation ensued. There was no way these blokes could outdo Joe in a fist-fight, even together, so, cursing over their shoulders, they walked off camp taking Banjo and Rankin with them and left Joe alone on a reserve with over a thousand head of cattle and horses.

And he thought, 'Shit, this is interesting!'

The four walked several miles into a small township nearby and complained about Joe's behaviour to the local policeman. On investigating, the officer soon understood the situation and he contacted the Cloncurry stock agents, who brought out Mickey and Rooster, another couple of Aboriginal lads, to assist Joe. But in Queensland,

Aborigines were under the control of missionaries. They required permits to leave their designated areas and the policeman immediately recognised them as mission runaways. Tension was rising as they sat with downcast eyes awaiting the outcome, but Joe reasoned with the officer, who thankfully turned a blind eye to this new dilemma and allowed Mickey and Rooster to stay on with specific instructions to return home when the drove was completed.

Joe planned to move the cattle even more slowly now in an attempt to feed and fatten them for a sale, and on 16 July he moved them on from Lake Nash and commenced the last stage towards Dajarra. The boys worked well for the remainder of the trip, but just two days from the railhead Mickey carelessly threw an empty tobacco tin away. It clanked loudly on the rocks and was enough to startle and rush the cattle. This could have wiped out the entire operation, not to mention the handlers, but each man knew what to do. With great agility and horsemanship the boys held the main herd together and, after a painstaking search, they eventually tracked and found those stragglers which had escaped into the scrub.

Because of their quality, it was difficult for the agents to find a buyer and the stock continued to be held on the road. Finally, in August, after four gruelling months of births, deaths and disasters, Joe delivered the original number of cattle to the Dajarra railhead.

For only three men to complete that epic journey with 1000 head of cattle was unheard of, particularly as the numbers had been delivered intact and saleable. It was a real testament to Joe's determination.

By comparison, life back at Mataranka was relatively easy as long as I continued to find joy in the little things. I loved my family and was fond of my little hometown with its unique characters. I tried hard to accept my position, spending my days working on the exchange or in the store, but after Melbourne I was lonely for people my own age. I craved a social life.

Sometimes, the Aboriginal women would invite me to sit with them in the dust under a shady tree and would show me how to split the leaves of the pandanus to weave them into traditional floor mats and baskets. At other times, Charlie, who was a very clever artist, would show me how he did his colourful, skeletal, traditional art works. There was little else to keep me entertained apart from work.

Mum was allowing me a little more freedom, but Dad had not changed, so my yearning to escape the confines of my home life at Mataranka never ceased. This branch was preparing to fall off the family tree. When I made my next serious break for freedom, I removed the connecting plugs from the post office switchboard and hid them where they wouldn't be found until I was long gone. With the exchange out of action, I had literally closed down the communications for the entire district. Then, early that morning as the sun rose and the little town slept, I hitched my final ride to freedom on a bus that had pulled up at the pub overnight, and I headed straight for the sanctuary of the church in Katherine and Father Ormonde, our very down-to-earth priest and family friend. He had been a priest for sixty years and now ministered to our huge rural Katherine district. He acted as mediator, pointing me in the right direction, and I immediately secured accommodation at a very well-policed young ladies' lodge and a job on the main telephone exchange.

Finally, my parents realised that I was unstoppable and reluctantly agreed to let me go. I had no clue where I was heading, but at last I was responsible for my own choices and had begun to walk on my own two feet . . . for a little while, anyway.

12

A load of bulls

With the droving done, Joe paid his men and they promptly disappeared. Tired and dusty, yet elated, he set his weary horses free on the reserve. Then he threw his swag onto the train that was hauling the cattle and rode in a carriage with them back to Cloncurry. From there, he hitched a ride to Mt Isa, intending to compete in the town's rodeo.

He had the stock agent book him into the swankiest hotel in town. By all accounts, quite a stir went through that hotel foyer as, smelly, dusty and tired, with four months' beard and hair growth, Joe strode through the lobby of the luxury hotel carrying his swag on his shoulder. The receptionist cast a few sideways glances at the apparition at his desk.

'Good afternoon, sir,' he said stiffly. 'May I show you to your room?'

While customers gaped, the porter quickly hustled him through the lobby and to his room, aware that this was not a man to be trifled with. Not only did he have a big cheque in his pocket, but Joe's reputation had preceded him. He drank, fought, rode, worked and played harder than most and, believe me, there were plenty of tough men in Australia's Top End back then.

Joe was brought up tough. As a child he had watched his grandfather, from a far tougher generation, set his own broken leg. Although it finished up jagged enough to hang a pannikin on the shin bone, he lived to ninety-five.

Nothing seemed to daunt Joe; he seemed to fear no man or beast, except snakes, and perhaps my mother. A man of his word, his handshake was a contract, but he also boasted that he was educated by some of the best men and the best cons in the industry. He worked for results, not accolades, and his usual retort to anyone blocking his way or disapproving was simple: 'Stuff 'em!'

Following his usual pattern, it took Joe just six months on the rodeo circuit with his mates to finally see him broke again and looking for work.

Along the way he had bought a flashy new Ford Customline which was constantly packed with his mates and their swags. His tattered dog, Bull (the first), was thrown up on the roof where he rode like an old surfer, and they would travel for days like that to get to the various rodeos on the circuit. There were no speed cameras or breathalysers then, so the boys usually made good time. But one night, after celebrating a particularly successful rodeo, they found themselves spearing off a sharp bend in the road and rolling into the darkness. They rolled five or six times and, with a sickening crunch, came to a grinding halt.

When the dust had settled, Joe slowly looked over his shoulder to discover his inebriated passengers sitting in a daze as if nothing had happened.

Brian Young finally muttered, 'Oh, no, not me bloody guitar!'

'Never mind your bloody guitar,' Joe growled. 'Is everyone all right? Are you other blokes okay?' And to his surprise, they were.

Joe thought he had killed old Bull, though. On the car's first somersault, the dog was catapulted off the roof and had become airborne, but to Joe's delight he reappeared, panting and limping through the long grass in the moonlight.

One by one the doors squeaked open and the men climbed out to survey the damage.

The car sat in knee-high grass with steam pouring from under the bonnet. Amazingly, apart from a few major dents and clods of dirt and grass that now decorated it, the car looked perfectly all right to drive and, what's more, Joe found that the motor still ran.

Astonished at their good fortune, they collected old Bull and gathered whatever possessions they could find. Then they climbed back in and prepared to embark on their journey once again, only to find that the car had lost its front wheels.

Now unable to follow the circuit, Joe found his way back to Moroak Station to trap the large herds of wild brumbies there. He was already planning to walk a herd of these wild horses, skirting the Simpson Desert, to Bourke in north-west New South Wales. These brumbies would be sold as pet meat for a lucrative five pounds a head, and he had employed six Aboriginal stockmen for this next venture.

He was several days into the laborious job of cutting bush timber and building the trap yards on a billabong where these brumbies watered when, unexpectedly, Mac's old Land Rover rumbled into the camp in a cloud of dust. Joe said that he had an uneasy feeling as the big grey-haired man lumbered towards him.

Mac called to Joe as he hung over the top rail of the half-completed yard, 'Do ya think ya could give a bloke a hand with a bit of a problem that I have?'

Joe replied suspiciously, 'That depends, old fella. Let's have smoko and we'll talk about it.'

After organising his men to continue the job, Joe walked over to stoke up the smouldering embers and to boil the billy.

'Joe, I've been talkin' with old Gus Trippe in Darwin and they're desperate for a load of bulls for a trial live shipment overseas. I told him you're just the man for the job.'

'Man's only got two hands,' was Joe's prompt reply.

This was when old Mac decided it was time to bring out the OP rum again. Slopping water from the water bag that hung from the bullbar of his vehicle, he handed Joe a drink and casually changed the subject.

Joe eyed Mac warily, knowing full well that the station owner was lubricating the situation for another approach, but he decided to stretch it out for a while.

They sat in the morning sun while the billy boiled and the other men came in for smoko, sat in the shade for a while and then went back to work again.

'Don't know if you really understand how much work is involved in this horse deal, Mac,' Joe said.

'Yeah, but the bulls will only take a week or so, matey,' Mac insisted.

'You realise, if we get any rain the horses won't come into the trap and our whole horse deal could flop?' Joe argued.

'Look at that sky, Joe. This is going to be a long hot dry season. We can always finish here later; just put the horses back a few weeks is all. This'll be a bit of a challenge for you. It'll be one of the first live shipments of bulls for that overseas market, so we're pretty keen to get a full consignment of big scrub bulls to make a good impression,' replied Mac, and Joe knew that he had just been baited with the word 'challenge'.

After much rum, cajoling and debate, Joe agreed to catch the bulls. He felt uncomfortable about the whole deal, though he couldn't quite put his finger on why. It wasn't long before his doubts were confirmed.

They had been mustering bulls for several days and were about twenty minutes' ride away from their coachers (main herd) when Joe spotted a particularly big ugly roan bull grazing in a gully off to his left, in the shade of some stringy-bark trees.

'You men follow those cattle tracks there and I'll catch you up later,' he said as they moved on ahead.

The bull's head jolted up and it snorted at Joe's approach. Then, lowering and shaking its head in challenge, it scraped the ground with its feet several times before charging. The horse sidestepped the attack on nimble feet and the bull galloped off down the dry, shaly creek bed to safety.

Giving chase at full gallop, Joe intended to shortcut over a rocky ridge, but the usually sure-footed brumby slipped into a hole and they tumbled headfirst into the ditch. Both horse and rider hit the ground with a heavy thud and, unhappily, the horse's body twisted and rolled over its own neck. They lay in a tangled mess, the horse with its head and Joe's leg pinned beneath it. Mercifully, the horse was unable to move as they lay there trapped for ages, with Joe's head between its back legs. Had the horse been able to struggle, it's likely Joe would have been kicked to death.

A boulder ground into Joe's thigh and he yelled for what seemed an eternity in the perishing heat but, apart from a few bird calls, the horse's laboured breath was the only sound he heard.

His men wondered why he was taking so long but, thinking he had a bull down, they finished working with their own bulls. Finally, two fellows tracked Joe to where he lay, exhausted and in excruciating pain. They rolled the horse to its feet and, as it stood dazed and trembling, they lifted Joe aboard another horse. He had a fair idea that his knee was shattered as he rode to where he knew there was an old truck in the neighbouring Beswick stock camp, about ten miles away. From there, they drove him about twenty-five miles into Beswick Station. George Bates and his wife were managing there, and they soon had him dosed up with whatever painkillers they could find, chased down with a very sizeable slug of OP rum. With Joe laid out on an old door, he was transferred onto the back of the station vehicle to be driven for another hour to the hospital at Katherine.

By that time Joe's leg was grotesquely swollen and the local medico decided that he should continue on to the Darwin hospital for what he secretly believed would be an amputation. So with a nurse by his side and finally full of painkillers, they set out to drive another five hours. The ambulance pulled up at each pub along the way for refreshments and by the time they arrived in Darwin, more than twelve hours after Joe's fall, nobody, including the driver, was sober or feeling much pain.

Meanwhile, over on Elsey Station, several hours away by road, Joe's brother, Ray, had been alerted earlier by his Aboriginal stockmen that Joe was in trouble. He couldn't understand what they were so worried about, but they were adamant. 'Boss, your brother, him in big trouble. You gotta go look out longa him.'

Ray knew nothing about telepathy and had no idea how the blacks knew, but on their insistence he went back to the homestead to telephone Moroak. By the time he got through he found that Joe was well on his way into Katherine.

Alone in the Darwin hospital, Joe fought desperately to save his leg against the will of the doctors who wanted to amputate it. They warned him that he could die but he argued, 'Without my bloody leg a man may as well be dead anyway!'

The expected outcome of such an injury under those circumstances would be gangrene infection but Joe had an answer for that. 'Gangrene? Nah. No bug could have survived the amount of rum we drank in the ambulance on that trip to Darwin.'

After many months of healing and learning to walk again, Joe was out of hospital and settling back into Territory life. His knee continued to give him trouble but he was surviving on workers' compensation and looking at the possibilities of taking over the management of a station out on the Roper River.

Then, out of the blue, we came across each other in Darwin.

13

An unromantic encounter

I never got used to the suffocating heat and humidity of Darwin, but in the early dry season, when temperatures sometimes drop below twenty degrees Celsius, Australia's most northern city can be a tropical paradise.

It was the middle of the dry season in 1963 and, unbeknown to each other, Joe and I were both staying in the heart of town at the Vic Hotel. This old building with its sandstone facade was Darwin's most popular watering hole and the only place I could find accommodation. Communal bathrooms were the order of the day and the bedrooms were furnished for the tropics, with open louvres and electric fans.

As luck would have it, early one Saturday evening I ducked across the road to buy a pie for dinner and, lo and behold, I found Joe only seconds from driving away from the hotel footpath with some friends. There were many people out and about so I didn't notice him until a familiar voice said, 'G'day, stranger.'

I was dumbstruck at this chance meeting. I hadn't seen Joe for over a year and he was the furthest thing from my mind.

He was going to have dinner at the home of a Mr and Mrs Berlowitz, so they invited me along. This couple was hoping to draw St Vidgeon Station in a land allocation and they wanted Joe to manage it for them, so the evening was spent planning their strategies.

After a great meal, we took our leave and explored the sights of Darwin in Joe's flash new Holden station wagon. Neither of us had seen the sea in years, so we followed the coast road out to East Point where, clambering down a rough, bushy pathway in the moonlight, we found our own perfect little beach. We didn't talk much as we walked, soaking up the romance of that balmy tropical evening. Then we sat on the rocks watching a few dark boats bobbing on the shimmering water, backlit by the glittering lights of the city. The waves were gently whooshing along the shoreline and the hermit crabs scuttled across the sand in their thousands, doing whatever hermit crabs are supposed to do. A few happy voices rose further along the shoreline as another falling star dropped to the horizon. We circled each other, intoxicated by the magic of the evening, neither wanting to make the first move, uncomfortable that this impromptu connection was all happening too quickly, but still unable to say goodnight. In the early hours of the morning, Joe threw caution to the wind and kissed me. And that was that!

The air had begun to cool so Joe rolled out his swag in the back of his station wagon. Then, overlooking the star-spangled Arafura Sea, we finally came together as nature had always intended and slept in each other's arms until the sun burrowed through the canopy above.

I had only recently found my independence. I had friends and a new way of life working on the telephone exchange in Katherine. I also had a special friend called Mac, who was about six years older than me. He was a tall, nice-looking man with a steady job. Together, we had decided that Katherine needed a laundromat, so we planned to start one, along with another girlfriend. My trip to Darwin that Friday was to purchase office equipment and I was also going to cheer for Mac in a football match the following day.

When he arrived the following afternoon, Joe and I arranged to meet him for a drink. It wasn't until we met up that day that I became aware that Mac was a serious contender for my hand. I fondly remember him breaking into song as we sat with drinks under the huge breeze battens (or punkahs) that floated to and fro overhead in the tropical lounge of the Darwin Hotel. I had never heard him sing before. I was amazed and embarrassed when he serenaded me with a beautiful rendition of 'You Belong to Me'. It was a brave and romantic gesture indeed, but far too late.

Joe, on the other hand, was never the romantic type, being clumsy and shy with words. I think the most romantic thing he ever said to me in those early days was, 'Woman, I'm gonna stick to you like shit to a blanket!' Thank God actions speak louder than words! The male-to-female ratio in the Territory was at least ten to one, and I guess if I had really wanted romance I should have chosen Mac, or Murray, or Harry, or Billy, or anyone but Joe. Apart from his animal magnetism and good looks, it is hard to say what attracted me to him. He was the strong, silent type and it was probably that mysterious, quiet strength of character, together with his old-fashioned values and insatiable spirit of adventure that appealed.

At this stage, I was still a free woman, albeit only eighteen, and I fully intended to return home to Katherine after the football match the next night. Joe had offered to give me a lift, along with his mate Gordon, who was one of the truck drivers I knew from Mataranka. Because Mac's vehicle had developed engine problems, Joe also offered, at my request, to take him and his mates along with us. On that Sunday afternoon we departed for that long trip back to Katherine with five big, hairy footballers squashed in the back of the station wagon. I sat sandwiched between Joe and Gordon in the front seat, playing music on Joe's battery-operated record player that was balanced on my knees. If I was not quick enough, each time we hit a bump or rounded a corner the needle would skid across the record with that awful, nerve-grating screech, but it was the best we had back then, and we were young and hungry for music.

We had gone several hundred miles, singing, joking around and dodging the many wallabies, emus, pigs, horses and buffalo that haunted the Stuart Highway at night. We were almost at the Hayes Creek pub when Joe turned to give me one of his special looks and – BANG! We were screeching to a halt with an unfortunate wallaby hanging out of the car's radiator.

There wasn't a lot anyone could do to fix things so, when the footballers' bus eventually caught up, Mac and the others piled onto it and headed for Katherine, promising to send out a new radiator. Joe asked me then if I wanted to stay or go on with Mac and I made my decision without hesitation.

No help arrived and it was after midnight, so in the wee hours we begged chewing gum from the Hayes Creek Inn and chewed frantically, and Joe patched the leaks with it. Then, stopping at every creek along the way to top up the radiator, we limped back to Darwin to have the car repaired.

We booked into Mayse Young's hotel overlooking the Nightcliff beach and the next morning we went shopping. Joe wanted to buy me an engagement ring. Twenty-one was the age of consent, so my parents could still prevent me from marrying. Regardless, Joe bought me a beautiful diamond and sapphire ring. There wasn't a lot of romance attached to the ring; it just seemed like a good idea at the time. He was a man of few words so, in my youthful exuberance, it never occurred to me to question why we never discussed marriage. I just thought it was a foregone conclusion. I guess his idea was to let the world know that we were thinking about it and, in the meantime, I was taken.

Joe wanted to take me out that evening but I had no proper clothes to wear so, because he would never be seen within cooee of a dress shop, he handed me his wallet and sent me off to buy a dress. This was quite an adventure for me. I had never been in a boutique before and I had little idea of prices, but I was determined to look stunning for my man.

I was so proud of the gorgeous black chiffon that the lady in the shop had sold me and I couldn't wait to show Joe. But his face paled when I told him that the dress and all the accessories had cost him sixty-eight pounds. In my excitement, I had spent all the money he had in the world.

'That looks great, hon,' he said as, ashen-faced, he slid slowly into a chair and gazed disbelievingly into the empty wallet.

Joe must have borrowed money, because we not only enjoyed that evening together but, wanting to show me off in town the following night, he sent me off again to buy a smashing red satin Chinese cheongsam dress that we had seen while window shopping. This time he gave me the exact money. Then we dined together in one of the many fabulous Chinese restaurants in Darwin. After dinner, we met up with Gordon again and proceeded to kick up our heels as only a bushie knows how.

The next day we packed our gear, rolled our swag and said goodbye to Gordon, and Joe and I headed bush for the first time together.

I was simply living for the present then. I don't know that either of us thought this thing would last, but we agreed to live by the motto of the hit song, 'We'll Sing in the Sunshine'. The words of this song warned us of the improbabilities of a future together but it finished with the line, 'We sang in the sunshine and laughed in the rain,' and that all sounded pretty good to me.

On our way through Katherine to Victoria River Downs Station, I phoned Mum from the post office.

'Hello, Mum.'

'Hello, Mary,' she replied in a reserved tone.

She seemed strained, waiting for whatever bombshell I was about to drop, so I continued nervously, 'I just called to tell you that I'm engaged.'

In a resigned voice, she replied, 'Oh, I expected as much, Mary. To whom?'

'To Joe Groves.'

The explosion that followed that announcement could almost be felt physically.

'WHAT? JOE GROVES!' she roared. I had never heard her respond like that before and it left me quite shocked.

I don't remember who hung up first, but I felt totally dejected as I walked slowly back to Joe, waiting in the car. Then, to my surprise, one of the telephonists ran out from the exchange and called, 'Mary, Mary, your father is waiting on the line to talk to you.'

Strangely, Dad seemed much calmer than Mum. 'I hear you're engaged,' he said.

'Yes, Dad.'

'Hmmm, that's nice. Who to?'

'To Joe Groves.'

'WHAT? JOE GROVES!' And a second explosion shook the post office.

Naturally my parents were concerned about our age difference and they probably knew more about Joe than I wanted to, but their response only strengthened my resolve.

Sad but determined, I hung up the handpiece again and, with a heavy heart, left my family behind to embark on a life of adventure. I was young and unafraid, but, then, I had no idea of the dramas that lay ahead.

Although Mum's health had been better for several years in this new climate, it had recently started to decline again, so, soon after that incident, my parents decided it was time to move – they had lost me, and to avoid losing any more children to the wilds, they left Mataranka. They figuratively cut me loose and headed back to civilisation in an attempt to keep the rest of the family safe from harm.

14

The Moolooloo mule

Our first experience of working together was horse-breaking on Moolooloo, an outstation of Victoria River Downs, some 250 miles south-west of Katherine. Once again, the trip was over rough dirt roads, with not another soul for hours in any direction. That first night, after driving for hours, we camped on the ground alongside the road. We slept heavily, snuggled up together in Joe's swag, and didn't wake until next morning, when the crows in the trees above began dropping small branches on us. They were checking to see if we were still alive.

We freshened up with water from the waterbag that hung on the bullbar in front of the radiator and arrived at VRD at around 10 a.m., just in time for smoko.

VRD was one of the larger Territory pastoral leases at 4772 square miles. The main station compound resembled a small corrugated-iron township with the manager's residence surrounded by several other homes. It boasted a general store and post office, a garage, blacksmith, butcher, bakehouse and even a movie shed. We sat with the entire staff and their families that evening, and watched a cowboy movie flicker in black and white across the screen. I remember this vividly because each time the cattle in the movie bellowed, Joe's old cattle dog Bull (the second) would attack the screen, much to the amusement of the audience.

George Lewis was the general station manager, a bachelor and a stoic old-timer who ruled the place with a gentle but firm hand. He showed us around the place and invited us to stay in one of the cottages for a few days while Joe secured his equipment and stores, then he accompanied us on our trip out to Moolooloo.

We left VRD mid-morning. I found the trip enthralling as we drove for ages through the flat, dry downs country, its open plains interspersed with groups of trees and anthills. Because there was no market for the tough scrub bulls that were beginning to overrun the land, George supplied Joe with a .303 rifle and heaps of ammunition to shoot as many bulls as he saw. Sure enough, we did come across a couple of wandering bulls that morning which Joe quickly dispatched. About an hour later, shaded by white gums in a dry creek bed, we boiled the billy for lunch and enjoyed the thick corned beef sandwiches that the station cook had prepared. Soon we were bouncing again across those open plains, until we finally reached our destination in the mid-afternoon.

It was early dry season, the weather was perfect and we were in love, so the days we spent on Moolooloo were idyllic. The little outpost was situated on open downs country. We were provided with our own cottage, sparsely furnished with a quaint old wood stove, wooden table, chairs and a couple of old beds, on which we unrolled our swag. The only lighting available was carbide lamps. These lamps were cylindrical, about the size of a soft drink can.

A thin pipe stood out the top, where the gas rising from the carbide and water mix would burn brightly when lit.

There was a stock camp on the property that employed about six other men. Joe spent many hours swapping yarns around the campfire with them after work while I sat listening, fascinated.

Joe had his own saddle. The station supplied only rough green-hide ropes and hobbles as breaking equipment. These ropes were made by the staff from the salted hides of animals that had been killed for meat during the year. To break in twenty-four horses and one jenny (female) mule in fourteen days, with such primitive equipment, was a big ask, but Joe was an expert horseman and, although it was difficult with his gammy knee, he managed remarkably well.

The obstinate mule, half horse and half donkey, hated Joe and the feeling was mutual. It was definitely a clash of personalities. He would only have to go near her yard and the mule would go insane. Standing out of sight behind her, he would toss a little tin and, like Don Bradman, she would boot it clear over the fence each time with great ferocity. But she responded favourably to me, so I decided to adopt her and I called her Baby. While Joe worked away in the main yard, I copied his example out the back with Baby and spent my days breaking her in. In hindsight, it's a perfect analogy for how I handled my man, with the gently, gently approach. Firstly, I had to let Baby know that I wasn't going to go away. Then, to commence handling her, I began by letting her know she was caught, lassoing and stretch-tying her legs to each corner of the yard and bagging her down. I would flick the bag at her, rub her down with it, and eventually lay it over her until she realised that I meant her no harm. The next day I slipped a bridle into her mouth. She objected to the strange feel of the cold, hard steel in her mouth, but I began driving her around the big yard with the long reins until we were both almost giddy. Finally, when she turned from her left to her right on command, I saddled her up and we were away. I had broken in my first mule, but my man was never that easy. Each day I would climb aboard Baby bareback and ride her up to our quarters to fetch the smoko for Joe. I would boil the billy, cook some Johnny cakes and then ride her back to the stockyards, carrying the hot tea and cakes. Now that's a quiet mule! I was chuffed and Joe was really quite impressed.

Handover day came and the stock camp arrived to collect the horses. I watched anxiously from the quarters as the men from the main station test rode each horse and they all passed inspection. But then it was my Baby's turn, and turn she did. She practically turned herself inside out, bucking, kicking, striking and snorting. She was my mule, and she wasn't going anywhere with any man. I don't know what happened to Baby, but I often think of her when someone is referred to as 'mule-headed'.

With Joe's work completed, we left Moolooloo and headed out to Hodgson Downs Station to visit his brother Ray and Ray's wife Colleen. This was my first experience of real domestic life on a cattle station.

'You wanna see my puppy?' a serious, soft voice from behind me asked as Colleen showed me to our bed in the barely furnished, corrugated-iron bedroom. I turned and there stood a little boy with a sleepy, fat-bellied, brindle puppy draped over his arms.

'Why sure. What's your name?'

'Well my name is Danny and I'm four, my puppy's name is Sandy. You wanna hold him?'

'Yes, I'd love to hold him,' I said, reaching for him. 'Where are your brothers?'

Danny pointed above my head. There in the rafters sat Phillip, smiling shyly down at me. His mother called in exasperation, 'Phillip! Get down from there. How many times have I told you? You'll break your neck.' And I could tell she had said that a thousand times before.

'And there's my baby brother Barry.'

Danny pointed at a hole in the corrugated-iron wall where a twinkly blue eye was peering through at me.

A tin shed home with happy children, mosquito nets, Potts irons, copper boilers and scrubbing boards, wood stove and hurricane lamps and the old kerosene fridge all added to this wonderful atmosphere. Sacks of sugar and flour, tins of butter, sides of beef hung in a meat-house. Fabulous stews, huge double-yolked eggs, thick steaks, corned beef, pies, biscuits and home-baked bread were always on the menu. All this more than compensated for the rough decor.

Joe and I slept on a single bed together as only lovers can do and, being reasonably slim, if we breathed in unison, it was quite comfortable.

I was introduced to my first 'flaming fury' at Hodgson. Unforgettable! This outhouse, or 'dunny', was a few hundred yards down the paddock. It consisted of a deep hole dug in the ground, lined with forty-four-gallon fuel drums sitting on top of each other, with a round hole cut in the top drum to serve as a seat. Periodically, it was laced with diesel and burned, and the nauseating stench of phenyle and burnt excrement simply had to be endured.

The old corrugated-iron shower cubicle wasn't much better, with its canvas waterbag and shower rose hung over a tin floor. It came as quite a shock one day when, covered in soap suds, I had an eerie feeling that I was being watched. Wiping the soap from my eyes, I spotted a little ankle under the wall. It belonged to the big blue eye that was peering at me through one of the many holes in the tin wall. I chased the culprit away, but I never really felt alone in the shower again after that.

Those three little boys had no fear and were as wild as the country they lived in. If you got on their good side they were a dream to look after. If you didn't, they were a real nightmare. They were very independent and the 'spare the rod, spoil the child' method I had been reared with had absolutely no impact on them. I offered to babysit the day their parents went to town with Joe and, to my horror, they ran amok. When I smacked Danny on the bum for cutting down his mother's pawpaw trees and running riot with a butcher knife, he marched off, roaring, 'I'm gonna get my father's gun and I'm gonna shoot you.' And he meant it! Believe me, it was a pretty nervous babysitter who welcomed the boys' parents home that evening. Usually, it is the children who throw themselves into the mother's arms in such circumstances, not the babysitter.

Regardless of how rough the dwelling was, it became obvious from watching Colleen that a good woman can turn any place into a wonderful home. Usually the Aboriginal women did the menial tasks, but I enjoyed sharing the workload, cooking or tending to the beds of vegetables or watering the brilliantly coloured zinnias that were growing around the place. After chores were done, there was plenty of time for riding, reading or target practice.

We spent ten days at Hodgson, getting acquainted with my new de facto in-laws and the uniqueness of station life. But Joe had to find work, so it was time to move on again. The Aborigines performed a goodbye corroboree for us on the morning we left and we headed off to Mainoru Station.

We travelled all day over the rough dirt roads. When a stretch of loose bulldust appeared too daunting, Joe would gun the engine and go at a speed that didn't give us time to bog down. This took some clever handling. But if he missed a gear and sank into the deep wheel ruts, we were in big trouble. Unless in the unlikely event someone came along, there was no help available within several days' walk.

Night fell quickly and we were miles away from anywhere, tired, dusty and hungry, when we noticed a campfire flickering through the trees. Most of the stockmen were busy settling in for the evening, while some lolled on unrolled swags around the fire, smoking and talking quietly as we approached.

This group of Aboriginal stockmen had just brought in a 'killer' (butchered a steer). The huge mound of red coals glowed welcomingly in the darkness and the billies boiled merrily away while the aroma of grilling beef tantalised our senses.

'G'day, boss. You wan 'im tucker?' was the cheery welcome as we walked into the camp.

'Too right, Bruce, we're starving! I thought you'd never ask,' Joe replied.

Joe knew the fellows who made up this camp, and he introduced me as his new missus. There was a united intake of breath as they exclaimed their approval.

This was an experience of genuine stock camp culinary expertise; my first real Aussie beef barbecue in the days before they were fashionable. The procedure was basic with both cooking implements and hygiene nonexistent. A heap of meat lay on gum leaves that were spread on the ground close by. As was customary, the offal cuts – sweetbread, curly gut, liver, kidney and brains – were the delicacies chosen first. Next, the rib bones were favoured. This was like a gourmet version of my walkabout days at Mataranka.

'Hey, Joe, you wan' 'im rib bone?' Bruce asked.

'That'd be great,' Joe replied.

Bruce selected a prize rib for us that was probably three feet in length. He had no axe to break it, so he tossed it whole straight onto the mound of hot coals to cook. As we sat by the fire to await our meal, a huge, chipped enamel pannikin of steaming sweet billy tea was handed to us and, while Bruce sat rolling cigarettes for the next day, Joe caught up on the local gossip. The rib bone sizzled away, and little flames ignited as the fat tried to escape the heat, illuminating the happy faces of the group who sat smoking and chatting in the dancing shadows.

Our host turned the rib bone with a forked stick. When it was burned to a crisp on the outside, he wrapped it in some paperbark from a nearby tree and handed it to Joe. I have never eaten the equal of that delicious bone. It must have looked appallingly primitive, but it felt very romantic, sitting together in the firelight and simultaneously devouring that huge bone from either end.

Later that night we took our leave and camped further along the road in the swag under the stars.

We arrived early next morning at Mainoru Station. This property was run by the McKay brothers and a lady who appeared to be their housekeeper. The usual laidback station atmosphere prevailed and, while Joe talked, I watched as the staff worked in the hot morning sun, digging holes out of the almost solid rock to plant an assortment of cultured hibiscus from Queensland.

After all the effort to get there, we spent only a few hours on Mainoru. It was not offering suitable employment, so we headed back to Darwin.

Frustrated at not finding work, Joe met up with a couple of his mates in Darwin and decided to hit the rodeo circuit. 'Come with me, love,' he said, 'and I'll show you how the other half lives.'

15

How the other half lives

Still short of cash, Joe sold his station wagon to his brother. He found an ex-taxi for sale in Katherine that looked like it still had some life left in it, and he bought it for 300 pounds. Then, with his two mates along, we packed our worldly belongings, pooled what little cash we had for fuel and food, and headed south.

I had very few possessions and all Joe had was a tired old Customline, thirty quid, two pairs of jeans and a cigarette swag (thin bedroll). But he shared it all with me. Oh, and there was Bull, Joe's big old boofheaded white dog, who rode up on the roof rack. My pet galah, Polly, travelled perched behind me on the seat, much to the annoyance of the boys in the back, but – rather suspiciously – she disappeared out the open window the first time I nodded off.

The third night out, we slept in our swags under the open sky outside the underground opal town of Coober Pedy. Although the canopy of stars above us was breathtaking, so too was the freezing desert wind. While we tried to sleep, it whistled and gusted by, dragging at our swag cover like some shapeless black monster. Romantically, Joe pulled me closer to him that night, and whispered in my ear, 'Gawd, woman, I'm glad I brought you along for a windbreak!'

The next morning, after we had eaten at the little cafe on the outskirts of town, we fossicked around for opals, but, realising that we were not cut out to be miners, we continued south.

There were very few road signs then as we pounded through the red bulldust for mile after thirsty mile, and we even managed to get lost at one stage. Due to my constant moaning that we were driving in circles for almost an hour on a track that kept disappearing, Joe finally pulled up to ponder our predicament. This was a wise move that probably prevented us becoming another miserable pile of rust and old bones. When Joe discovered big, barefoot tracks of some wandering Aborigines, we realised that we were really lost. Nevertheless, it became a memorable episode, because after following those tracks for a while, we came across a group of nomads at a water trough. They were dressed in their traditional naga, or loincloths, and sported hunting spears, woomeras and boomerangs. They spoke no English, so we didn't talk much, but sign language instigated an exchange of cigarettes for two killing boomerangs and some general directions. We turned around and backtracked until we came to the junction where we had so carelessly overshot the highway.

The old taxi was a plodder which we christened Bessie. It had half a million miles on the speedometer, but the old girl had a heart of gold. We used to top her up with petrol and fill her up with oil at each stop along the way. Apart from the pack rack and the bullbar falling off, old Bessie carried us all the way through the desert without a hitch. She broke down for the first time just on the outskirts of Port Augusta. So we pushed her the last few miles into town.

While the boys did some running repairs, we stayed at the same caravan park where my family had stayed when we had first ventured north. This brought on a rush of nostalgia and I stood in the laundry that faced the northbound Stuart Highway with tears blinding my eyes. The huge chasm between my family and me was now apparent. I hoped that I had made the right choice; there was no turning back.

We secured a carburettor and, two days later, left Port Augusta, arriving in Adelaide after several hours, just on sunrise. Stores and cash were low and we were getting hungry. We needed to find work urgently. Being able-bodied, social security was never an option. We planned to stook wheat, pick and pack fruit, paint and do whatever we could to provide nomination and fuel money to get us around the rodeo circuit for the next six months.

The four of us sat on a bench in that unfamiliar environment in the early morning sun, scouring the newspaper for work. The locals were already setting off for their day and we could only gawk when one of the town's socialites drifted by, teetering on her ridiculously high pink stilettos, with her bright pink hair piled into the fashionable beehive hairdo. Beside her, on a bejewelled lead, strutted a bright pink poodle, the likes of which I had never seen. It almost seemed that we had landed on a different planet overnight. The boys' eyes rolled, but they managed to contain their mirth, while I sat comfortably in my rolled-up jeans and rodeo shirt, wondering if this was what Joe meant about showing me how the other half lived.

Gordon nudged me and whispered, 'Hey, kiddo, reckon ya could walk a mile in 'er shoes?'

But Johnno let out a whistle of approval, muttering aloud, 'Gawd, the sights ya see in a big city.'

With that, the pink lady and her dog threw their noses further into the air, then, turning, she shot a look of total disdain directly at me and teetered on her way. That's when we all burst out laughing at the absurdity of the comparisons. In her defence, it was considered uncouth for ladies to wear jeans in those days, but I loved them. When I had paraded my first pair of treasured blue denims for Grandma, on one of her visits to Mataranka, she had been horrified, saying, 'Mary, only wharf labourers wear jeans.' But jeans and Akubras were a symbol of who we were now and Joe loved me in jeans, so I brazened it out. Goodness how things change! Now jeans are an essential wardrobe item. I like to think that back then I was the Germaine Greer of ladies' fashion!

It was late October when the boys secured various jobs in the little country town of Clare, South Australia. It was about an hour's drive from Balaklava, where our first rodeo was to be held in the following weeks, so the excitement was mounting. Joe could boast an array of unusual friends all over Australia. Consequently, we slept in some extraordinary places, from our swags rolled out in sheep pens at the show-grounds one night, to a millionaire's mansion the next. In Clare, we had been given accommodation in an abandoned farmhouse. Although we lived frugally, I was trained as a child to be a proud housekeeper, even to the point of deco-rating the old farmhouse with little jars of pink roses that I scrounged from the climbers over the back archway. Usually the boys went off to work and I would have dinner ready when they came home. With no refrigeration, what meat we had was hung down the well in an old boiler to keep it cool. One afternoon, as I began to retrieve it to cook dinner, the rope broke and the boiler, with its contents, plummeted to the bottom with a sickening splash. That left me with nothing to feed three hungry men.

'Hmmm, what's a girl to do?'

I grabbed the rifle and went rabbit hunting. But the few rabbits I saw scuttling through the long grass were riddled with myxomatosis, so that idea was soon abandoned.

I flopped down on our swag by the window that afternoon, really worried that I was letting down my side of the bargain as camp cook. Suddenly, I heard a rustle in the leaves outside and *voila*! There stood a huge fat sand goanna, just begging to become dinner. I grabbed the rifle and, with a quick shot, I bagged this bonanza. But how was I to disguise it? I sat for ages, skinning and chopping it up, and made a curry with the limited ingredients that were left in our tucker box.

The boys arrived home late, tired and hungry. I was able to keep a straight face while I served their meals. I intended to tell them the truth after they had eaten, but Joe smelled a rat – or, should I say, a goanna.

'What is this, woman?' He always called me *woman* when I was on the mat.

'Oh, it's rabbit,' I replied.

But although the other boys devoured their meals ravenously, Joe, not trusting my poker face, pushed his plate aside. Gordon and Johnno enjoyed it so much that they took some to work with them the next day to share with their workmates and, even though he went to bed hungry, I scored high marks with Joe for ingenuity.

Joe, always the boss, made a point of never drawing payment until the job was completed. In reply to our hungry moaning, he would say, 'Just pull in your belt and call it a meal.' It was tedious work in those dry wheat fields. From daylight to dusk, the sheaves of wheat had to be stood on end in clumps, ready to be thrown onto the trucks for threshing; but at least we had work.

On one occasion we had set up camp in the old shearing shed on the property. The two boys camped down one end, and Joe and I at the other. There was a small stove installed, where I would prepare the meals.

When my few chores were done, I would sit alone most of the day, knitting my canary yellow, cable-stitch sweater. I had never been in this country before and the noises that rose intermittently from under that hollow shed were quite spooky. To make matters worse, a heavy rope swung from the rafters, drifting to and fro for no apparent reason.

'What's that for?' I had asked the boys that first evening.

'Oh that's where a bloke hanged himself,' was Joe's nonchalant reply. 'The place is supposed to be haunted. But nobody has ever seen the ghost, so don't worry about it, love,' he added quickly, sounding very concerned.

So for three days I nervously watched that rope swing and listened to the strange bawling of what turned out to be straying sheep under the shed.

On the fourth day, I was packing to leave and the shearers were moving into the shed. Trying not to sound too sooky, I asked the head shearer, 'Fred, what's the story with that rope?'

'Oh, they use that to swing the wool bales,' he replied.

I'd been sitting all that time in trepidation due to a fictitious ghost! That was probably my first and best lesson in dealing with Joe's laconic sense of humour.

Feeling pretty stupid, I drove old Bessie to deliver the smoko of billy tea and damper to the boys in the paddock that afternoon. After toiling in the hot sun for days, the boys were quite proud of the acres of wheat standing in neat rows. We were all delighted. Finally, we would be cashed up again and we were all looking forward to a big counter lunch at the local pub.

'Hey, Joe! Why did you lie to me about that swinging rope?' I asked, handing them their pannikins. 'I've been worried for days.'

They all began to laugh to the point of collapse. Totally outnumbered and embarrassed, I took off in a huff, which of course is a girl's prerogative; but disaster struck. When I jumped into old Bessie and put my foot down to reverse, the accelerator fell apart.

Why, at that very moment, in a paddock of newly stooked wheat, and after all those thousands of miles? Why now?

Suddenly the joke was on them. It all happened so fast. The three boys stood transfixed, watching with dismay as Bessie took off out of control. I was not an experienced driver. There I was, weaving through that paddock in reverse at what felt like a hundred miles an hour, desperately trying to avoid the wheat stooks and heading for the barbed-wire fence. Eventually, I thought to reach over to turn off the ignition, pulling up in a shower of dust and grass. By the grace of God, or ghost, I had somehow managed to miss every stook in my path, but Joe had lost his sense of humour. In shock, I sat stunned and alarmed at Joe's anger as he jammed his Akubra on his head and came stomping down the paddock towards me. He thought that I had been having a tantrum until I sheepishly produced the collapsed accelerator. But I did notice that the boys had stopped laughing at me and my ghost story. Hmmm, perhaps it was the work of a ghost after all!

16

The rodeo circuit

Saturday 2 November 1963 saw us well on our way to Balaklava for our first rodeo. We had intended to be there the night before, but after the boys were farewelled with many rums and beer chasers they were in no condition to drive, so we camped on the side of the road. With great expectations, we rose early and drove through the rain, arriving just as the announcer was calling Joe's name for the bull ride. After all that anticipation, it looked like Joe would miss out on a main event. We pushed through the crowds at the gates where the six-shilling entry fee was waived because we were competitors. While Joe coaxed the chute boss, who was organising the riders, to give him a break, the boys struggled to organise their riding gear and I parked the car near the riders' enclosure. The atmosphere was charged and I settled in for the time of my life.

Reluctantly, the chute boss gave Joe three minutes to present at the chutes, and with no time to prepare himself Joe slid onto a bull. Within seconds, the gates were flung open and an enormous roan bull with huge twisted horns burst into the arena with Joe on its back. I had no idea what to expect. I had watched Joe ride broncs in the travelling tent shows back in the Territory, but with only a rope between man and beast, this was something else altogether. With one arm thrown in the air, Joe spurred to make points, but lost his balance, slipping down the side of the bull and touching down a second before the bell blared time. Joe's gloved hand was caught in the bull rope. As bull and rider scrambled across the arena together, I hardly breathed. Finally, Joe pulled free, leaving that murderous beast, distracted by the other riders, snotting and snorting and looking for blood.

Joe had been within seconds of winning and the frustration was evident on his face as he headed back to the chutes. Gordon and Johnno were mediocre riders, but Joe was professional and was expected to bring home the moolah.

Joe always expected success. Nevertheless, he took me aside after that ride and instructed, 'Hon, if I ever come off and get hurt, don't come into the arena, whatever you do.'

'But what if you get hurt really bad?' I asked, beginning to understand the risks we were taking and how serious things could get.

'Just wait outside the gate and jump into the ambulance, but don't come into the arena.'

I figured it was obviously a man thing, a loss-of-face thing, and I pushed down the little voice inside that wanted to know, 'And what happens if you get killed?'

But then the announcer called his name for the open saddle bronc. Buckling up his chaps again, he headed for the chutes. He looked totally fearless, pulling his hat down as he strode across to the arena, and I was a very proud girl indeed.

The horse he had drawn was a sixteen-hand high, Roman-nosed bay gelding. He was, as Joe put it, as rough as guts to ride, and he certainly earned his keep that day. Joe put up a very determined ride and stuck it out for the full time but finished out of the money in that event also.

Hmmm, this way of making money was certainly not as easy as I had been led to believe.

The last chance for petrol money was the open 'surcingles' or bareback event. As Joe pumped himself up for this at the back of the chutes, he became very focused, and by now I knew enough to keep clear. Old Bull and I sat watching anxiously from the car park as he lowered himself onto the horse and the announcement blared over the speakers: 'And from chute five, ladies and gentlemen, we have the runner-up champion of Australia, Joe Groves, on this as-yet-unridden gelding. Let's see if he can ride time without hitting the dust.'

The arena went quiet for a moment, then the gates swung open to a roar of approval from the crowd and Joe exploded into the arena on the big dappled grey. The horse gave his all, twisting and bucking, but Joe's ride was flawless. Then, on the whistle, the crowd went wild again as Joe dismounted beside the still-bucking horse and bowed. He was quietly confident that it had been a top-class ride. We were all disappointed when he was awarded only second place, but the seven pounds prize money went into kitty and I kept the ribbon. There was a reception held after the presentation, we helped ourselves to the free food and drinks for the competitors, then headed straight for Cootamundra in New South Wales for our next rodeo.

The language of rodeos was changing rapidly.

The sport originated in Argentina and America, so naturally those countries' influence and terminology gradually took over here. Americans pronounced it 'rodao', while we said 'rodeo'. Rough riders were replaced by rodeo cowboys, moleskins by denim jeans, Cuban heels by top boots and the good old Akubra went into competition with the Stetson. But after all that international influence, rodeos in Australia remain very Australian.

The thrill of the rodeo kept the riders coming back year after year and each township looked forward to the annual arrival of the cowboys. There were Brian and Bonny Young, Barry Crawford, Col McTaggart, Ron Lacey, Len Purse and Arthur Grant, just to mention a few in our little group. The small towns boomed when the riders appeared, so they were treated like celebrities. There were some gorgeous guys among them and, consequently, the rodeo left a trail of broken hearts. Joe always expected that some younger cowboy would win my heart and steal me away, but given his 'alpha male' reputation the boys always knew to keep their distance. I didn't find being around them daunting because I was used to handling my brothers and most of them treated me like a kid sister. Well, except for Arthur, that is.

I met Arthur one day in our flat at an orchard when we were picking fruit in Ganmain, just north of Wagga Wagga in New South Wales. A group of Joe's mates were preparing saddles and equipment for a rodeo. I was clowning around, imitating the boys, dressed in Joe's chaps and high-spurring on one of his saddles. In a world of my own, I looked up and connected with an intense pair of dark, smiling eyes. I don't remember what colour they were, just the intensity. If I had known about soul connection then, I would have put it down to that, but it was the 'eyes across the room' syndrome, and I was gone, hook, line and sinker. I guess he caught me off guard. Arthur was a good-looker, closer to my own age, who came from a cattle property in Queensland. He was a great little rider but should not have been, because, as Gordon explained later, he had a brain tumour.

He was not expected to live, but he figured that he might as well go out doing something he loved.

Overwhelmed by this connection, I slid over and sat beside Joe, who was now talking to him, telling him that he could have any of the droving horses that he had left on the Dajarra reserve if he could catch them. And then, after a meaningful glance in my direction, Arthur was gone. I ran into him several times in the street in town in the following weeks, and we politely passed the time of day, carefully avoiding any further discussion, but it was quite obvious that the feelings were mutual. Soon, Arthur disappeared, but like an old song, the memory lingers on. I wonder what story I would be writing now if we had acted upon our attraction.

We arrived at Kyabram in Victoria just before Christmas and secured a rather cute little caravan in a shed, with a toilet and laundry outside, for five pounds a week. It was a lovely spot with an apricot tree at the front door that was laden with fruit, so I began to settle into temporary domesticity.

Unaccustomed to the usual camaraderie on the circuit, I could only watch in wonder over the following week as Joe's rodeo mates descended upon the place. They stripped the apricots from the tree like a plague of locusts and left a veritable flood in the laundry as they washed their clothes and primped and preened to be ready for the local rodeo ball. Joe didn't dance and I was very disappointed not to be going, but I ironed shirts and straightened ties and stretched the steak and kidney pie I had prepared for our four among fifteen hungry cowboys. That night, I lay trying to sleep against the throb of the distant dance music and I just ached to be there.

The next day Mr Smith, our exasperated landlord, asked us to find alternative accommodation and I wasn't surprised. So we moved to a caravan park, but it wasn't long before we again had swags rolled outside our van, with happy cowboys strumming guitars and singing to the encouragement of the local residents.

Christmas and New Year were spent around the Myrtleford and Kyabram rodeos. To add a bit of Christmas cheer to the day, under very trying conditions, I was able to make one of my famous puddings and a fruitcake. We bought a couple of live hens somewhere, which I had to kill, pluck and clean. In those days, chicken was eaten on special occasions. They were not the hormone pumped-up feather pillows they are today. No matter how meagre the offering, it was again shared among many hungry cowboys between rodeo events.

Our three men competed in most events, including the pick-up teams and the wild cow-milking contests – anything to earn a quid. Depending on the mood of the local judge, some days were good and some pretty ordinary. When anybody won, the prize money was put into our kitty, but we made sure Johnno never got his hands on it because he was prone to shouting some lucky girl to a good time at our expense. To attract these girls, he would hobble through the crowd wearing bandages on the outside of his jeans as if he had been wounded in action, looking for a soft bosom to cry on, and like bees to a honey pot they would fly.

I had turned nineteen that November, but I still could not legally marry without my parents' consent. Although I waited patiently for Joe to bring up the subject of marriage, for some reason it never arose. But he did mention, to my surprise, that he would love a blond, blue-eyed son. I took that opportunity to suggest that we should be married first. It was then that he sheepishly dropped the clanger that he was already married. My mind went blank. This scenario had never occurred to me. I couldn't get angry because he had never lied to me but still I felt deceived. He went on to explain, 'I was only seventeen at the time. She was in serious trouble, pregnant to some guy, so I married her.'

What chivalry! Visions of that pregnant girl I had met on the train all those years ago flashed through my mind and I finally realised the enormity of her situation – and, for that matter, my own. I was talking to a totally different man now, a man who had secrets. I had never asked him about his former life and I didn't really want to know, but I was hurt that he hadn't shared something so important with me. Finally my parents' concerns were becoming a reality. Joe had a son who was almost as old as I was!

'So what happened to her?' I asked.

'I was working on stations around Collinsville an' some old bloke came on the scene and she took off with him.'

I was now expected to believe that he had simply ridden off into the sunset like all good cowboys do and had never seen her again. He said he had never looked back or bothered to divorce her and he had no idea how to go about it. He suggested that if I could sort it all out we could get married. In my situation I had absolutely no hope of doing that.

Our days were busy. There was a rodeo somewhere most weekends that the boys would travel to, while I mostly stayed behind to work. I picked or packed fruit in the cannery, while the boys did whatever they could between each rodeo to keep the tucker bags full. At one stage we all picked tomatoes, a back-breaking job, bending for hours in the hot sun, and I became very ill. I vomited from morning till night and we figured that I was sunstruck. I eventually saw a doctor who gave me an injection. It had me immediately vomiting into his hand basin and I left his office with no answers. As long as I didn't eat, I could get through my days reasonably well. I lived on pineapple juice and icy poles while I waited for the bug to pass. It was six weeks before I was properly diagnosed; I had never dreamed that this could be twenty-four-hour-a-day morning sickness. In fact, even though I had six younger siblings, I knew little about pregnancy and Joe knew even less. It was definitely women's business as far as he was concerned. Suddenly life became more serious. After travelling the circuit through the southern states for six months, it became obvious to Joe that we had to settle down to a more responsible way of life.

In the weeks that followed, we put old Johnno out on the side of the road somewhere in South Australia for some misdemeanour, and Gordon was offered a permanent position driving trucks back home, so Joe and I were travelling on our own again.

We traded Bessie Ford on a later model ex-taxi and headed north again with two girlfriends we had met on the circuit. Once again, our new second-hand taxi was loaded to the hilt, now with our two dogs travelling up on the roof rack.

My pregnancy was hardly showing, but I was so ill that Joe left my pup and me with his parents at Longreach in Queensland. With a lot of trust and a twinge of pregnant jealousy, I had no option but to wave him goodbye as he continued north with the other girls. They were continuing on to the Darwin rodeo and Joe figured he would be there in two days. Immediately after the rodeo, he planned to try and make some money mustering wild bulls from horseback again for Old Les MacFarlane. Meanwhile, I had to be content to stay with Joe's parents. They were a wonderful old country couple of Kilkivan pioneering heritage. The family were of genuine convict stock. While Pop was a descendant of an English customs officer who arrived in Australia with his Irish bride in 1885, Mum was of

German and Spanish descent. Her forebears were deported to the colonies in the 1840s for stealing a loaf of bread and a dress. Later, they received a land grant for good behaviour and service to the Crown and became highly respected pillars of the Kilkivan community. Joe's great-grandmother became a well-respected midwife for the district. These were definitely survivors.

Mum doted on Pop, to the point where she would sit between us when we went on country drives, corking his beer bottle with her thumb so that it didn't go flat between mouthfuls while he drove. I think I began to realise then what was expected of me as a successful bushman's wife!

I was missing my mate so much I almost went out of my mind with despair. I wrote almost every day and waited eagerly for Joe's replies. I pleaded with him that I was well enough to go on up to join him in the stock camp, but really I was wretchedly ill. Joe's mum would fuss around me, exasperated, trying to get me to eat simple meals, but nothing could be done to ease my constant vomiting. I wondered if I would survive it.

After several months of pleading, Joe finally relented, and I took the old, low-flying DC3 back to Darwin. It was my first flight and, as excited as I was, I never let the sick bag out of my hands. It was a long, slow, bumpy trip with many stops along the way for deliveries and to refuel. Arriving in Darwin, weary and sick, I was able to rest overnight at the Vic Hotel before heading bush. As I lay on the bed under the thumping fan blades, I remembered our romantic encounter there and wondered what I had let myself in for. The humidity sapped my energy and I spent ages retching into the toilet but, with comforting words from Eileen, the hotel manageress, I gradually pulled myself together. Next morning, fighting off waves of nausea, I boarded a Greyhound bus for the long trip back to the Mataranka hotel.

Joe was pleased to see me but he was obviously worried. He had left the camp preparing to move out the next day and he was in a hurry, so, after a quick kiss and a hug, we immediately headed back out to join his crew on Moroak Station and to my first experience of life in a real stock camp.

17

Piccaninny daylight

I was almost mid-term and still able to conceal my pregnancy, but my constant morning sickness had to be endured silently so as not to upset the stock camp equilibrium. I was a round peg in a square hole, but I had begged to be there. It never helped that mornings on Moroak would start with the breakfast bell sounding at around 4 a.m. Like it or not, a breakfast of liver and onion gravy, curried mince or baked beans would be provided, and then we would sit around on the stockyard rails until the sun rose to give us enough light to work the cattle. But I came to love this magical time of day that the bush folk call piccaninny daylight. With a background of waking bird calls, I would watch enthralled as the darkness gave birth to the light; when the mauve-pink or yellow hue on the horizon would gradually burst into a new day, full of promise and exciting opportunities.

That camp was made up of five Aboriginal stockmen and two young rodeo riders from New Zealand, who had just finished shoeing the horses for our next muster. We had boiled the billy and were congregated around the fire, almost ready to move out from the station, when an apparition suddenly appeared from nowhere. It was a myall (wild Aborigine) called Bingo and he strolled boldly towards us. He was dressed as a ringer, in greasy jeans and a scruffy shirt, but wore no riding boots. He simply told the boys that he was coming with us and Joe, desperate for all the help he could get, agreed.

Like most of the men in Joe's camps, Bingo could speak very little English. He was a bit of a novelty, so Joe introduced him to me and I said, 'Good morning, Bingo.'

With a big, yellow-toothed smile he replied, 'Good fucking morning, missus.'

This nearly floored me, as bad language was never used in front of women, but it was probably the extent of his English.

Bingo had a distinctive smell about him that was probably stale goanna oil, or perhaps his rancid hair. He had to give a little jump to put his old Akubra hat on top of the smelly black hair that was coiled high upon his head. He wrapped a couple of spare bull straps around his lean body, then he stuck a huge, ugly, cracked bare foot into the stirrup, slopped into the saddle and, in his gangly fashion, rode off towards the cattle coachers with the others. Boy, was this a sight!

He was probably only interested in the food, though, as within the next few days he disappeared just as quietly as he had appeared.

After that, Bingo was like a phantom. We never saw him again, but we knew he was around. The boys were always windy of him and I kept close to Joe. Bingo had always been considered a bad blackfella and lived alone up in the hills between the front gate and the Moroak homestead. Among other things, he would sneak into the station camp at night to steal young girls to keep as slaves. He must have had some special magic, because he was always treated with a healthy respect by the other blacks. I believe he was the area's *kadaitcha* man or devil-devil man.

I was over five months pregnant but because of the times, and the fact that I was not married, was keeping my condition a secret. As the boss's missus, I was privileged to be in Joe's camp, and as long as I acted like one of the boys I was totally accepted. Like the old sailors, who were hesitant about taking women to sea, Joe was always happier without women in his camps. He used only male horses in his plant to curtail sexual challenges and I guess the same applied to his staff, and they all seemed happy enough. The boys worked long hours. They enjoyed the hunt, and they were usually ready to crash, exhausted, at the end of the day.

Being June, it was the dry season, and the weather was mostly hot with cooler evenings. Without the horrid, tropical humidity, I coped with it reasonably well. I was naive enough to think that no one had noticed my pregnancy; at least, they never broached the subject with me. To mount up, I would use a log or anything I could find and carefully ease myself into the saddle. I took this precaution because I was concerned that I could do harm to my baby. I couldn't eat the stock camp tucker, so I secured my own tin of rolled oats and would cook a little on the camp oven lid each morning to keep me going. The black billy tea would make me retch. I would carry the unappetising, soggy damper in my shirt pocket just in case I got hungry, but it was usually rolled into balls and flicked away to the birds as I rode along after the cattle. During the day, I would ride off to hide from the men and vomit from where I sat in the saddle. But apart from all that discomfort, I was deliriously happy to be with my man and in his swag under the stars.

It didn't matter what time we arrived in camp at night, it was a cold dip in a nearby creek to bathe, while I prayed there were no man-eating crocodiles nearby. I was constantly reminded of the time that one of the station's old stock camp cooks had weaved his way down to the river to get some water at night, and come within inches of being taken by a large crocodile. He staggered back to camp, wet and covered in mud and with his clothes torn. Trembling and as white as a ghost, he kept muttering, 'Help me, help me, that big bastard's got me rum bottle,' so everyone figured his story must have been true. Joe later shot a monster croc in that same area, because it haunted the river where the station children used to play.

There were no vehicles in the camp. Everything was carried on the pack horses that tailed along behind the cattle with an Aborigine who not only looked after the horses but also doubled as camp cook. About once a fortnight, Old Mac would rendezvous with Joe and deliver more stores, mail and any news of the outside world. The rations were always the same: flour, baking powder, sugar, tea, salt, tomato and Holbrook sauces, plum jam, syrup, dried vegies for stews, potatoes, onions and soap. Oh, how I craved fresh salad sandwiches, but alas! I had to accept things as they had always been, pregnancy cravings notwithstanding.

The bush camaraderie and living under the stars had a magical effect on me. The vision of those huge blue skies melting into the distant tree line, and the warm morning sun on my back, is etched in my memory. We would ride up red, rocky ridges, our horses' shoes flinting off the loose stones, through the sweet pungent smell of cattle and grass left hanging in the air. Although it was no place for a pregnant woman, it was exhilarating to know that I was an accepted part of this wonderful bush existence.

Although the mustering was completed satisfactorily, it seemed that we were never going to get the horse stud that Old Mac had promised us on an outstation of Moroak. I was entering my third trimester and living conditions were still primitive, so we left there and Joe started mustering horses and shooting the wild donkeys that were overrunning Mataranka Station.

For a while, I stayed at the homestead, which was also overrun by the pets owned by Betty Martin, the manager's wife. With her only son away at school, she had developed an excessive love for animals, to say the least. The bantam hens and pigeons shared the open kitchen freely with the bread dough that was set each morning. To this lady's amusement, I often grappled for my breakfast, while her cat sat on the table attempting to swipe the egg off my plate, but I was certainly not in a position to scold or complain.

Betty had a huge pet kangaroo that was as spoiled as any child. I watched it one afternoon standing bolt upright, seeming to read a comic book that it had picked up somewhere. It looked hilarious so I went to investigate. It dropped the book and loped off a little way. By now, growing more uncomfortable with my pregnancy, I had slowly bent down to pick the book up when this monster came flying high through the air like a kickboxer, with me its intended target. I stood up quickly, sidestepping as it slid past, its huge clawed feet missing the middle of my back by inches. Trembling with shock, I turned quickly to confront its challenge. With the arrogant air of a wilful child, it eyed me off, but, luckily, as if nothing had happened, it decided to lope off to lie in the afternoon sun. Only by the grace of God went my baby and I!

Soon after that, Joe decided that it was too big a risk to have me out bush any longer, so we looked for accommodation in town.

18

The honeymoon is over

While Joe went chasing bulls again, I stayed alone in a railway fettler's cottage that we rented in Mataranka. I had no telephone or radio and my only company was a tiny naked budgerigar that I was rearing, whose little green pinfeathers were just beginning to blossom. Colleen would visit occasionally when she could get away from Hodgson, and I became friendly with the publican's wife, who kept a close eye on me during that lonely period.

It was early August and I was enduring the wet season build-up. The added heat of my pregnancy was unbearable. To cool down, I would sit fully clothed on an old wooden chair in the shower recess, while the tepid water streamed over my swollen body. However, the temperature inside the shower recess was not all that different from the usual 104 degrees outside.

Now nearly eight months pregnant, I was constantly vomiting and most of the time I felt wretched. I read a lot, helped my friend at the pub sometimes and was generally bored out of my mind as we headed towards October – the beginning of the hottest, driest, most humid and debilitating month of the year. It was usually referred to as suicide season in the Territory.

'If only we can make it through October,' I thought, as I lay awake at night, my hands searching for the feeble movements of my little unborn companion.

As none of today's amazing technology was available, pregnancy was a process of trial and error and I really had no idea when I was due. Eventually, the doctor took pity on me and I was admitted to the Katherine hospital for observation. I waited anxiously as women came and went with their new babies. The hospital was a louvred, colonial Queenslander structure with a large closed-in veranda all around. The men's ward was on one side veranda opposite the women's ward. These wards were separated by a room in the centre that served as the operating theatre and the labour ward. The office and outpatients' clinic were at the front and the communal toilets at the back. The only relief from the constant heat was provided by a couple of shared fans between the beds. The building was not soundproof, so when a woman went into labour, it was hardly a private event. The fellows must have had difficulty sleeping with the commotion each time a baby was born, and they often sent shouts of encouragement or discussed developments with us on their way to the showers next morning.

Beside myself with boredom, I became the unofficial ward entertainer, but after about three weeks my patience and my jokes began to wear thin; so thin, perhaps, that the doctor suddenly decided to break my waters to induce my baby. Right there in my bed on the veranda, an ether mask was placed over my face to knock me out. To the amusement of the other patients and the doctor's embarrassment, I woke up during that clumsy procedure, swearing at his bald head that appeared between my legs. I must have been using my father's bad language, because I never consciously swore, but the sister attending was tut-tutting, saying, 'Mary! Mary! Enough of that language!' Never mind poor Mary!

The doctor, who was appropriately named Hugh Dunnit, panicked. Announcing that I was having twins, he ordered an emergency air evacuation to fly me to Darwin in the middle of a monsoon storm. My head was spinning with this sudden activity and with the unaccustomed air travel. I was feeling very alone and frightened indeed.

When the matron of the Darwin hospital met me at the airport, she immediately put my mind at ease and was amazed that I didn't appear to be full-term yet. Obviously my baby – one baby, not twins – was happy where it was and the general consensus was that when the apple was ripe it would fall.

Darwin had a much grander hospital than Katherine, but still had only one fan between two beds, so in the October build-up it was extremely hot and humid. To some extent I was acclimatised to the heat, but I never got used to the humidity in Darwin.

Another three weeks was spent waiting in Darwin away from everyone I knew. I had no communication with my own family, who had settled in Port Augusta; my parents considered that I was living in sin, not unlike that girl on the train all those years ago. I waited in mortal fear of the birth process and I listened to the cries of agony again and again drifting from the labour ward. I promised myself that I would be strong like my mother, who I assumed must have been Superwoman in labour, and I vowed that I would not utter a sound when my time came. This would be my initiation into real womanhood!

When, as a youngster, I had quizzed Mum, her only words to me on the subject of childbirth were, 'Mary, the pain of childbirth doesn't bear remembering.' Those words kept echoing through my head although I had no idea what they meant.

In the three weeks I waited and walked through the corridors of the Darwin General Hospital, I welcomed newborns and farewelled the dying. I was beginning to wonder if my baby would ever be born. In fact, its movements were becoming weaker and I was worried.

The matron ran the ward like a military base, but I had become her favourite. Every day she clucked around me in her brisk manner until at last, without warning, she stuck a drip in my arm and announced that she would induce me. Nobody explained to me what that meant, or what to expect; I assume they thought I knew.

They eventually took the drip out of my arm, but nothing seemed to be happening. I was young and, by then, totally bored, so, of all days, I chose that morning to slip out of the hospital to go for a long walk along the beach that was adjacent to the hospital. The hospital was apparently in an uproar as they searched for me, and I was totally oblivious while they worried that I was in labour somewhere. Naturally, I was severely admonished by the matron when I reappeared, my slippers covered in sand and my pockets full of seashells.

But my luck held out and my baby was still as snug as a bug in a rug. After much pacing of the corridors, I finally went into labour at seven that evening. I remember clearly when my waters broke. I was embarrassed because it was visiting hour, and the ward was full of my roommates' many friends and relatives. Among the happy chatter, they wheeled me off to the dreaded labour ward, clutching my mother's rosary beads.

The pain was just as bad, if not worse, than I had feared, but after eight hours and an unusual delivery on my side, a tiny baby lay across my ankles, and I experienced the joy and the wonder that only a mother could know. She looked like a miniature of Joe. I couldn't believe it when they said that she was a girl. Although we had planned for a boy, who was already named 'Little Joe', to my total surprise our first-born was this tiny five-pound, fourteen-ounce girl, born on 30 October 1964, and I named her Paula.

My life was now filled with responsibility. After a week, I left hospital with Miriam Hagan, the girl in the bed next to mine, and booked into a small motel before Joe finally arrived from Mountain Valley. Until that morning he was unaware that his little girl had been born. He was on his way into town to visit me, when he finally received the telegram that the hospital sent a week earlier. He was excited but totally unfamiliar with parenthood. He lovingly referred to Paula as 'fish bait' because she was so tiny, but on our trip home, he wouldn't allow me to put soiled napkins in the boot of his car. As expensive as they were, I had to throw them away. I can see the funny side of that now, perhaps, but sadly, in his macho world, babies were women's business alone. Men sowed the seed and women reaped the harvest. He was so nervous that it was almost comical. Too nervous to even hold his daughter, he was more than happy to leave the child-rearing completely in my hands as we headed for our new position on Mountain Valley Station.

19

Mountain Valley Station

Joe had secured further mustering on Mountain Valley and we arrived there in early November. It was a well-run establishment operated by the Hood brothers, Ray and Neville, and their wives, Helen and Mary, two couples in their late thirties. I had often served them in the shop at Mataranka.

The Aborigines there were still quite primitive. They did not have a good grasp of English and the elder tribesmen still had numerous wives. One elder had fathered two babies who were born on the same day from two different mothers. They looked like identical twins and were plump, healthy, shiny black babies of about six months, with big black eyes and beautiful smiles.

Another of the elders had twelve wives, the youngest of whom was the lovely Jenny. Not long after we arrived, there was a commotion in the camp when it was discovered that Jenny had been seduced and taken away into the bush by a young outsider called Bruce. He was a handsome young man who, together with some relatives, was working on the station at the time.

Late that afternoon they bravely returned to confront their respective relatives and to accept their punishments. The scene at sunset was surreal and a hush fell over the station as the young lovers walked towards the camp. Everyone watched with bated breath as the handsome Bruce, dressed only in a naga, or loincloth, his head held high and his spears slung over his shoulders, strode arrogantly back to the camp to return his stolen love to her rightful owner. Jenny, on the other hand, followed submissively, eyes downcast, carrying their swag on her shoulder.

The affair was a huge affront to the tribal elders and payback was inevitable. This warlike encounter between two clans would usually involve the throwing of spears and boomerangs. It was imperative to draw blood, to wound or even kill the offending party or his relatives. Ray, Neville and Joe armed themselves with revolvers and rifles to ensure that things didn't get out of hand, but this was blackfella business and they would not interfere. In the bush, bush law prevailed. All the whites could do was stand back and tend to the wounded. Helen, Mary and I manned an emergency ward that we had set up in the homestead kitchen.

As night fell, the opposing sides congregated in the compound outside the homestead and soon the ruckus erupted. We women were not privy to what went on, but spears, woomeras, boomerangs and killing sticks were all used in the fight that ensued.

In the kitchen, we patched up representatives of both sides as best we could. Then, amazingly, the combatants went back out and joined in the fracas again. The wounds we treated were certainly not scratches, but the participants seemed immune to pain. One big, gruff, middle-aged man walked sullenly into the kitchen. I gestured to a chair and he sat silently in front of me with his arms crossed, present-ing an immense, bloody and gaping head wound that ran from his forehead to the back of his skull. I swear I could see his brain!

What to do?

We were many hours' drive over rough dirt roads to the nearest medical assistance, so there was nothing I could do but bandage my patient's skull tightly. Then, without a word, the gruff old warrior rose to his feet and strode back out to battle. I can still remember my shock and amazement as I watched his big, broad back disappear into the night and once more into the fray.

The white men didn't need to interfere. Happily, no one died that night and I never heard any more about the incident. I can only assume that the wounds healed in their own time.

It was generally agreed that it was not a good idea to interfere in tribal matters. They were usually left to run their course, so I was intrigued when the station owners' wives chose to interfere in the marriage of a young girl of about fourteen, who had been promised to one of the older men. The girl came running to the homestead late one night, terrified, and protesting that she did not want to marry the old man she had been promised to at birth. She was taken into the homestead for the evening and I was told she was later sent away to school. Faced with that decision, I probably would have done the same thing. It may have demonstrated a lack of tolerance of Aboriginal ways, but assimilation had commenced and change was inevitable.

Our days were punctuated by exciting events such as when one of the Aboriginal elders went hunting and came across a water buffalo bull near Policemans Point, some twelve miles from the homestead. Buffalo were not usually found in this country and this was our first sighting. They usually spooked the inland Aborigines, but this brave hunter, on his own, wounded the beast and walked it all the way back to the homestead. This was an Aboriginal version of a butcher making a home delivery. By the time it had arrived back at the station, the poor animal was peppered in shovel-nosed spear wounds and was pretty darned angry. He came charging and snorting into the station compound, head down and nose out. Water buffalo are normally gentle and intelligent animals, but when stirred up and fighting for their life, they are to be avoided at all costs. This powerful fellow, with his huge set of dangerous horns, was looking for something to use them on. Nobody knew what to do with him. Almost all of the blacks scrambled up the nearest tree they could find to dangle there, giggling and laughing. The three white men loaded their .303 rifles and headed out to the stables to protect the prize racehorse Armac, which was in the path of the rampaging bull. The unfortunate bull was halted mid-charge by a well-placed bullet, and the hunter was finally able to deliver his prize to the camp.

That night around the campfires, after eating their fill, the blacks honoured the bravery of the skilled hunter with another corroboree. As always, I was thrilled by the sound of the didgeridoos and clap sticks. Their happy songs and throbbing music kept the night alive. It echoed for miles, floating from rocky outcrops and out into the night skies.

My time was mostly spent tending to the needs of my baby, washing napkins, cleaning and helping in the kitchen whenever I could. There was little to do after dark and I would read when the generator was going, but generally I would lay awake peering into the darkness, listening to Paula's gentle breathing, wishing I could share her more with Joe, while all the time craving to be held in his big, strong arms. I was often alone for days with only the blacks on the station. Although this didn't concern me unduly, I will never forget the fear and isolation I felt when Paula, at about six weeks, became constipated and quite ill with a distended stomach. The station owners were away on holiday and Joe was out in the camp. Every couple of days, I would contact the flying doctor over the radio and he would assure me that her symptoms would pass, but after nine days my baby was weak and showing signs of distress. Driving to town in the middle of the night on my own was not practical, but something had to be done to bring relief to my tiny girl. Hoping desperately that I was doing the right thing, I gently administered a warm soapy water enema with an eyedropper and prayed, and we were both relieved when the angels answered my prayers.

We would eat at the main table with the family and always in our set positions in order of priority. It was all very proper and civil, but I always felt that I was an encumbrance, or just part of the price that management had to pay for Joe's services. Joe always seemed popular wherever we went, particularly with the ladies, and I learned to ignore the fluttering eyelashes. Here, the family were pleasant to me, but distant, and I always felt that I was being ostracised for not being married. But despite the lack of a licence I considered myself Joe's wife in every sense of the word.

I had been left alone with Paula on one occasion when the management and staff were in town. I had beef fat and caustic soda boiling in the laundry copper to make washing soap when I heard yelling from the compound yard and went to investigate. Two teenage boys were pouring petrol onto a dog and preparing to set it alight. I went to the dog's rescue and chastised the boys. I made them sit on a bench outside the kitchen so that I could keep an eye on them while I worked in the laundry, but it soon became apparent that as a strange white woman I had no authority at all in this camp. I noticed the boys smirking and looking up; I was startled to see what resembled a lynch mob assembled at the back of the laundry. All the adult camp residents, it seemed, were hanging around the garden fence and glaring at me.

I was only nineteen, the only white person on the station, and I was scared half to death. I stood my ground for a few minutes but soon scuttled back to the kitchen to find Aida the cook. She was an older Aboriginal woman, proud and well educated by the standards of the day. I hoped she would know what to do under the circumstances. Wiping her floured hands on her apron, she confronted the group and after some serious talk among themselves they slowly disbanded.

These boys had just been initiated and were now traditionally men and the tribe obviously resented any white, female interference. With feigned authority, I told the boys that they could go now, but I would be reporting them to the boss men when they returned from town! Nothing more was said about the incident and I don't know whether they continued their cruel sport or not, but I decided that it wasn't my business.

We had an old Kodak eight-millimetre movie camera, and that year Joe was privileged to be one of the first white men invited to attend to film a circumcision ceremony. There was a young half-caste boy in the camp at the time who had also been through the ordeal. He had apparently cried during the process. Sadly, he was lambasted by the same two boys who had hurt the dog. They were intent on letting him know that he was an outcast. Because he had not passed that cruel initiation, they taunted him. My heart went out to this lad, caught in the situation of not being white enough to be considered white by white people, but not accepted as black by his black peers. Rusty was considered a 'yella fella'. Tribal law forbade interbreeding and they did not consider a coloured child worthwhile. It was customary in those days for station management to prevent 'coloured' children in their care from going walkabout with the tribe because often, due to neglect or unforeseen circumstances, they did not return. So the boy was cared for by the station owners and lived his life between them and his full-blood relatives.

Cohabitation between races was illegal and both government and tribal laws regarding breeding and relationships were strict. Penalties for breaking them appeared harsh, but it seemed that tribal laws of kinship had obviously played a large part in the successful preservation of their race for millennia.

We were reasonably happy at Mountain Valley. Joe worked for about six months there, coming and going from the main homestead between mustering, and I did what I could around the homestead to earn my keep, but over time I had developed pain and swelling in the abdomen. After several radio contacts with the doctor, it was decided that the flying doctor's plane would be diverted late one afternoon and I would be flown immediately to Darwin. Joe and I waited in vain on the airstrip until night fell for the plane that never came, before returning to the homestead. With no telephones or after-hours radio reception, we were not able to find out what had happened to it, so we drove several hours that night, bouncing over the rough dirt roads to the Stuart Highway, then on through to Mataranka and Katherine. We left Paula with Joe's parents, who had since moved from Longreach. While Joe returned to the station for work, I took the bus to Darwin alone, where I was eventually operated on for the removal of a small tumour.

Meanwhile, I had become disenchanted with our living arrangements in the homestead back at the station. I believe that I was easy to get along with but, being so much younger than everyone else, there was not a lot I could do right. Consequently, I was becoming increasingly bored and lonely. The better living quarters we'd been promised hadn't eventuated and, when Joe was at home, we were still crammed into one small bedroom, which allowed us very little privacy. We knew it was time to move on when the grumpy head stockman, who slept on the other side of our thin bedroom wall, complained about me talking in my sleep. Our patience was gone so, after the operation, I agreed to stay in Katherine with Joe's parents until Joe found another position. I never returned to Mountain Valley.

20

Mount Sanford Station

Dry season 1965 saw us back at Victoria River Downs on the Mount Sanford outstation, where Joe had accepted the position as head stockman. We were excited about the position because it offered a house and, we thought, some normal living conditions – but that couldn't have been further from the truth.

I was twenty then and Joe was thirty-seven, a cattleman to the core, and he was happy to be earning a living the only way he knew how. Although we now had reasonable accommodation, he was still going to be away mustering with the stock camp for weeks at a time. Again, I would have to live alone at the homestead with my baby as my only companion. I had no way of contacting him and the morning radio session with the main station was my only contact with the outside world.

It was a lonely place out there on the red soil flats. The wind would break the silence, moaning through the eaves and whistling through the flyscreened verandas. After a while, I began to enjoy that mournful sound.

Apart from the rifle, I was pretty defenceless. One afternoon, while pulling some carrots from the little vegetable garden that struggled beside the house, my dingo pup pricked its ears and looked into the distance, whimpering. When it disappeared to hide down a culvert under the road, I knew something must be coming. It would have been half an hour before my ears picked up the hum of a vehicle approaching. I wasn't expecting anyone so I was pretty nervous and felt like joining the dingo. Finally a grader appeared, pulling up in the compound in a cloud of dust, and the scruffy driver came to the locked screen door looking for directions. He was an unexpected stranger and I was certainly apprehensive, but little Paula was overjoyed to see someone. She toddled to the door with her arms outstretched crying, 'Dadadada!' This certainly broke the tension. He blushed and I giggled as the poor fellow took my directions, and I don't know who was the more embarrassed as he scuttled away to go about his business. I soon became accustomed to dealing with such unexpected situations. Luckily, the typical outback bushmen usually turned out to be rough diamonds.

Outback stations were generally supplied with well-equipped medical kits and station people were expected to be able to use them. This was not a problem for most families because the majority of station owners and managers were married to nurses, familiar with the kits' contents. The rest of us guessed their uses or followed instructions received by two-way radio from the Royal Flying Doctor Service base in Wyndham. Without this system, I am sure there would have been many more dire results. However, there were times when bush people survived even without orthodox medical assistance. Because of my position as the boss's wife, or *kudjiri*, it was often assumed that I had formal training, but my medical education was limited. I joke about it now, but we wives had to learn quickly, so over time my knowledge became pretty comprehensive. Medical emergencies were common and could be quite frightening to a young woman trying to cope alone.

George Lewis was still VRD's general manager. A few weeks after we arrived he departed for holidays in the south, leaving Joe fully in charge of the Sanford outstation. After pulling together a ragged camp of unusually reticent stockmen, Joe set out on his first week away mustering, while the remaining staff planned to play. Joe was oblivious that this secretly planned revelry was the reason his own men were so unwilling to leave their women at the station camp.

George had his favourite staff and one of these was his distant cousin, who acted as his horse trainer. Elmore was a rugged, scruffy fellow who was addicted to booze and women, and he arrived to party at Sanford before the dust of Joe's departing camp had settled.

The mechanic was a white man with a full-blood Aboriginal partner called Thelma and two young sons. The party raged in his quarters for the first day but, apart from the racket, they kept to themselves, leaving me with no option but to ignore the goings-on and hope that we were safe.

The first day passed without incident, but on the second day the young woman who usually did menial tasks for tobacco and rations did not present on time to clear up the kitchen. I was beginning to get annoyed with her for being late when she burst breathlessly into the house with her clothes askew and a look of sheer terror on her face.

'What on earth is wrong, Maggie?' I asked.

'Oh, Jesus, help me, *kudjiri*,' she replied. 'That Thelma, I'm gonna kill him me-fella. She 'im got him axe!'

Within minutes, the screaming Thelma began circling the house. I locked the screen doors and hurriedly prepared a plan of action. The problem was that Maggie had attended the ongoing party, where she was caught by Thelma in a compromising situation with her man.

Thinking rapidly, I put Maggie to work in the kitchen and tried to placate the intoxicated Thelma from behind the locked screen door. But the enraged woman with the axe meant business and insisted, 'Him blackfella business, *kudjiri*.'

As Maggie whimpered behind me in the kitchen, Thelma continued, 'You gotta send 'im that Maggie out for punish, or me fella gonna come right in an' pull him outside.'

She continued to circle the house, ranting. In desperation, I used the only delaying tactic I could think of and, through the locked screen door I told her, 'Thelma, this Maggie been late back to work, now him got him big job to clean up. Soon as him finish up, what about I send him out, then you can punish him?'

Her respectful acceptance of my request seemed to defuse the situation for the moment and she muttered something under her breath in reply as she wandered away.

Maggie performed her minor chores in slow motion that afternoon and by the time she returned to the camp Thelma had calmed considerably, although there was still some screaming wafting back from that direction. Thankfully, the axe was never used.

However, we hadn't finished with Elmore. As horse trainer he would ride the racehorses each day to train them for racing, come what may. The day after the axe incident I became concerned when Thelma told me, 'That Elmo, missus, him no good. Him properly drunk bugger an' him riding that horse longa airstrip. Too bloody hot, missus, ain't it?'

Although the heat was tremendous, there wasn't much I could do to intervene, so I carried on with my own business.

Sometime later, the bleary-eyed mechanic knocked on my door. I hadn't done more than say hello to this fellow before. He was pale and he swayed where he stood, unshaven, dishevelled and reeking of alcohol.

'G'day, missus,' he slurred. '*Hic*! You got some cotton wool?' He was almost incoherent but he looked concerned and was trying hard to focus, so I knew something serious must have happened.

'How much do you need and what's it for?' I asked cautiously.

'Ol' Elmore's came orf his 'orse on the airstrip, missus.'

I left Paula with Maggie from the camp and, grabbing whatever I could find in the medicine chest, I headed over to the quarters to see what I could do to help.

I found the smelly, unshaven Elmore lying on a bed in the mechanic's house, covered in blood and gravel rash, with his ear torn out of his head and hanging down his neck by a piece of skin. It looked like an unhappy plant torn from the earth, roots and all – a gruesome sight indeed!

'Do I snip it right off or stick it back on?' I wondered.

I wasn't sure whether he was conscious or not until I leaned over to inspect the damage and felt a gnarly old hand reaching for my leg.

'Is it really me own Florence Nightingale?' he mumbled before I slapped his hand away.

Elmore was intoxicated and certainly not feeling much pain, so I swabbed the wound with disinfectant and hot water. Still trying to avoid his groping hands, I cleaned the wounds, but I was interrupted by the wailings of the mechanic's wife. One of her young boys had jumped off the stockyard fence and gashed his foot on a sharp rock. The wound was deep, jagged and bleeding profusely. So now I had a drunken, groping horse trainer *and* a panicking mother with her bleeding son. The rest of the party was stumbling around being more hindrance than help and, as the group were all still quite drunk, I knew I had to take control.

I told the mechanic to load mattresses into the back of the station's four-wheel-drive truck. Then I proceeded to tourniquet, disinfect and bandage my way out of the predicament; but what to do with the dreaded ear? After cleaning it up as much as possible, I carefully stuck it back into the gaping wound in his head! I had no stitching equipment, so I firmly bandaged the ear into place.

With my running repairs done, I ordered the mechanic to drive them to the main station where there was a medical centre. It was almost dark and they had at least eighty miles to drive on the rough shortcut track. If they made it through on this route, it would cut a considerable distance off their trip, but it was going to be a big night for all of them.

I watched as the tail-lights disappeared into the darkness and I could only pray that the intoxicated driver would not roll the vehicle in one of the rough creek crossings on that seldom-used track.

Wandering home alone through the dusty yard, I watched little dust eddies rise from my feet like ghosts in the torch light, and I chilled a little as my dingo pup howled a lonely reply to an evening chorus of dingoes somewhere off on the horizon. Maggie went home and a quiet calm finally settled over the deserted station compound.

The next morning, the nurse from the main station came onto our radio session to tell me that the wounded had just arrived there okay, adding that the horse trainer was not making much sense. She had tended the little boy's wounds and he was fine, but she was unable to find out the extent of Elmore's injury because he had made it clear that she was not to remove his bandages under any circumstances. Consequently, his ear healed exactly where I had put it.

When Joe arrived back from camp about a week after the ear incident, he almost came to blows with the battered Elmore over the disruption he was causing to the running of Mount Sanford. Finally, because Elmore was never disciplined by VRD, Joe decided that working conditions had become impossible and he resigned as head stockman. I remember the day distinctly because I had just finished the laborious job of developing a huge vegetable garden. It was almost twenty feet long and a yard wide and was dug out of hard rocky soil. The house girls and I had extracted the rocks using a sort of chain-gang method. We stood for ages, heads hanging, tossing rocks through our legs until all that remained was this lovely, even loam. We were justly proud of the garden bed that eventually evolved after hours of hard work, but as I planted the last corn seed and stood up, Joe braked at the gate in a shower of dust and gravel to announce, 'Pack up, woman, we're leaving.'

So we packed and left that day. My heart sank as I left that labour of love behind and I can only hope that someone else watered the seeds and reaped the benefits of our days of toil.

It was probably fifteen years before I saw Elmore again, lopsided ears and all, in the beer garden at the Katherine hotel drinking with the ringers. I'm not sure if he remembered me when I said hello, but he was totally recognisable to me, with one ear sitting almost half an inch lower than the other.

21

Little Joe the Wrangler

We left Mount Sanford, heading east of the Stuart Highway. Two enterprising Territorian mates of Joe's, Gus Trippe and Ray Townsend, had bought a livestock ship between them to transport stock into Asia. Finally, there was a market for those scrub bulls that were being shot and left to waste, so Joe easily found work catching them on various stations in the Roper River area. He was like a man possessed. The only time he would take a break from his work was for Christmas, a rodeo or when the wet-season rains made the roads impassable.

By then, Joe was no longer catching bulls from horse-back. He had developed a technique of catching them from four-wheel drives. These vehicles would be stripped almost bare, to the seats, tray and chassis. To catch a bull Joe would drive alongside the animal at full speed, and he or the boys would catch it by the tail. Flying out of the vehicle, they would throw it off balance, flinging themselves across its flanks to strap its hind legs together. When contained, the animal would be unstrapped and tied by the horns to a tree until the boys were ready to load it onto a truck. To load, the bulls were slid up a metal ramp with a winch and cable, onto a four-wheel-drive truck that would deposit them into a set of mobile steel yards. From there, they were laboriously reloaded onto a larger truck and sent, about ten at a time, over rough bush tracks to the main station yards. Speed and efficiency were always essential to avoid bruising and stress.

Dogs used to play a large part in the capture of these animals and they were bred for the purpose. Many times I watched Joe's old dog Bull pull out from chasing an animal to roll and chastise a younger dog for not doing its job properly. He probably saved Joe's life on several occasions. Joe still had a weak knee and it would collapse on him at the most precarious times, but old Bull was always right there to turn away any charging animal.

Joe caught bulls on Elsey, Hodgson, Moroak and Roper River stations, while Paula and I stayed on and off with his parents or with old Joan in Katherine. Joan lived by herself in an old corrugated-iron house on the corner of Second Street, in the heart of town. She was one of those colourful characters who constituted the older Territory population. These tough pioneers lived a hard life without comfort. In a lot of cases, it was all they knew. In other instances it was a necessity because they were on the run from spouses or the law.

Joan never failed to astound me, but she was my buddy and could do no wrong. Having been brought up with very proper parents, it was always a shock for me to find this old lady sprawled asleep on the cool cement floor, stark naked, picking up the airflow through the passageway of her home. That was not a pretty picture and I certainly couldn't look. It was quite common for her to be in the same state of undress out in the street at night, swearing and cracking her stockwhip to quiet the local dogs. But Joan had a heart of gold and I stayed with her for about eight weeks until we took up a position at Delamere Station.

With promises of great remuneration, Joe became assistant manager on Delamere until the new American owners arrived. The Americans were intent on taming this 'last frontier', and teaching us all they knew. They came with family and belongings until the homestead bulged at the seams. We took an instant liking to the newcomers, who were full of new ideas. They were rodeo people, so we had something in common, but they were pretty soft by our Aussie standards. Instead of being armed with six-shooters, as portrayed in America's Wild West stories, they would not walk out of the house without being armed with a can of fly spray. They had no concept of how difficult the country was or the huge distances involved. Otherwise, I am sure they would not have had men risk life and limb to swim flooded creeks, simply to fetch delicacies for their traditional Christmas dinner. They soon realised that the ranching they had been used to in the States was a whole different ballgame to the Australian wilderness.

My twenty-first birthday came and went at Delamere without much ado. My only present was a set of rosary beads from my parents, who probably hoped that prayer would save me from my uncivilised existence. But it was on my birthday that I realised I was pregnant again, and for me that was gift enough to make it a special day.

Thankfully, this time I suffered only a regular amount of morning sickness, so I managed to look after Paula and to earn my keep as the cook for the three families who now lived under the same roof. Joe was shouldering the station responsibilities, again for minimal wages. Once again the promised accommodation and conditions never looked

Me as a baby with my mother, North Fitzroy, 1944

Mataranka General Store and Post Office, 1960

Women's corroboree, circa 1962

Boys' farewell corroboree, Hodgson Downs, 1963

Joe and stockmen, Mataranka, 1961

Tipping a scrub bull's horns in the stockyards, early 1960s

Joe rides on the southern rodeo circuit

Me, aged 19, at Kyabram Rodeo, 1963

Dinner camp

Crossing the Victoria River, Coolibah, 1966

Joe and I at our first race ball, 1969

Baby Mary-Lyn, three days old, 1973

Me, my house girl and a friend in the stock camp at Roper Valley, 1970s

Joe, me, Paula and friends at the Timber Creek Rodeo, mid 1970s

Paula, Joey, Mary-Lyn and Stephen doing their chores at Fitzroy, 1975

American owners visit Fitzroy, 1975

The family at Fitzroy, 1975

Buffalo muster, late afternoon, Woolner

Prices Springs, 1980

Around the campfire, catching camp on the Marrakai Plains, 1981

Paula after winning on Kidlat, 1981

The original Woolner Homestead, 1982

Me and Joe after a muster at
Woolner

Joey catches a bull with
the bionic arm (note Joey's
broken arm), Woolner, 1983

Stephen, 17 years old, driving to an early morning muster, Woolner

Last cattle muster at Woolner, 1988

Me and Jilly, Alice Springs (minutes before the disaster), Cannonball Run, 1994

Blazer, Katherine Hospital, 1997

Joey and me with part of the truck fleet at Twin Rivers, 1996

Steve and his chopper with the one that didn't get away, 1996

Mary-Lyn, me and Paula, 2000

like eventuating, so, after about six months, we reluctantly moved on.

I spent the latter part of that pregnancy in town with Joe's parents on their little farm near the high level bridge over the Katherine River. Once again, I almost went crazy with the boredom of waiting. I filled in my days tending to little Paula, sewing or knitting, and helping where I could around the farm. I had formed a friendship with a girl from VRD Station who was living in town, and I visited with her quite often. On the afternoon of 19 July, I knew my time had come. I had her take me to the hospital for my regular weekly visit and, although the doctor insisted that I should go home and be patient, sure enough that afternoon my water broke and I went into labour.

There were no complications, so after a little happy gas and eight hours of that unbearable pain of childbirth – that pain which doesn't bear remembering – we had our little boy.

During all this time, Joe was catching bulls somewhere way out towards Arnhem Land. When he hunted stock, he followed cattle pads that would track the movement of feral stock over vast areas, so he never knew where he would be catching. This always made contact very difficult. His only communication was via the station manager's irregular rendezvous so, with our limited communications, I devised what I thought was an ingenious way to let him know the outcome of my pregnancy. I asked Joe to listen to *Party Time* every Saturday night on his little transistor radio. He was a very private person and didn't want our life publicised, so I told him that if we had a girl I would have the DJ play the song 'Maryanne Regrets'. If it was a boy, he would play 'Little Joe the Wrangler'. At least that way Joe would know the sex of our new baby and that it had arrived. With this all in mind, I had written to the radio station telling them the situation. I asked them to have these songs ready and I specifically asked that the compere not say anything about the baby. But on the night the call went out, the DJ completely blew our cover. He made a celebratory announcement, probably more suitable to the moon landing. I cringed but, at the same time, I felt really proud as he announced, 'So tonight we have a special request for Joe Groves, who is somewhere way out in Arnhem Land catching bulls. Joe's wife Mary has presented him with a beautiful, healthy six-pound, two-ounce baby boy, born on the nineteenth of July at the Katherine hospital. We are to let you know, Joe, that both mother and baby are well.'

But, unbeknown to that wonderful DJ, Joe was definitely not supposed to be *in* Arnhem Land catching bulls! That was illegal. He was supposed to be working his way towards the Arnhem Land boundary. There were no boundary fences over those huge areas and wild cattle roamed freely. I could visualise every manager on adjoining stations in that area galloping out to protect their boundaries.

Anyway, with much fanfare and ado, the song 'Little Joe the Wrangler' was played to announce the arrival of our son. It seems the only one in the Territory who didn't hear it was Joe. He was well out of radio range and, whether he was in Arnhem Land catching bulls or not, he would probably have a good deal of explaining to do.

Anyway, it was a unique way to announce the arrival of our first son to the world and, after that announcement, he was known for years, all over the Top End, as Little Joe the Wrangler.

22

Coolibah Station

Joey was three months old when we moved to Coolibah Station late in 1966. The Coolibah homestead was a three-hour drive over gravel roads from Katherine. It sat at the foot of a monolith called Wondoan. With its ragged red escarpments, Wondoan was always treated respectfully by the Aborigines of that area as 'devil-devil country'. The original stone homestead that had featured in the classic Australian film *Jedda* was still in use. I had been moved by that movie as a young girl in Melbourne. Even then, I had noticed the starkness of the stone walls in the living room, particularly in the scene where baby Jedda was handed to the grieving manager's wife. That movie is still the most accurate portrayal of Aboriginal life of those times that I have seen recorded. That same living room still served as the main dining area in our time and I'm sure it witnessed many such intriguing real-life tales.

Joe had secured a position on Coolibah as a contract bull-catcher. We set up a camp outside the little cottage by the airstrip where the mechanic and his wife lived, to enable us to use their ablution block. It was meant to be a temporary arrangement as they were leaving, but the days turned into months before the mechanic moved on and we were able to move into the cottage. An English couple, she was a pleasant woman who did the cooking at the homestead, but he was a crude, rude man who was never easy to get along with. Still, we needed the job. So as not to upset things, Joe persuaded me to pretend he didn't exist.

Tony was an Aborigine and Joe's top man, and his wife Nita was my faithful companion. Nita spent most of her days between the Aborigines' camp and mine, but she always seemed to be around when I needed her most. That year, we endured a particularly hot and humid build-up, with spectacular storms but, initially, little rain. The huge grey clouds would roll in low, bringing deafening thunder and dazzling lightning and the occasional stinging rain. These storms would gust through the station compound, wreaking havoc on our little camp. Nita would be grappling with tent poles and flapping canvas, while I scurried about saving the children and items of value from the threatened torrential downpour. At the same time, it would be a battle to ensure that our little cooking fire stayed alive for the next meal. Paula was almost two then and, during one of those late afternoon storms, she ran and slipped in the mud, rolling across the top of the campfire grill plate. Thankfully, she was immediately swept up by Nita and hardly burnt. Our adventurous life was full of little miracles. Living in the tent was certainly not comfortable, but I was young, still in the bush and close to the man I loved.

The property was managed by an older fellow whose nickname was Leggings. He and his wife were stoic, old-school managers; the type who rang silver bells for the maids to attend the dinner service. But, as lovely as Leggings' wife was, that type of culture was definitely lost on us.

Joe was soon away after cattle and, again, the only contact I had with him for several weeks at a time was letters, when old Leggings would visit his camp. For Joe to write a letter by the campfire at night, after a hard day chasing cattle, was a labour of love. I still treasure these letters . . .

Well Hon, We have been shoeing [horses] *and my back thinks it's broke in a dozen places. Have changed my mind about mustering towards the station and am going back where I was last time as I know there are plenty of cattle there. Will be gone about four weeks so look after yourself. All the boys have bad colds, so have I, hope you and the kids don't get it but suppose that's what you get for going to town. Hope everything is going well with you, just grit your teeth and put up with everything, as I think I can make a few quick quid here . . .*

P.S. Don't take the car over the river as I only just made it through. You might hit a rock . . . See you when I get a mob – wish me luck.

When, after two long months, the mechanic finally left, we moved into the little house by the airstrip and I turned it into a wonderful home. We were only contractors, so it was never meant as a permanent residence. The management willingly supplied paint, so I set to and painted it a pretty green from top to bottom. Eventually, it became my dream home, with curtains I sewed whenever the generator supplied enough power to run my treasured sewing machine. Mum had given me the machine as a present for a wedding she despaired would never happen. This had been the first sign of her accepting our relationship.

I established a little vegetable patch, of which I was very proud. I would fill my days looking after the kids, decorating the little cottage, working in the garden or sewing for a little pocket money. I had learned to make the colourful body-hugging rodeo shirts for the staff. Aborigines love bright colours and these shirts, and the little outfits that I made for their children, were an array of all the vivid colour combinations imaginable. Today, they would probably be considered haute couture, but even then those rodeo shirts were considered collectors' items among the staff. Nobody could go incognito wearing an M.G. special shirt. There was a cook who went missing after a local rodeo that year. We thought he may have met a sticky end, but we finally discovered that he was okay through the bush telegraph. We heard that a redheaded guy, with a flamboyant red-patterned cowboy shirt, was last seen hitchhiking somewhere in Queensland. Although he had stolen the treasured shirt from one of the boys, that, along with his red hair, had helped to identify him, so at least we knew that he was still alive.

We managed Coolibah for four months that year while Leggings went on leave – and what a period that turned out to be!

We had a wonderful Irish bookkeeper called Joel. He was probably in his late fifties, which seemed ancient to me in those days. He was a city bloke who was not used to the ways of the bush.

I was sitting on my veranda in the dark one evening when I heard the frantic scramble of a couple of stockmen as they ran by with something obviously chasing them. As I watched they seemed to disappear towards the stockyards. On closer scrutiny, I noticed, by the glow of their cigarettes, that the long, skinny fellow lay along the top stockyard rail, while the short, dumpy fellow melted into the shorter, rounder upright post.

'What on earth could be frightening these usually fearless fellows?' I wondered, when suddenly old Ruby came staggering through the darkness in pursuit.

Ruby was one of our regular hard cases from the camp. She was in her sixties but had a penchant for the younger men, particularly when she was inebriated, as she was that evening.

As she lurched and searched through the darkness, she had no idea where the men were hidden. She pleaded with them to show themselves, wailing in exasperation, 'Where you two fella gone? I only wanna luv him yo' two fella!'

As alcohol was not permitted in the camp, we couldn't for the life of us work out how the camp-dwellers were getting drunk. No alcohol was sold at the station, and the staff had no way of getting to town undetected, so it was an absolute mystery.

The mystery was finally solved one evening at dinner when Joel the bookkeeper, who also helped me intermittently in the store, said in his charming Irish accent, 'Yer know, I'll be beggared if I can keep up the medication to the camp.'

'How's that?' Joe replied.

'Well, ta be sure, I'd say that every soul in the camp is got arthritis.'

'What makes you think that, Joel?' I asked.

'Well, I have never seen so many folk needin rubbing med'cin.'

As I controlled the medicine cabinet, I asked suspiciously, 'So what are you selling them as rubbing medicine?'

'Well, only the usual methylated spirits that they've always used.'

Joel was a gentle man; so different that I wondered how he had made his way to this rugged part of the world. I was certainly glad he did, because he would enthral us all at our shindigs with his brilliant fiddle playing. He had been married to an Irish lady who passed away and left him floating, like a leaf in autumn, just waiting for the turn of winter. We talked a lot together and he often confided in me his concerns at having lost contact with his wife's twin sister. He was worried that because she was identical, she would also grieve and pass away but he had lost all hope of finding her.

It was pretty late in the year and Joe had let the cook go because of pilfering. Cooking for the main homestead, organising the station business and running my own house and family was more than I could handle, so Joe decided that it was time to give the boys a break in town while he went looking for a new station cook. Six happy stockmen climbed onto the back of the Toyota tray-back at five o'clock one morning, and with Joe, Joel and young Keith the head stockman in the front, they began their long drive over the rough gravel road to Katherine for their big day out.

During the heat of the day the boys had enjoyed some considerable time in the pub and, as usual, Joe managed to find a cook there among the patrons.

Later that afternoon, on the journey home, Joel was sitting cramped between Joe and Keith. He complained that he was not feeling too good. There was no air-conditioning then, so they pulled up briefly in the shade of a tree by the side of the road for a spell. Joe then decided, as they were loaded to the hilt with stores and inebriated staff, it was best to head for home. Joel dozed on Keith's shoulder as they bounced over the corrugated roads, arriving back at the station just on dark. Joe left the boys to unload the perishables and returned, exhausted, to our little cottage. He was just pulling off his boots when there was a knock on the door. I opened it and Keith stood there with a look of absolute shock on his face.

'I jus' tried to wake up old Joel,' he said, 'and 'e's not movin'. 'E's stiff 'n' cold and I reckon 'e's bloody dead, right where 'e's sat in the Toyota!'

Joe quickly pulled his boots back on and went to investigate. Sure enough, quietly and without a fuss, Joel had simply passed away, just as he had lived, without being a bother to anybody.

The only thing Joe could do was leave the body where it was and drive the ninety miles to deliver it to the police station at Timber Creek. It was a harrowing drive with the corpse bouncing along beside him until it slid over and came to rest on his knee, where he nervously let it lie for the rest of the journey.

There was a beautiful full moon on the evening that Joel died. It was one of those crystal-clear evenings when the stars hung like jewels from black velvet. Such evenings were to become synonymous with the passing of special people in my life. It felt mystical, not necessarily a crying time, but more like an 'All's well and God's in his heaven' type of evening. Joel had obviously felt his time was near, because he had repeatedly doodled RIP on a pad in his office. I knew now that his prayers were answered and that he was happy somewhere else.

On returning to the little cottage much later that same evening, Joe was in the act of pulling off his riding boots for a second time when another knock came at the door. Again, Keith stood there, now with a look of total confusion on his face.

'What's the problem now?' I asked.

'Struth, missus, this new bloke is locked in 'is room at the quarters and 'e's throwin' an almighty fit. He's bouncin' off the walls an' I reckon 'e'll kill 'imself if we can't stop 'im.'

Poor Joe! The look on his face was ashen as he sat, still tugging off his boot in slow motion.

'Hurry up, hon,' I urged. 'Better go before someone else dies tonight.'

There was a moment's strained silence before Joe exploded in exasperation, 'If the bastards want to die, let the bastards die!'

Then, slamming his feet back into his boots, he stormed off to sort out this new problem.

It appeared that the new cook was having some sort of fit. It was probably self-induced. For a heart-starter, the old bush fellows would sometimes take a tiny bit of deadly strychnine off the tip of their pocket knives. The secret to survival was in the measurement. It was like adding high-octane fuel to an old T-Model Ford. Instead of a slow crank start, these old fellows used to erupt into a frenzied fit and, if they lived through it, they would simply brush themselves off and start all over again. We suspected that this was the cause of the ruckus.

The fit finally wound down and peace once again reigned at Coolibah. I was ready to step in and cook breakfast, but the new cook showed up on time at four o'clock the next morning as if nothing had happened. Then it dawned on me that, although we now had a cook, we were down a bookkeeper, but at least that wasn't as trying a position to fill as that of the cook.

Believe me, the way to a bushman's heart is definitely through his stomach and, without the camp cooks, the camps did not operate. We had become used to the varied temperaments of station and stock camp cooks. Most of them were prised out of the pubs, clutching the promised supply of rum. It was subsequently grappled out of their grubby arms and smashed before their horrified eyes at the first sign of trouble, usually on the long trip home. These men were quite often in a putrid condition of self-neglect, so they were literally hosed down and left to dry out before they commenced their mostly temporary new life as a camp cook. After a forced period of cold turkey, these characters were usually quite grateful to Joe for his firm-handedness, becoming model citizens for a time before they again began to crack. They would find some reason to go to town and the pubs would invariably reclaim them.

Because of necessity, these cooks used to get away with hell but they were occasionally good at what they did. We once employed a cook with a wooden leg who had the habit of surprising unsuspecting visitors to the stock camp by unzipping and dropping out his 'old fellow' to show the world his pride and joy. Thankfully, I never endured this exposé, as it could well have turned me off both sex and food for life. His pride and joy was the fat blowfly that was tattooed on the end of his penis. Very modern for those days, I think, but the pain endured during that art work surely must have been more awesome than the result.

That cook didn't last too long because he got on the booze with the one-legged grader driver who had come in from another station with some rum. These two fellows had chummed up quickly because they had so much, or so little, in common. I smile remembering the night they crept past my place after a highly sackable binge in the blacks' camp. As they quietly wended their way home in the moonlight, they clung onto each other like Siamese twins. The only giveaway was their shushing and their squeaking wooden legs as they staggered, left, right, left, right, away into the night.

Bush cooks were definitely a strange bunch, with a scattering of wonderful characters, like Basil. During the war, Basil had been a sniper, and he would handle any 'insubordination' in his camp with impromptu demonstrations of sharpshooting. Not surprisingly, there was never a hint of bad manners, dirty hands or crowding around Basil's cooking fire. As a treat, he would often boil up his special plum duff in a cloth, in a drum on the campfire, and he could make the most wonderful potato bread and spotted dick.

We didn't get to know most of these men well, as there was seldom cause for any in-depth conversation. I had learned long ago not to question where they had come from, because most of them, although pretty harmless, were either running from the law or ex-wives. It was best for all concerned if we never knew.

Time went by and life was good on Coolibah. The little cottage was just across from the stockyards, and the comings and goings of the cattle and horses were always a cause for excitement for my little family. As soon as we heard the first jangle of the hobbles, or bellows of the cattle, we would be forming our welcoming committee along the top stockyard rail.

Late 1967 saw me well on my way with our third pregnancy. My house girl, Nita, was determined that she and the other women were going to take a mattress and me down to the river at Coolibah for the birthing of our next baby. But Joe went catching cattle again on Moroak and, at his insistence, I moved back to his parents' home in Katherine.

23

Benny

Again, it was a long, monotonous wait for my baby and the days ticked slowly by at the little farmhouse. I had quite a few friends in town, but there is nothing like having your own partner around to share the few joys of being pregnant. I never got used to that particular loneliness, but by now I knew no different. I guess I was learning to live with few expectations and, consequently, with few disappointments. But still, ever so slowly, I was breaking my bushman in to parenthood.

Our Stephen, a beautiful, peaceful baby, was born a healthy six pounds, seven ounces, on 2 December 1967, two days after my twenty-third birthday. Pop, with his trousers inside out, had run me to hospital in the wee hours, where I had my usual eight-hour delivery. Bearing in mind that a baby's arrival date was all guesswork then, and although his intentions were good, Joe was again elsewhere. But during those eight hours of excruciating pain that bonds mother to child, nothing and nobody else really existed anyway.

This time, Joe had planned to be close at hand for the birth, and I think he was really looking forward to being around. Still, he did not arrive at the hospital until the next day. It was really through no fault of his own. In the past, Joe had undergone ear surgery that was causing major problems. The motto in the Territory then was: 'When in pain, catch a plane.' Being wet season, work had slowed, so he grabbed this chance and flew to Adelaide for surgery. After the operation, he was supposed to recuperate for six weeks before flying to avoid further damage to his hearing, but, being a professional risk-taker, he chose instead to fly home immediately.

Joe had been offered the relief manager's position back at Coolibah, with a contract for further catching as soon as the new manager arrived. So Joe visited us in hospital straight from the airport, then drove the three hours to the station to take up his new position. To his amazement, he found that the retiring manager, Leggings, had got sick of waiting and had left the store keys with the cook. Of course, this was a recipe for disaster. Naturally, the cook took advantage of this rare opportunity and, when Joe arrived, he found a full-blown drunken spree underway in the homestead. This involved the entire staff and their wives, who had taken alcohol and anything else that they wanted from the store.

Joe took control of the situation as usual and, single-handed, tossed the drunks out of the homestead one by one. During the struggle that ensued, the only punch that connected with Joe was on his newly mended ear. Sadly, after all the pain, suffering and expense he had just gone through, his hearing was back to square one. But life went on as usual and within a fortnight our expanding family was together again in our little cottage by the Coolibah airstrip.

It was well into the wet season and the seasonal maintenance had begun. With the mustering over, we were now able to spend some well-earned quality time together and we began to enjoy a normal married life. Over Christmas and New Year, we celebrated in grand style in the old stone homestead with staff and friends. I had to admit, though, that between the office, cooking for the station and tending to our little family, I was being run ragged. I would cook and organise the stores and the homestead maintenance, while Nita would watch the children. Then I would hurry off home to organise the kids and collapse on the bed, with my head swimming, to breastfeed Stephen. But I grew stronger as the days passed.

After two months, the new manager and his wife arrived. They were the Shannons, a younger couple than the previous managers and, although they were seldom on the property, we all got on well together. It was such a relief for me to have another white woman my age close by. As the wet season subsided, life reverted to the usual, with me happily tending our little family and Joe off chasing wild cattle again on the outstations, but now at least I had someone to talk girl-talk with, and I certainly made the most of it.

It wasn't long before the Shannons went on holidays and Joe and I were again left to manage things. One day, I found a tiny tin of salmon secreted away in a dark corner in the storeroom and decided that it was mine. We very seldom saw tinned fish and it was a real treat, so I made a sandwich. It seemed a little dry but, not knowing what it should have been like, I ate it for lunch. Luckily Joe came home later that day. He found me lying on the bathroom floor, with the shower running, while I vomited continually down the shower drain. Too ill to stand, I had been in that condition for hours and I didn't have a clue what was wrong with me.

Joe scratched his head and offered me a cuppa, which was his usual solution to a problem, but the thought only made me retch all the more. After a little soothing discussion he coaxed me to my feet. He could see that I was really ill, but he had no idea what to do with me and I was in no state to decide. By way of encouragement he cooed, 'Never mind, hon, you're probably just pregnant again.'

Just what I needed to hear!

'Here, we'll go for a drive, that'll make you feel better.'

That was the last thing I felt like, but I was too weak to object. So off we went, driving into the twilight, with the kids and me packed into the front of the truck, me bouncing along beside Joe with a chronic case of food poisoning.

The days rolled along peacefully enough as I waited in the little cottage for Joe to return from his latest muster. I minded my own business, tending to the children, the garden and whatever sewing was in progress. But living so close to the stockyard was not always an advantage. The new manager had employed a fellow to break in some horses to renew Joe's horse plant numbers. This fellow was a tough, flashy man commonly referred to as the Show Pony, though never to his face. He had a few of his own Aboriginal staff from elsewhere. The memory of one of these young men still haunts me today.

One afternoon, as I watered my garden at the cottage, I heard a commotion from the yards where the horse-breaking was in progress. I watched one of the young ringers crawl through the stockyard rails to sit slumped against a post in the dry grass. His mate hovered above him, hat in hand, and I had a sense that something was very wrong, but the horse-breaker showed no concern. He was the only other white person on the station at that time. I was always reluctant to interfere in men's business – I risked upsetting station protocol by doing so – but I could sense this boy was in trouble, so I wandered over to ask if I could help.

The second fellow told me that his mate Benny had been kicked by a horse. I asked him to show me where and, shyly, Benny showed me the outline of a savage, hoof-shaped swelling on his solar plexus that was becoming angrier by the minute. He was still walking and coherent, but was obviously in a lot of pain, so I suggested that his mate take Benny to the camp to rest while I radioed for medical assistance. Meanwhile, the horse-breaker had driven off to town for the evening.

Unfortunately, it was too late for the flying doctor to land that afternoon. He told me to monitor Benny and said they would come out first thing in the morning if we still required help. Night was falling and there was nothing more I could do, but an unfamiliar feeling of help-lessness enveloped me.

Later that evening, Benny's mate came to me for pain-killers and seemed worried, so I went to the camp to try to help them. Benny was a long way from his own people and he seemed lost and alone. Although he appeared uncomfortable, he hid his pain. He had an unnerving air of fatalism about him. He never complained, but I guessed that he was still in considerable pain and I radioed the doctor again first thing in the morning. The doctor told me to look for signs of blueness around the face or pain on the shoulder tips and they were both apparent, so we finally flew young Benny out that morning.

I heard afterwards that Benny had died several days later of peritonitis. Sadly, due to his embarrassment, he had not shown me the hoof mark on his lower abdomen that had burst his gut and actually taken his life. I felt totally frus-trated when I learned that Benny had died, and wondered what I could have done differently. I consoled myself that I had done the best I could but I am still frustrated to this day.

The total area of Coolibah, with its outstations Bradshaw and Wombungi, was 3964 square miles and Joe mustered all of those areas between 1966 and 1970. The only mail and perishables service to the station was by air. Obviously, that was only if the airstrip was open.

The padre from the Salvation Army offered an invaluable service with his little plane. He was famous for his risky flying and we often joked that he flew extremely close to God. Something was definitely watching over him. In the long wet seasons, when no other soul would be moving about, the drone of his plane was always welcome. At considerable risk, he would land on the muddiest airstrips among the tall spear grass to deliver newspapers and supplies, and would then set up his projector and show black and white movies, accompanied by just enough preaching to his captive but grateful audiences.

The airstrip was between the Victoria River and the homestead billabong. Crocodiles were a constant hazard in Territory rivers. We had been presented with the skull of a twenty-two-foot monster croc from the Aborigines at Bradshaw that was so large it would not fit into a forty-four-gallon fuel drum. On one occasion, when the mail plane was due to land, I had to make a mad scramble to the two-way radio to contact the incoming pilot to abort the landing. I had gone to await the plane's arrival and noticed that the airstrip was literally teeming with migrating crocodiles of varying sizes. They would have been totally unexpected and almost impossible to avoid as they lay sleepily in the morning sun and I had no way to disperse this unusual invasion. It was an amused radio operator who scrambled the airwaves that morning to warn the pilot that the plane must not land at Coolibah because of a crocodile swarm.

The following wet season was particularly long, so Joe had to make what was meant to be a quick trip into town for some desperately needed supplies and a new gas stove for the cottage. My parents had introduced gas stoves and portable gas into the Territory all those years ago and now finally I would benefit. But Joe was trapped in town when the Victoria River flooded. After almost a week, he finally made it to the opposite bank of the river, but he could proceed no further. We were like White Dove and Running Bear stuck on either side of that huge, raging river, until finally the manager felt sorry for us and sent the boys across in rubber tubes to retrieve Joe. He was a non-swimmer, so this must have been a terrifying experience for him and I was petrified that he would drown, or be taken by a croc. As it turned out, the crocs had probably dispersed into the nearby billabongs to wait out the raging flood waters.

Joe rode that wild river on a car tube towed by his Aboriginal stockmen. Tossing about on the turbulent waters, he held aloft a beautiful sewing case that he had brought back for me as a gift. Now that's love!

I was excited. The station was exchanging the old wood burner and things were becoming more civilised. After a few days, the river subsided and the team went back to retrieve the four-wheel drive that sat loaded with the stores and the long-awaited gas stove. It was a supreme effort to get that vehicle back across the flooded crossing. Although the river height had dropped, the current was strong and the water almost over the bonnet. We held our breath as Joe slowly rolled the vehicle into what had been a rocky crossing before the flood. The boys walked ahead through chest-deep water, feeling out for traps in the riverbed. Then, finally across and with all hands on deck, they pushed the vehicle through the waist-deep silt that now smothered the road on the station side. I am still amazed at the tenacity of Joe and his men. I often saw them succeed at many such near-impossible tasks that were well above and beyond the call of duty, just for the sheer hell of it.

24

On Bradshaw's Run

It seemed that Joe's dream had come true when we were sent out to manage Coolibah's outstation, Bradshaw, in the latter part of 1968. This station was situated in rugged escarpment country near the junction of the Victoria and Angalarri rivers that ran west into the isolated Joseph Bonaparte Gulf. To get to Bradshaw's Run from Coolibah, we had to drive roughly ninety miles over rough escarpments, through sandy creek beds and across rocky tidal riverbeds. Crossing the Saddleback Range was always a risk, as it was a sheer drop from a rough track that seemed almost vertical. We had a tucker box and swag on board and were prepared to camp that night if the tide was not in our favour at the last major rocky creek crossing.

Our day travelling to Bradshaw with our heavy load of supplies was spent handling flat tyres, ploughing through miles of either bulldust or corrugations, and using rocks to chock the wheels of the old four-wheel-drive truck as we slowly inched our way over the Saddleback jump-up in low gear. Dusty and tired, we forded the river just in time as the tide was rising, and we finally reached our destination.

The basic, but almost new, homestead backed onto a red escarpment basin that overlooked a valley leading off to the Angalarri River. There was no garden, but we excitedly made plans to develop one, and to spend the rest of our lives together in this intriguing place among those rugged ranges.

Being close to the mouth of those two huge rivers, Bradshaw's wild country is the backdrop to some amazing stories of the voyages and the characters who settled the area.

As history has it, in 1894 Captain Joe Bradshaw had owned his own steamer, which he called the *Red Gauntlet*. Not only a capable seaman, he was also a serious horse and cattle man. He had sent Aeneas Gunn, made famous in the book *We of the Never-Never*, to prepare things for a large herd he had intended to take into Western Australia from Queensland, but instead, due to prohibitive government charges to cross the border, Bradshaw moved these cattle down the Victoria River and took up Bradshaw's Run. It is said that 11 000 of his animals were speared by blacks as he tried to settle into the Territory, so it was not proving to be a very economical venture, particularly after the months of incredibly hard droving that went into landing them there in the first place. Not only was Bradshaw finding settlement almost impossible, his good friend Gunn from Elsey Station had died during this period. But still this determined man persevered.

At one stage, there had been an attempted massacre in the area by the blacks, at which one of the Bradshaw men was killed. Ivan Egoriffe, Bradshaw's then manager, had narrowly escaped with his life. There had been an investigation and trial, and a man from the local tribe was hunted through that rugged country. Eventually he was caught and, as a warning to others, he was hanged for murder from a tree at the Bradshaw homestead by Ivan Egoriffe.

Ivan Egoriffe was Russian. Supposedly a cruel man, he was known as Ivan the Terrible. He had managed the settlement of Bradshaw all those years ago, and had used water pipes as a framework to build the original homestead. The old homestead still stood and we used it as machinery shed. This old shed was always known as the 'singing homestead' and the blacks still held that shed in awe, testament to the terror that Ivan had instilled in their grandparents. Each wet season, the many green frogs hiding in the hollow pipes would become active. A single croak would erupt, followed by hundreds. Reverberating through the pipes that amplified the cacophony of frog song, it would soon become deafening. This fearsome noise was something the likes of which the blacks had never heard before, so this commotion was always referred to by them as the spirit of Ivan the Terrible.

Ivan Egoriffe was eventually killed by Aboriginal raiders aboard the launch *Bolwarra* at the beginning of the twentieth century, along with Captain Bradshaw's brother, Fred, Ernest Dannock and Jerry Skeehan, a young stockman from Auvergne Station. The unfortunate Jerry had broken his arm at Auvergne, and had ridden twenty-five miles towards the Katherine hospital. Riders were sent after him to give him a message to return. Management suggested that he instead take the doomed launch back to Darwin. Sadly, his employers thought this mode of travel by sea would be easier on him.

Some time after the *Bolwarra* set sail, a telegram was received at the main centre for telegraphic communication at Brocks Creek post office, near the thriving community of Grove Hill. It read: *Terrible tragedy, feared massacre of white men all believed dead at Bradshaw's Run.*

Police and trackers were sent to that isolated area and eventually, after much investigation over many months, what was left of the bones of these men was found, and the perpetrators were hunted down.

I believe that Captain Joe Bradshaw eventually died in Darwin in 1916 from gangrene complications. After failed attempts to send his remains to Perth by sea, they were finally entombed on the escarpment at Bradshaw that has become known as Bradshaw's Lookout.

While we were at Bradshaw, the Aborigines in the area gave us a seafaring map that I now realise was probably of great historical importance. Marked in red up the Queensland coast to Cape York was the voyage of the map's former owner. The map was on thick yellowed parchment, and it was written in old-style Spanish or Latin and was dated sometime in the 1700s. What a treasure I had in my hands! Aware of its probable value, I trustingly sent it off to Adelaide for verification, where it mysteriously vanished. How frustrating this is when I recall the old carvings of the tall sailing ships that we discovered on the trees along the Victoria River. These ships were obviously etched into the bark of the white gums as a record by some mariners making their way along the Victoria River. It would have been exciting to trace the map owner's voyage and to relive his adventures through that wild terrain so many years ago.

We quickly settled into our isolated life and, with Joe spending more time around the homestead, we were content and very happy. We had employed a white mechanic and his wife. I found she was good company, but she soon tired of the isolation and they left. I cooked for the men and organised the stores, medicines and station operations, while Joe worked the men and the cattle. There were about forty Aborigines in the camp and, in truth, it always felt like Bradshaw belonged to them. The Bradshaw women taught me the power of the moon. They showed me a spring quite high on a hillside. For most of the month it was dry but, come full moon, it would become a lovely freshwater stream. To me, it symbolised the female cycle which the Aborigines referred to as their 'moon', and so that spring became our special 'woman's place'.

No alcohol was available on Bradshaw, so this was a very happy camp. These people were definitely children of the earth. They spent most of their free time fishing, hunting or performing corroborees. I have attempted to paint this scene, but doubt that any artist could ever depict the essence of those clear starry nights, in a clearing in the scrub. They were particularly attractive people and the vision of their almost naked bodies dancing in the firelight still lingers. I can still see the old music-makers with their didgeridoos and clap sticks seated beside a blazing fire, black, bare-breasted women doing their feminine ankle-driven jig while the lithe black bodies of the men glistened as they pounded their dance into the rising dust, wafting orange in the firelight. It did not seem to matter how long their days had been, their nights seemed to go on forever. Night after night, that haunting sound of the didgeridoo, the clicking sticks and their hypnotic vocal rhythms echoed through the surrounding hillsides. How I miss drifting off to sleep to that comforting sound.

I actually experienced the call of the didgeridoo and I felt, at times, that I had been hypnotised by it. If I had not had babies, I imagine I would have been drawn to dancing with the girls around those fires at night. But even though they would have made me most welcome, I had learned to respect this as truly 'blackfella business'.

Bradshaw Posie became the wife of Tambo, one of the Aboriginal stockmen. She was about sixteen and the sweetest young woman you could wish to meet. Her father, Old Billy, had apparently swum the river at some point where the river was not so wide, and had walked many miles to visit and do business with Tambo about the betrothal. Over the months that followed, on Tambo's request, I sent money, riding boots and a regular supply of tin tobacco to Billy as payment for his daughter's hand.

Tambo was one of four brothers, whose names all started with 'T'. They were good-looking men, all around six feet tall, very fit and athletic and great stockmen. They had worked for us in various places on and off over the years, but their home country was the Bradshaw and Port Keats area.

One Saturday afternoon, following their successful negotiations and at Tambo's behest, Joe offered Posie's old father a ride home by boat. Back down to the junction of the Angalarri and Victoria rivers was a trip of roughly fifteen miles. Tambo was going along and Joe asked if I would also like to come for the ride with the children. We could catch fish on the way home. I was delighted to do this, as any break from the homestead was always welcome. It was not until I got out onto that huge expanse of shark- and crocodile-infested waters that I realised what a risk we were taking. There were no life jackets and neither Joe nor I could swim. I don't think Joe realised how dangerous those waters were. I clasped the children to me that afternoon in mortal fear and my blood ran cold as the boat, with its little twenty-five-horsepower outboard, bounced us over the waves heading towards the isolated, far-off shores of the Victoria River. Trying to relax, I glanced up at what I thought was a huge log floating on the water. Suddenly, it lurched, splashed and disappeared beneath us. This crocodile must have been over eighteen feet long! It was much longer than our little tin boat and I felt that we probably looked like a can of sardines to him.

After what seemed an eternity, we beached at our destination to put Billy ashore. He waded through the shallows, wearing nothing more than his naga, and carrying his spear and his medicine bag. A proud, gruff old man, he headed off alone, with no more than a nod, to walk the many miles along that deserted beach back to the Auvergne Station camp. How lonely and brave this tough little bushman looked, melting into the landscape and gradually disappearing from our view as we pulled away from the shore.

My fears had subsided somewhat and we fished along the way, arriving home safely late that afternoon with several monster barramundi and catfish on board. We were tired, but pleased with our catch – and, I might add, decidedly relieved to have survived our initiation into the wilds.

Our days on Bradshaw were happy, even though we worked extremely hard for only basic conditions and wages. We were so isolated that any social interaction was always welcome. Visitors had to cross the tidal saltwater inlet on the approach to the homestead and a rifle was usually fired to alert the station of an impending arrival. This bang would reverberate around the surrounding red escarpments and a sudden burst of excited activity would erupt within the camp in anticipation. I would cook up a storm and usually a fishing trip or corroboree would follow for the visitor's entertainment.

I would spend hours writing letters home but the turn-around time for replies could sometimes take weeks. We needed a real love of the bush to do without the simple convenience of electricity and telephone that others took for granted. To do without these things when working for ourselves seemed feasible, but working for wages for the betterment of absentee station owners who lived in faraway luxury was always off-putting to me. There were always empty promises of better things to come from the station hierarchy, but we had learned not to expect too much from them. At least we had a roof over our heads. We simply made the most of our primitive conditions and lived in hope, waiting for that elusive breakthrough.

When baby Stephen almost died of dysentery, we decided that we were far too isolated for safety. Because the roads were impassable, the only vehicle available for the dash to hospital was an old ex-army, four-wheel-drive Blitz truck that was used for fencing. There were no doors and no springs or padding on the single passenger seat. While Joe drove us over that horrific road back to Coolibah, I sat with legs stretched to the dashboard to cradle the baby, while holding Paula and Joey under each arm. As we bounced and struggled over the rough terrain for hours, all I could do was pray and keep Stephen as cool and as hydrated as possible.

On arriving at the main station, we took our own car and drove the next few hours to the Katherine hospital. Stephen, now critically ill, was admitted immediately and placed on a drip for several days. We decided that it was a call too close for comfort.

Although we hated leaving the people and the area, sadly, after only six months, we decided to look for better working conditions and we left Bradshaw. We finished off the season catching bulls again back at the main station. Our job was finished and we were anxious to get to town for a much-needed break and to look for more work. The monsoons were arriving at regular intervals and the airstrip was almost too wet to use. We were packed up and excited about leaving that day, but it looked as if there was more rain coming and, if that happened, we would not get out for weeks. In desperation, we finally talked a pilot into landing to pick us up.

The pilot was an older man who did not have a lot of bush experience and, it seemed, not much spirit of adventure. He had landed, but was unhappy about taking off loaded under those conditions. After a bit of cajoling from Joe, he finally agreed. The plane was loaded to the hilt with nappies, babies and the usual family luggage. We settled in and buckled up. But my heart sank as I watched our dapper pilot nervously tweaking his moustache while he studied the airstrip's condition. Soon, Joe was on board and we were tearing down the runway. Huddled in the back seat with the children, I was a nervous newcomer to flying, particularly in small planes, so, like a mantra, I repeated, 'He doesn't want to die, either; he doesn't want to die, either,' as the end of the airstrip loomed. I could see the pilot begin to lose his nerve and I held on tightly to the children and prayed harder, while, above the roar of the engines, I could hear Joe yelling at him, 'Lift the bastard, lift the bastard!'

With a rush of relief, I started breathing again as we circled into the blue skies above and the homestead slowly disappeared beneath us.

25

Eva Valley Station

We were like herders anywhere in the world. We constantly hunted those renegade animals, always on the move to make a living, but always with the promise of a happy home just over the next ridge. In the interim, we had to be happy wherever the work was. While the children were too young for schooling, this didn't present too much of a problem.

Joe was never long out of work and was soon offered a job managing Eva Valley Station, which was situated just north-east of Katherine and bordering Beswick and Arnhem Land.

Eva was a property of 1130 square miles and it was as unique as the old fellow who had owned it. Old Bob had run the place for twenty years and had made the station's buildings out of mud. With no doors or windows to close, this quaint station compound looked more like a Mexican village. The main homestead was built beside a spring that was full of snakes. In fact, the whole sleepy area was full of them. The bathtub stood behind a sheet of corrugated iron on the spring and was filled by bucket directly from the stream. Snakes would often slither over the end of the tub while you soaked, and we quickly learned to shake the towels out well before we dried off.

Bob was an educated but very simple man who spent his days reading. His feet had rubbed deep grooves into the cement where he always sat, exactly in the same position, year in and year out. When we first met him, he had sent his men out to get a killer for lunch. That usually meant shooting a beast for meat. It was a shock even to Joe when they arrived back carrying a large kangaroo, butchered and ready to grill.

Being a shrewd man, Bob had planned to stay put until the new owners delivered his final payment, a new Land Rover that was part of his sale agreement. That and a cruise on a ship were the only plans Bob had for his future away from Eva. He was actually planning to sleep in the back of the Land Rover when he went to live in town.

Eva's main homestead was sparsely furnished but tidy. It seemed grey and colourless. When Bob finally moved over to the men's quarters, I couldn't move fast enough to toss out all the old saddles and equipment that he had stored in the bedrooms – much to his displeasure. With lots of effort and little money, I soon turned the place into a home. Then we initiated it with our customary Christmas and New Year celebrations, with plenty of friends, loud music and much revelry. But still, despite all this intrusion, old Bob was not leaving.

Stephen was just beginning to walk and we enjoyed some lovely family times together at Eva, but as the weeks rolled on, we waited impatiently for Bob's settlement to happen and for him to leave. We could do nothing on the property until then, so we decided to go to South Australia to visit the family I hadn't seen since I had left Mataranka. It was wonderful to see them all again and, after four years, they were thrilled to catch up with my three little ones.

Nothing much had changed within the family apart from them now living under more civilised conditions. Mum was running the post office at Port Augusta and Dad was a whitegoods salesman. Our family had split in two, with my kid sister Kate the eldest of the younger children. My parents were still rigid and stressed as they dealt with this second generation of kids. It was obvious that the tenets of the Catholic Church still controlled the family, along with the underlying volatile energy of my father, but we had all learned to tiptoe around that. Mum made it quite clear that, even though Joe and I shared a bedroom with the children, it didn't mean that she condoned our relationship. In the eyes of the church we were living in sin and so were a bad example to the rest of her family. It must have been difficult for them. It was impossible to explain to her that Joe and I lived with high Christian values. In my eyes, I was living in love and my God was a compassionate one who gifted me my beautiful children.

If anyone deserved to be canonised a saint, Mum did. Although free love and the hippy movement were rampant, age had not wearied her, and she still tried to shield her kids from the outside promiscuous influences. One evening, as the family sat watching the news, an item came on about sex and contraception. Mum actually got up and, in disgust, turned off the TV. I knew little about the subject then, other than when my sister-in-law Colleen took me aside and suggested that I look at prevention. Although my jury was still out on contraception, we were in the middle of the sexual revolution. The pill had been introduced in 1961 and the average family had 3.5 children. I looked at my mother, still bringing up children, still fighting to survive with her asthma and still weathering the control of the church, and I thought, 'What a contradiction!'

While we were in Adelaide, Joe had decided to look for a pick-up horse for the rodeos. He was not riding the roughies any more, but he would pick up the riders who were not bucked off. He found a beautiful grey thorough-bred filly at the Tudor Vale stud that he just had to have. The stud owner's sons were away in Vietnam and his workload was too much to handle, so he agreed to sell Joe this lovely 'Buck's King' filly for $200; but this was only on the proviso that we take eight of his old breeders and give them a good home. We gladly agreed and as we prepared to truck our first little group of broodmares back to the Territory, we had visions of finally having that horse ranch we had always dreamed of.

As happy as my parents had been to see us and to mend fences, they were almost as happy to see us go. An influx of five into a household that size is considerable, and so we were also relieved as our departure drew near.

The Eva Valley owner was a car dealer in Darwin, so on my birthday, against his better judgement, I had talked Joe into exchanging our old Ford for our flashy new Monaro. Joe hated it. During the trip down through the desert, it had sucked in the fine red bulldust like a vacuum until we could see the kids in the back only if their eyes were open. We also found that the dealer had overcharged us, so, furious with him, Joe traded the Monaro on a flashy new Ford GT and he was happy again. Just quietly, so was I.

The mares had all gone ahead by truck and train. We had bought a new horse float to tow home the two stallions that we had also purchased. Soon, with the stallions in the float, the three kids nestled in the back seat and the new car loaded to the hilt, we again headed back out across the desert, arriving home just in front of the wet season's deluge.

When he was finally paid in full, Bob went on his cruise and, as unlikely as it seemed, while aboard the ship he met a couple of extremely wealthy sisters. In order to claim their inheritance, they had been forbidden to marry by their benefactor. They say that good things come to those who wait, and Bob the bushie was claimed by both sisters. Perhaps they never married and, hopefully, they all lived happily ever after.

Although Joe sorted out his differences with Eva's owner, it was never going to be more than a hobby farm, so we stayed only until after the wet. Coolibah wanted us back again to catch bulls, so we sold the old broodmares to Eva Valley and headed back to the little green cottage on the airstrip with only the grey filly in tow.

26

My Dream

We called the grey filly My Dream. She was still Joe's prized rodeo horse, but things began to change rapidly when people recognised her class. Soon, Joe was reluctantly persuaded by his mates to race the filly at the next Queen's Birthday carnival in Katherine.

The excitement of a new challenge was in the air but, to race, the filly's diet had to become serious. This beautiful, leggy filly had become a family pet and could often be found raiding the stores with her black muzzle buried in a drum of flour up to her huge brown eyes. If you didn't keep a close eye on her, she would devour the daily bread I turned out to cool. We kept her in the stockyards and, while Joe was away mustering, I exercised her, supplementing her forage diet with lucerne hay and fresh eggs. She thrived.

I had always been frustrated with Joe for never taking me to the race ball, but he was just not interested. Now, finally, it looked like we would at least be going to the races! Race week was always crammed with activities and Katherine would explode with the influx of people as owners, managers and staff from stations near and far descended on the town for a well-earned shindig. Each station would set up their own camps and campfires around the rodeo, show arena and racetrack. With sideshows and fairy floss, show rings and gymkhanas, races and rodeos, it was always a memorable occasion and the revelry continued from one weekend to the next.

With the impending activities, the manager's wife and I had decided to do a bit of titivating prior to the big week. When I was a child, bleached blondes were frowned upon as wanton women, but Marilyn Monroe was my idol, so, against convention, I bleached my hair regularly. That morning, without a modicum of sense, we agreed that for such a big occasion we should perm and blonde my hair again, both at the same time! This, of course, is a definite no-no. Suffice to say it was an unmitigated disaster. So, with hair like straw, I anxiously awaited the return of my man.

Joe had been away in the camp for two weeks and was due to return the day before our departure for town. He and the boys arrived late that afternoon with a good mob of cattle. He handed the stock to the manager then, tired and scruffy, Joe walked into the cottage, gave me a hug, delivered some huge catfish and some baby crocs for the kids and collapsed in a hungry heap.

I cooked a wonderful three-course dinner for Joe and his offsider Keith, while I anxiously waited for some comment on my hair. Dinner came and went with no indication that he had even noticed. Finally, in total frustration, I blew a fuse. Without a word, I ran into the bedroom, and with typical female logic, I razored off the offending hair, muttering, 'I'll show him . . .'

When I re-emerged Joe looked at me, bemused, but still made no comment. I guess he realised that was his safest option. Then my blood drained into my feet when I remembered that we were due to leave for the big shindig in Katherine the following morning. Shock, horror! Finally, our first big race week and I had a completely unfashionable, inch-long, mangy-looking razor cut. So much for my female logic!

I could do nothing but brazen it out. Arriving in Katherine the next day, we stabled My Dream at Joe's parents' little farm and prepared to celebrate, come what may. During the frenetic ten days that followed, I hid my hair under hats.

All the activities that week were relatively new to me. I was run ragged trying to keep up with the preparations but, amid the turmoil, I did stop one morning outside the chemist shop window. I was like a kid at a lolly shop. There on display were all the sparkly silver trophies and blue race ribbons for both weekends. I had never seen such beautiful silverware! I had no idea how it would happen, but a thrill ran through my veins as my angels whispered, 'They're all yours, kiddo.'

Joe led the rodeo procession that Saturday morning, proudly riding the grey filly along the main street through town. The whole family, including his brother Ray, his sons and our kids looked fabulous on their horses and ponies in procession, wearing the iridescent turquoise-blue team shirts that I had made for them all.

By the time I had fed, clothed and reorganised Joe and the kids for the races that afternoon, I was running late as usual. Joe had asked me to back My Dream for him with a bookmaker, but I had no idea how to do that. By the time I arrived at the track, the filly was streaking to the line in the Katherine Bracelet for her first win, at twenty-five to one! My heart sank. Although I have never been allowed to forget it, the thrill of winning our first race in such a splendid manner certainly overshadowed any money we lost on the punt. But, needless to say, I was never trusted with his punting again. Not only did My Dream win the Bracelet, she went on that same day to win the Katherine Cup. The mood was euphoric and the crowd went wild when our first cup was presented to us that afternoon. It was a popular win so we really had to celebrate. Finally my prince was going to take me to the ball! But alas, I had practically no hair to speak of, and I couldn't possibly wear a hat with my evening dress!

God was not just smiling on me that day – he must have been in sheer hysterics as I rushed around the small town looking for a wig. What a joke!

In desperation, I stumbled into a toy shop that happened to be open and found some doll hair rollers. So I rolled and cajoled each tuft of hair, and happily the results were reasonable. One of my favourite photos was taken that night, with my gorgeous man finally wearing a suit and tie and me wearing that expensive black dress that I had bought in Darwin. That was the first of many of our popular race celebrations over the years that followed.

That was in 1969, and what a week it had turned out to be. These were not yet registered races and the horses often raced twice in a day. Not only did My Dream win the Katherine Cup and Bracelet on that first Saturday, but also the Larrimah Cup and Bracelet that were held in Katherine the following weekend. So my premonition had been right after all, and the trophies in the window *were* ours.

Soon, though, other quality thoroughbred horses began to arrive and it wasn't long before the Territory joined the official racing industry. The following year we loaned My Dream to a trainer to run in the prestigious Darwin Cup. The race started, but most of the gates didn't open and half the horses, including My Dream, were left standing in the barriers. The race proceeded but chaos ensued among the punters and, before the presentation, members of the public ran off with the trophy in protest. Obviously there were going to be many teething pains in Territory racing as it came of age!

27

Life on the Roper River

With the thrill of racing coursing through our veins, we took the grey filly bush with us again. We had secured a bull-catching contract east of Mataranka on Roper Valley Station. It was managed then by Rob and Anne Gifford. The Territory seemed to be filling with young, ambitious, exciting people and these two were no exception.

We set up our first camp and caravan not far from the main station. Anne was about my age and her children were the same ages as ours, so we soon became good friends. Everyone involved got on well together and we made our own fun. The combination of hard work and even harder play was having great results.

My forte was always target shooting and Joe was proud of my prowess. He would boast that I could shoot the eye out of a needle at a hundred yards with my rifle. One lazy, hot Sunday afternoon, the policeman from Roper Bar and some mates had dropped into our camp for a casual visit. While I made scones, they shared a few beers along with the gossip of the area. To pass the time, they were doing a bit of target practice with their revolvers and making a hell of a racket. They were aiming for a bird poop on the top of a huge termite mound about forty feet away and having no luck. The noise went on for ages. Joe finally wagered that I could hit it with one shot. All eyes were on me as I left the cooking, picked up the .38 Smith & Wesson revolver and blew that poop to smithereens. Joe won a bottle of rum. I was keen to keep shooting, but the boys quietly put their guns away. I guess being outshot by a female was a bit confronting for them!

After several months we moved further into the bush, about twenty miles away from the main station, and we were well into work mode when we received an offer that I thought we couldn't refuse.

It was one of those fresh, golden, dry-season mornings that Territorians wait all year to experience and I was alone with the kids in the camp. Our black and white bitser dog lay in the sun, lazily watching my pet duck and three bantam hens clucking and scratching around while the little red rooster squawked at them from the caravan step. I was having a pretty sloppy morning. Country music was blaring in the background and I was shuffling through the usual Saturday chores. The bread was set and I had just finished building up the campfire with another load of snappy gum to burn down for coals. The holes were dug and the camp ovens stood greased at the ready for the baking.

In the bush, you learn to expect the unexpected and, sure enough, the children soon came running over, squealing with delight. They had found a baby galah that had fallen out of its nest after a crow attack.

'But why can't we keep him, Mummy?' was the chorus, in competition with the constant wailing of the pathetic little featherless bird.

'His mother would be heartbroken,' I explained as I kicked my shoes off, 'and besides, I have enough to do without having to feed it.' With that, I tucked the bird down the front of my shirt and commenced to climb the big coolibah to reach the hollow where I could see the parents stressing out.

I had weaved my way cautiously three-quarters of the way up towards the high nest when I heard a little voice say, 'Mummy, someone's coming.'

I could hear the vehicle approach, but I decided to complete the operation and slipped the baby back into its hollow. Down below I could hear a deep male voice saying to the kids, 'Hello, kids. Where's your mum?' To my total embarrassment, I heard them reply, 'Oh, Mummy's just up in the tree with the galahs.'

When he walked around from behind the caravan, I was mortified to see that it was Big Jim Killen, as he was affectionately known. Jim was a well-respected man in Australia and the president of the woolgrowers' association, among other things. He had dropped in for a cuppa on his way through to the station on business.

Finally, after a slow, awkward descent, I dropped to the ground with a clumsy thud and stood barefoot, my jeans and shirt covered with a mess of flour and bark from the tree. To make matters worse, as I reached out to shake his hand, I noticed that mine was still covered in bread dough and bird fluff. Embarrassed, I hurriedly wiped it off on the leg of my jeans.

'Good morning, Mary, I just dropped in to see if Joe was about,' Jim said, laughing. He handed me a copy of the latest Darwin newspaper.

'No, Jim, he's away but I'll try to raise him on the two-way radio if you like,' I replied, as I stoked up the billy to offer him a cup of tea.

Jim talked to the kids while I tried to connect with Joe on the midday session to see what his movements were. 'Romeo Juliet Tango, this is base. Can you read, Joe?' I repeated the call sign over and over, but there was no reply.

'Never mind, Mary, can't talk over the radio anyway, but you might give Joe a message when you see him. Tell him there's a manager's position on offer in Queensland and to send us a telegram if he's interested.'

My heart leaped with joy! As we drank our tea, he hungrily devoured a slice of fresh damper with treacle, and we nattered about everything in general, while my mind was away sitting on the veranda of some palatial manager's residence in Queensland. I couldn't keep the smile off my face. Then, after planting a kiss on my cheek, he was gone again, and I was ready to start packing to move. That was until Joe arrived home several hours later in reply to the telegram I had sent.

'What's going on, woman?' he asked, smiling as he jumped out of the bull-catcher to give me a bear hug.

'Wellll, Jim Killen was here and wanted to know if you want to manage a property for him in Queensland,' I blurted, unable to contain myself.

'Not likely,' he answered, like he thought I was joking. My heart sank.

When he saw I was serious and how excited I was about the prospect, he told me, 'I'm not going back to Queensland, hon. They'll lock a man up there. A man's got everything he needs right here. I can't let Robbie down on this job and, besides, I'm my own boss here. I don't need no bloody fancy-pants manager's job. A man does best to stick to what he knows best. Anyway, something will soon come up here in the Territory.' And, with that, the subject was dropped and never brought up again. So my childhood dreams about living on a station in Queensland were dashed. It knocked the wind from my sails a bit. But Joe was the man earning the money. I figured he was older and wiser and presumably knew what he was doing, so life rolled on as usual.

We were still battling financially. To make good money we needed our own bull-catching equipment, so we took a gamble and applied for our first loan. The finance was for a second-hand D600 truck and crate, and a new four-wheel drive, which we secured on hire purchase. These basic four-wheel-drive vehicles were relatively new in Australia and had been imported originally for the Snowy River Scheme. Our application was successful and we began what was to become an extensive, mechanically driven cattle-catching operation that ran successfully for another thirty years.

The catching vehicles were set up with old tyres wired onto the front bullbar to serve as buffers. These tyres enabled the drivers, when in pursuit at full speed through the bush, to swerve and bump the animal and tip it off balance. When the animal flipped, the tyre on the bullbar acted as a cushion and was parked on top of the animal to hold it down until the boys could secure its hind legs with their straps. Naturally, the more gently these animals were handled, the better their condition when they arrived at the meatworks. Joe always insisted on the best men and equipment that he could afford and always achieved excellent results. Led by his example, others soon followed suit and this way of catching feral animals soon took over in the Top End.

Before work one morning, we were listening to the world news on the radio and it was announced that St Christopher, the patron saint of travel, had been demoted from sainthood and axed from the Catholic church. We weren't particularly religious, but I had previously glued a St Christopher medal under Joe's dashboard, so, in jest, it was removed with an axe that morning. Following that little ceremony the boys piled in, four to a vehicle, and left to run bulls well outside the huge paddocks. They were gone only an hour or so when Joe returned alone unexpectedly. I could see that he was really shaken.

'What's wrong, hon? What's happened?'

But he was head down in the rubbish drum.

'What'd we do with that medal?' he muttered, searching through the bin.

Then, elated, he held the medal aloft like a trophy and explained, 'Me and the boys were swinging a bull through the scrub flat-chat. I had three guys in the four-wheel drive with me when we hit a log hidden in the grass. The catcher was airborne, spearing us over a deep gully that would have killed us had we gone into it. It was twenty feet wide. Jesus, we should have all been killed! I reckon old St Chris was giving a man a warning, so he's stayin' put with me.'

Axed from the church or not, St Christopher remained in his place on the dashboard of the lead bull-catcher for years to come. Call it what you will, either the power of positive thinking or prayer, but Joe continued to have many miraculous escapes. Considering how many bulls that were caught in such conditions, it was amazing that nobody was ever seriously hurt. During all those years catching, the only serious accidents were two broken arms, a broken leg and a few minor gorings.

As usual, my role was to look after the family and run the camp, stores, medicines and bookkeeping, but now I also had the new horse to train for racing.

We still fed the filly on lucerne and eggs, and why not? It had worked well in the past. But racing was becoming a much more serious occupation and, although I pre-trained her while Joe was away working, closer to the race days Joe's father took over and put the finishing touches to her preparation in Katherine. They were heady days and the little mare seemed unbeatable. We were justly proud of her many trophies and ribbons. Then she had to be registered under the South Australian Jockey Club or SAJC racing rules. The name My Dream was not available, so we registered her as Roper Queen. It is said that changing a horse's name brings bad luck, and this change proved to be no exception.

The Queen's Birthday race, rodeo and show week came around and we closed up the camp and headed to town around the 13th. By this time we had bought another horse called Charter King and both horses were already stabled in town. As we left the station, I felt an unease that I couldn't explain. Joe had left ahead of me in the truck with the staff. The kids and I followed in the sedan, loaded up with camping gear and the pet duck, and pulling the horse float with the kids' pony on board. The kids and the pony loved the fun of the gymkhanas, which usually included peg, barrel, flag and pick-up events, and they were usually held in conjunction with all rodeos and shows.

About five miles from the station on that winding dirt road I narrowly missed having a head-on collision with a station vehicle being driven erratically. It later collided with a grader, causing the driver to be rushed to hospital. Soon after that, I came to a sharp turn in a deep creek crossing, but it was too severe for the horse float. My heart sank to see the float bounce off the tow bar with a sickening crunch, to sit, miserably, nose down in the creek bed.

There was no help for miles. There we sat, the three kids, me and the duck, with the pony sitting in a tangled heap in the front section of the horse float. There is a lot to be said for the convenience of mobile phones nowadays. I could have done with one then. Pondering the situation, I decided the only way to get the float back onto the tow bar was to jack up the trailer. I scrounged around and found enough rocks to support its weight in the sand and commenced the laborious task. After unloading our week's supplies and the bedding and suitcases that I had so diligently packed, I found the jack. Then I muttered and cursed until the job was done. More than an hour later we were on the road again.

While all this was going on, Joe had been pulled up at Mataranka by the local policeman. He was investigating poddy-dodging (cattle-stealing) charges against Joe, which had been lodged by a frustrated neighbour. These charges were unsubstantiated and Joe could prove that he was not near that particular boundary at the time indicated, but although the charges were subsequently dropped, it was a sour note on the day.

Finally, after all these dramas, we arrived in Katherine only to find that Roper Queen was ill with a terrible flu-like virus.

The following day, the vet injected her and advised us to race her in order to stimulate the medication. I must admit this sounded strange to me. But the big-hearted filly raced to the best of her ability that day and was well in the lead when she ran into a strip of twisted railing and broke her stifle.

Devastated, we took her back to Pop's and searched for any way possible to save her. Sadly, there was none, so Joe had the vet put her down with an injection. She was like a member of our family and I cried like a baby when she died. And so we were introduced to the hard reality of racing.

But our rotten run of luck was not over yet. We arrived back at the racetrack in time for Charter King's first race for us. The club was short of equipment and for some unknown reason he carried saddlecloth number thirteen in the four-horse race. This beautiful chestnut gelding was in the lead against the running rail, when suddenly the jockey's leg caught on that same broken rail and he was dislodged, falling heavily. Now we had one horse down and although they had only minor injuries, we had two jockeys in hospital.

We were determined not to be superstitious, but that truly horrendous week was the start of a sequence of events that confirmed that number thirteen was indeed a number not to be trifled with – not by our family, at least.

We returned to Roper Valley without the grey mare, and we buried ourselves in our work again. Life went on as usual. After another few months of bull-catching, it was time to head to town for the annual Mataranka races and rodeo. It was the usual good fun event and, after the rodeo, I was privileged to present all the winning trophies to the riders. I had never kissed so many gorgeous guys! But the following day, I became terribly ill and was admitted to the Katherine hospital, swearing never to kiss another man in my life. It eventually turned out that it wasn't the riders' fault at all; I had contracted Hepatitis A from contaminated drinking water. Apparently, the blacks had been swimming and washing in the spring that supplied the drinking water for the station, so the outbreak was inevitable.

Anybody who has had that awful disease will know how terribly depressing it is. I was a miserable patient. For years I had been hinting about never receiving flowers, so Joe decided to cheer me up and he gave his mother money to buy me some roses. When Mum proudly delivered them to the hospital, I managed to hang on until she left before I broke down in tears. Joe's poor mum had bought a pot of awful pink plastic roses because she thought that they would last longer. Talk about depression!

While I was in hospital, a commotion broke out on the ward late one night. The nurses were jubilant because a set of twins had been born, but the alarm bells went off in my head when they added that they were Aboriginal babies. I knew that for the tribes, the birth of twins was not a happy occasion and that one would surely die. Usually, one baby was considered good, but the second was not. I knew what this meant and could not comprehend why more consideration was not shown to the mother's situation. The next morning, I wandered down the corridors and, to my dismay, found that the new mother was my little friend Posie, the wife of Tambo from Bradshaw. Posie was weak and distraught and, although my heart reached out to her as one mother to another, I felt helpless. I had a contagious disease and Posie was haemorrhaging and in a state of shock, so I was in no position to console her. Reluctantly, I had to leave her in the hands of the medical staff. Sadly, although I did meet one twin years later, I never saw Posie again.

Our children were being looked after by Joe's parents at the time, so when I finally got out of hospital, only half well, I loaded the car with stores and headed for the camp to surprise Joe. He had moved camp after the rodeo and had left me with crude directions. I had to go to Elsey Station and then follow a track for about ten miles. Then, when I came to a certain tree, I should follow that next track for so many miles, and so it went, until I came to a creek with a hairpin bend and a burnt ghost gum. Well, that's where I stayed. It was stinking hot and I was still ill. I had lost my fighting spirit. I had grounded the car on the rocks in the bulldust, and just sat there sulking in the shade. With tears of frustration running down my cheeks, I cursed Joe and anyone else I could think of who was unfortunate enough to cross my mind at that time. Yes, even though he didn't know I was coming, it was all Joe's fault! I guessed that I was about five miles from the camp, but I was certainly not well enough to walk. I had no water and no idea what to do next. After about an hour sitting in the heat, I heard the welcome rumble of a vehicle and soon Joe appeared with his men. Finding me stuck in the creek was definitely not the surprise I had planned for him, and, to make matters worse, he seemed to think my predicament was hilarious.

It didn't take Joe long to get me unstuck and back to his camp, where he had our caravan set up beside a shady billabong. When I had cleaned it and arranged it to my liking, I brought the three kids out and life again returned to normal.

The kids hunted and fished with the Aboriginal women whenever the opportunity arose. Nita was still with us and one day she and Joey came to me with a lovely surprise. She had been teaching Joey to dive for mussels and to hunt for turtle eggs. They were proud of their catch, which Nita had prepared, placing them on a tray and presenting them to me in grand style. So as not to offend, I graciously accepted, but because I was still squeamish and the mussels were not cleaned, I was planning to dispose of them when Nita was not around. Joey could see my hesitation and popped one into his mouth to show me how delicious they were. He began chewing away with much gusto, smiling merrily with the green gritty guts dripping down his chin. My stomach heaved. I persevered with the turtle eggs, but they were just as bad. No matter how long I boiled them, they never lost their slime, so, days later, I buried them under the campfire when nobody was looking.

28

Mustering Elsey

After several weeks, we moved from the billabong and had set up camp at Number 10 Bore on Elsey Station, with their staff assisting with the bull-catching. This increased the mouths for me to feed from five to ten ringers, but it was always fun to have this jovial competition around. The Elsey boys had arrived on the first morning and we were all enjoying breakfast around the campfire when little Joey, who was then four, spotted the Aborigines throwing a goanna into their fire. Like a shot out of a gun, he was gone. After a bit of a tussle, I carried him squirming and protesting back to our camp and, to my embarrassment, in front of all the visitors, he cried, 'But, Mummy, we haven't had our goanna for breakfast yet!' I was mortified and the whole team burst into laughter with someone suggesting that I try feeding the kids baked beans.

The men left and that day passed slowly. I was bored and, because we had no river close by, I took Paula bird-watching that afternoon. I had left Nita showering the two boys at the water tank to cool down, and Paula and

I wandered off through the scrub trailing some beautiful iridescent kingfishers that we had seen. We wandered far away that afternoon and, because it was overcast, we soon became disoriented. It was late in the year and the monsoons were building, bringing occasional heavy storms, and we were caught in a downpour as we headed through the scrub for home. In more than thirty years I had never felt the likes of that stinging rain. It was cruel. It pelted down on us like needles. I knew we were lost and when our tracks were obliterated in the downpour, nobody would stand a chance of finding us. I could only guess the way home in the blinding rain, so, amid the thunder and bolts of lightning, we ran as fast as we could in that general direction. As we ran, I imagined how much trouble our disappearance would cause. After a worrying time the water tank loomed up in front of us and, with great relief, I knew that we were safe. When we eventually straggled into camp, looking like a pair of drowned rats, we found the camp awash with everyone still lying low. Nobody had even missed us.

After the storm passed, with Nita's help I got everything shipshape and ready for the return of the catchers, who were due in at sundown.

The fire and wood had been covered with sheets of tin, so when evening came the billies were happily boiling on a roaring fire. The huge camp ovens were loaded with rich beef curry, rice and vegies, there was freshly baked bread, and tinned fruit and custard for dessert, all ready and waiting for the hungry hordes. But the men were unusually late. Darkness fell as I fed and put my children to bed and waited by the fire, worrying that something dreadful might have happened.

The storm that passed was still a distant rumble. As I sat in the quiet, studying the inky night sky and thinking how lucky I had been that afternoon, I noticed a flashing, like sheet lightning, way off in the distance. The silent flashing through the trees went on for almost an hour, until I realised that it was headlights and that the boys were also lost. Soon, I could make out a low hum of motors and, eventually, the first headlights appeared out of the thick scrub.

A bushman takes pride in his homing instincts, so there were some very embarrassed men that night as they sat around the fire drying out, each one trying to blame the other, and even the stars, for their inability to find their way home. I winked at Paula and we never mentioned that we had also been lost in the storm.

Tony and Nita had returned to their people and Bandy and Glenys were now our head Aboriginal couple. They had worked with us before. Bandy, a big, brawny man with a mischievous twinkle in his eye, took no nonsense from anyone. He kept an eye on the politics in the camps, and peace reigned when he was around. It was well into the dry season and the men were all away bull-catching. We had moved camp again to a big billabong and I had a caravan set up about thirty yards from the water's edge. The five Aboriginal women had their camp in a scrubby area not far away from my camp.

Fishing in the Roper area was a unique experience because the water was usually crystal clear. If I sat quietly over the water on a log, I could watch the big rifle fish, with their black-spotted sides, swimming below. Long-necked turtles swam to and from the bank, while lazy, fat black bream and big silver barramundi would nudge my pathetic dead bait before moving on to better pickings. They would much prefer to lie in wait to feed on any flying fox babies that dropped from the clusters hanging in the branches above the pandanus trees.

The fish were really hungry only at certain times of the month. The rest of the time we had to outsmart them with the tasty grasshoppers that we caught in the tall, dry river grass. We women spent most of our spare hours together hunting and fishing. As no other temptations were available, I became very fit and healthy on a diet of boiled rice and fresh fish that I cooked on the hot coals of the campfire that always waited at the ready.

Over our many years together, the only time that I had a falling-out with Glenys was when I spoke to her about her little boy acting indecently towards another boy. To emphasise my displeasure at her son's behaviour, I told Glenys to tell her boy that if it happened again I would report him to a policeman. Not a wise choice of words!

The next thing I knew, one of the other girls told me, 'Glenys him proper mad one, missus.' Glenys was at that moment going through a thickly wooded area, measuring up tree branches to choose which one to use on me as a killing stick. In some cases, the women's ritual to sort out serious disputes was to burn sticks until they were red-hot charcoal. The combatants would then climb out over the water on a fallen tree to whack each other with the smouldering branches until one of them was defeated and fell into the water. I assumed that this was in store for me and it certainly did not appeal.

There I was with my three littlies, alone, to face the rage of this slighted woman. I tried to maintain my composure on the outside, as sheer panic invaded my innards. How would I handle this? I wondered.

I did the only thing possible. I went to the cupboard and pulled out the trusty old equaliser. I had been taught from a very early age never to pull a gun unless I intended to use it and, as I sat on the bed in the caravan with my .22 rifle, I was horrified at the thought that I might actually have to shoot dear old Glenys. But a confrontation seemed inevitable.

I reckon I must have been having some pretty heavy conversations with my ancestral guides, because my prayers were answered. Right when I thought a showdown was imminent, I heard the distant rumble of a vehicle coming towards the camp. As I stepped outside, lo and behold I saw the men coming through the trees in a cloud of dust, all piled onto one bull-catcher. What a wonderful sight they were, returning by chance for an unscheduled break from their work – or perhaps this was just another case of telepathy!

It didn't take Bandy long to sense what was going on, so he took Glenys aside and, under his command, peace was restored. Joe was never comfortable discussing women's issues, so little was mentioned about the incident and, after a respectable time sulking, Glenys was her usual happy self again. Believe me, I learned a valuable lesson in how to approach such delicate subjects in the future.

Meanwhile, having limited radio reception, we really looked forward to our rare visits to town to stay in motels, just to watch black and white television and catch a glimpse of the 'outside' world. Life in the civilised world was careening forward at breakneck speed. During the previous ten years, there had been the launch of the first Sputnik, with its eerie beep-beeping, when people honestly feared that we were trespassing in God's domain. Soon man walked on the moon and, with the shock assassination of the American president, John F. Kennedy, universal innocence began to fade. Television was in most homes in the big cities and computers were introduced and being mooted as the way of the future. The world was changing rapidly, but none of it seemed of much relevance to us, ensconced in our idyllic way of life, blissfully isolated in our own world.

29

St Vidgeon Station

Still constantly on the lookout for a place to settle and rear our little family, Joe finally relented and gave up contracting. We took over the management of St Vidgeon Station for a Mexican family on New Year's Eve, 1970. This was the station that Joe was looking to manage when we had met in Darwin.

St Vidgeon is situated close to Port Roper, which is at the mouth of the mighty Roper River in the Gulf of Carpentaria. The New Year's revelry was a sign of things to come, warning us that our time at this station was to be yet another unforgettable experience.

During a very wild party that was thrown by the departing owners, Chico and Margarita, I found myself waterskiing for the first time on the huge waterhole beside the homestead. This was very exciting for me, and I figured it was safe enough because they knew what they were doing. Wrong!

I had managed to stand up and ski well into the centre of the waterhole, about half a mile from the ramp, when I was dumped into the muddy brown water. Being a non-swimmer, the sensation of floating in that most vulnerable of positions put the fear of God into me. I tried to stay calm. The boat motor had conked out. I could feel the creatures from the deep congregating for the kill by the time the boat finally circled and came back for me. It was only after I had been unceremoniously dragged back into the boat that the locals pointed out the huge slide into the water. This slide belonged to a monster seventeen-foot resident crocodile in whose kitchen I had been floundering. Perhaps he had not been hungry, or was shy of the boat noise or, as Joe joked, I probably looked a bit tough!

The Mexican cowboys flew their own Piper plane, which was in pretty much the same tired condition as everything else on the station. It was certainly Cobb & Co'ed like everything else. Cobb & Co was a famous pioneering delivery firm that was renowned for getting the job done, even if it meant tying broken parts together with wire, and there wasn't a vehicle on the station that didn't sport a wire twitch somewhere. The plane's condition was so basic that the passengers could actually interfere with its controls by pulling wires under the floor in the back seats.

These were wild pilots, to say the least, and radio communications that day were, not surprisingly, out of order when we flew over to Roper Mission to pick up our mail. I was in the back seat as we lifted off and circled the airstrip to leave the mission. As I looked out of my window, I saw another plane circling to land. It wasn't more than sixty yards away and was on a collision course with us. I am sure that pilot saw the look of shock on my face, because I saw his as he frantically climbed away. I am positive our pilot never knew how close we had come to disaster that day, but I knew better than to cast aspersions on a bush pilot's abilities. It really was a case of sit down, hang on and shut up, and that's how we survived.

The Mexican owners were broke, but Joe made arrangements for a share of the cattle catch. Things went well for quite a while, with life at St Vidgeon reverting from a Mexican way of doing things to a very Australian routine. We spent most of our days running cattle and repairing equipment or fencing. Joe was still mustering the paddock cattle on horseback and he roped each animal that needed branding to the bronco rail. The invaluable bronco horses were held in high esteem for their ability to quietly hold the cattle. It beats me where they got their name. Once lassoed, the rope that was tied to the saddle would slide into a slot in the bronco railing and hold the animal tight, while they were quickly castrated and branded. But things were going through dramatic changes and this method would soon slip into bush history. Joe had always been a forward-thinking man and four-wheel drives were beginning to take over where horses were once used. This was to be the last place I saw Joe use a bronco horse.

Joe had told the Mexicans about an overgrown area on the property where the blacks had found evidence of an old plane crash. The American military plane, apparently with a considerable payload, had gone down during the war and was lost with everybody on board. The actual crash site had never been found by whites. The Mexicans eventually located some aircraft parts, fuel tanks and coins from the area, but whether the wreck was ever located always remained a mystery to us.

St Vidgeon was definitely wild country, miles away from civilisation, but we were happy and doing what we did best. I was overjoyed when, out of the blue, my little sister Frances and brother Gregory arrived on holidays. We enjoyed many fishing trips together to the Roper and Little Towns rivers. We would be mesmerised by the phosphorescent waters at night and thrilled as we watched stingrays and all manner of fish swim under the boat in the morning light. We would lay our catch of trevally or barramundi straight onto rocks that had been heated on the open fire at the river's edge. The white succulent flesh, eaten straight off the bones, was a pleasure never surpassed in any restaurant. Both Greg and Fran fell in love with the Northern Territory all over again and it wasn't long before they too absconded from home for wilder parts.

The fishing was huge on those rivers and some of the fishing stories are almost unbelievable. For instance, Jimmy, our mechanic/handyman, was a very big bloke with a huge heart, the strongest man I'd ever seen. He was also a dedicated fisherman. One evening, we had decided to set chains and cables as fishing lines and tied them onto the winch of a nearby truck. Jimmy had baited his cable line with the tail of a monster hammerhead shark that some professional fishermen had left floating nearby. He was definitely after a big one. He settled into his swag for the evening between the truck and the jetty's end and went to sleep while waiting for a strike.

Joe and I were camped with the kids some distance away when, during the night, there was a commotion from down at the jetty. The groper struck at about ten o'clock. It was so huge that it slammed Jim into his swag, trapped by the half-inch cable that held him tight across the chest. He lay there, pinned to the jetty between the truck and that huge, frantic fish snared on the end of his line. I dare say this would have crushed the chest of a lesser man, but Jim's strength enabled him to lift the cable and extricate himself. He eventually landed the 800-pound monster. The groper still had the tail of the shark protruding from its mouth in an evil, serpentine grin.

When we weren't fishing we would be exploring the wild terrain with the locals. It was during one of these trips that we were introduced to the amazing cave of the Rainbow

Snake. This is one of the most feared and respected creatures in Aboriginal mythology and I thought how peculiar it was that our own biblical Garden of Eden story also involved a snake. The cave was on high rocky ground and seemed to me like a small and primitive cathedral. It looked somewhat like a frozen wave, opening onto a view of the surrounding countryside. Its high walls and ceilings were inscribed with some ancient Aboriginal art confirming that this cave was truly a dwelling of this fearsome and vengeful creature.

Old Harry, an elder from that area, explained, 'Missus, this Rainbow Snake him got plenty arms an' legs an' heads, an' him can't die. If you cut one off him head or something, 'nother one gotta take him place straight away.'

Harry said that the tribal medicine men actually took their power from the Rainbow Snake. The coloured stars in the night sky were considered its eyes, which are not to be gazed upon at any cost. He explained that the serpent devours the storm, hence the rainbow – the serpent's belly being the top colour of every rainbow that you see. I figured that this Rainbow Snake mythology was their tribal social guideline, equivalent to our Bible, as it represented the forces of good and evil. If certain rules were respected you would avoid the snake's wrath. It is said that the snake disappeared physically because it refused to share its shelter with its sister, which perhaps teaches that the community will survive only through sharing, which, as we know, most Aborigines do so generously.

Meanwhile, it was wonderful to have a roof over our heads and some home comforts available. The homestead was quite basic, with red poinciana trees and a nice green lawn within its dry compound yard. The women from the Aboriginal camp helped with the gardening, but I handled most of the other chores myself. However, it was a great help when they watched the kids from time to time. When they all left for ceremonies without notice, I was forced to employ Anita, a babysitter from town, to help with the children. We had only the two bedrooms, so for the short time she was there, she had a bed in the children's room.

It was about ten o'clock one evening and we were both preparing for bed. The men were away and the children were already sleeping soundly. I was brushing my teeth when Anita called, 'Mary, quick, there's a plane coming into the airstrip!'

The airstrip was almost adjacent to the homestead and I knew this was not possible at night.

'It's red and blinking and moving real funny,' she added.

I listened, but heard nothing.

'Nah, you must be seeing the evening star or something,' I told her.

'No, there is definitely something coming!'

'Don't worry, hon, it's okay. Your eyes must be playing tricks on you. You go off to bed now,' I replied.

So she went off to bed and everything was quiet, but when I eventually wandered onto the veranda, I was immediately alarmed by a flashing red light that seemed to be descending towards the far end of the airstrip. At first I thought that it must be a plane in trouble. It appeared to be the size of a man's fist, and its colour pulsed ruby red as it slowly travelled in an ever-descending arc closer and closer to the line of trees that formed the horizon in the night sky.

It was difficult to tell the object's distance without knowing its size. It could have been coming down at the end of the airstrip, or it may have been coming down over the Roper Mission, about thirty miles away. Then again, it might have been 1000 miles away. It was on an agonisingly slow descent as it swung from side to side like a pendulum. When it hit the earth, there was a silent flash, like a visible explosion, that lit the night sky for two or three seconds. Then the strangest thing happened, simultaneous with the flash or crash – every dog on the station ran out in that direction, barking furiously.

By now I was seriously alarmed. 'Should I grab the kids and run or should I lie low?' I wondered.

It's a strange thing how real fear doesn't kick in until after the fight-or-flight instincts have activated.

With a pounding heart, I went out to the airstrip to see what I could in the dark, and I was amazed to find that there was nothing to be seen or heard but the thumping of the station's diesel engine. I turned off the generator so that if it was an invasion of some kind we would not be so traceable. Then I stood for a while in the quietness, scanning the dark airstrip and the black treeline, praying that I would not see anything. Now everything was silent, apart from the thumping of my heart, and I jumped as a cool breeze wafted past my cheek.

Still watching over my shoulder, I hurried back to the homestead to write a note to Joe on the only scrap of paper I could find in the torch light.

Dear Joe,
  I believe we may have invaders. If we are not here when you get back, know that we love you.

In an attempt to make light of the situation I added:

PS: I hope they are good-looking.

With this done, I checked the children and Anita and found all of them asleep. The dogs had quietened down now and nothing appeared to be moving. After sitting in the darkness for some considerable time, I decided we were probably safe and that I might as well go to bed – with our .38 revolver close to hand!

I don't know how long I slept before I was sprung awake by a strange snorting and grunting. The sound seemed to come from everywhere and it was accompanied by a loud scratching and scuffling in the roof. These were noises the likes of which I had never heard before. I froze. Slowly, I reached for the revolver and pointed it at the ceiling. The noise stopped. I thought if it recommenced I would fill the roof with holes, but immediately I thought of how I'd explain the damage to Joe later. 'Stay cool, girl,' I whispered. 'What if it's just some animal?'

At last I began to drift off to sleep again, only to be startled awake by the same sounds. Whatever was in the ceiling sounded as large as a young child. Walking quietly below it, I tracked the scuffling along the veranda, waiting for an opportunity to shoot. Then, from the children's bedroom area, came that fearsome grunting and snorting. I burst into the room with my gun at the ready, only to find Anita, deep in sleep, suffering a bout of severe sleep apnoea.

I was so relieved that I almost laughed aloud, but instead quietly backed out of the room, preferring not to wake the children. Still, the mysterious scuffling in the roof was yet to be accounted for. After a short time, it recommenced and I slowly crept under it, tracking its movement to the far corner of the house, where it seemed to just leave the roof. Poof! As simple as that, it was gone.

I never really found out what it was, but I assume it was a visit by a huge possum at a very inconvenient time. I still couldn't account for the descending light in the night sky that had startled the dogs, though.

It was our responsibility to report strange activities, so the following day I reported the incident to the Department of Civil Aviation. Military planes were sent to explore the area, but we were never privy to the results of the search so, as bush people do, we just got over it. We heard later that other people in the area had witnessed the same phenomenon, but without the accompaniments that I had endured.

We had similar experiences over the years in different places, and although they were always quite unnerving, we were never beamed up. At least, I don't think we were!

We had become good friends with the Mexican family who were now living interstate, but eventually they sold everything and went back to Mexico. The new owner did not suit Joe so, as much as we had enjoyed the place, once again we packed and continued on our wandering ways in search of our dream horse ranch and homestead.

Joe's elusive former wife had finally signed divorce papers and, later that year, he suggested that perhaps we should get married. This was now just a formality and not a memorable event. To keep my parents happy, I practically begged the bishop to allow us to marry in the church, but initially, as Joe was a divorced man, that was out of the question. He finally agreed that we had extenuating circumstances and consented to marry us, with a couple of witnesses, at the side altar in St Mary's Cathedral in Darwin on 24 September 1970.

30

Katherine was a cattle town

November 1971 was the year that both of Joe's parents died. Grandparents were few and far between in the Top End in those days and Mum and Pop filled that role for many families. At any time, visitors could pop in and find Mum in her pinny or apron, baking one of her delicious shortcake apple pies, while Pop sat rolling and smoking his tobacco, ready for a cuppa and a chat at any time of the day or night.

Pop was hard of hearing and Mum had become his ears, so they were inseparable. Apparently, Pop had been kicked in the groin while shoeing a racehorse and had subsequently developed bowel cancer. It was a long time before he was diagnosed, but their cats knew. Each time Pop would suffer a bad bout, those cats would be sitting on him, pawing his stomach and purring heavily to console him.

After a lengthy period of suffering, he was operated on in the Darwin hospital on 13 August, and he died thirteen hours after Mum, who died of a coronary occlusion. She was found dead in the laundry by their thirteen-year-old grandson, Philip, whom they had practically reared. So, especially after our past experiences, we were naturally becoming increasingly uneasy about the number thirteen, because it always seemed to herald a time of chaos for us. Both had been born on 13 December, Mum in 1895 and Pop in 1898. They had both died on the third and were buried together on the tenth. They were well loved in the Katherine district, as evidenced by the huge crowd at their funeral, and their headstone with the two hearts entwined still stands in the Katherine cemetery as a testament to their lasting love.

Joe was hit hard by the loss of his parents and, to compensate, he worked all the harder, catching bulls again over the months that followed. By now, Joe was contracting around the Roper again with his young offsider Dave Hanson, a ringer from Queensland who had joined Joe at Roper Valley. Dave became an excellent cattleman and close family friend over the years. But our children needed schooling, so we decided that it was time for a change. We took over a farm on the Florina Road, just outside of Katherine, which we planned to buy eventually.

Most of the time, I lived alone at the farm with the children, but I had become used to the status quo. There was lots of work to keep me busy between the kids, the horses, feeding stock and general maintenance, but I was a healthy woman with normal desires and my long days and lonely nights were becoming tedious. Paula and Joey had commenced primary school by correspondence while we were on the Roper River, but now I was sending our three children twelve miles into Katherine each day on the school bus. It was a sad day indeed when I lined up my last baby's school shoes and the three of them left home for their first day away at a regular school. The house was now totally empty.

To compensate, I buried myself in my work, but I became really clucky. I wanted another baby. It hit me with an unbelievable urgency. Unexpectedly, I began to crave a dark-haired, dark-eyed daughter, just like my little sister Frances had been. The Aborigines say that a child chooses its parents and I strongly believe their theory. The urge was so strong that I left the kids with my sister-in-law one afternoon and, taking tablets to keep me awake, I drove for several hours to the camp where Joe was mustering. To his surprise and delight, I had only one thing on my mind. It didn't take much seduction as I fluttered my pretty blue eyes and discreetly rolled my unsuspecting, but very willing, husband into his swag. Apart from an interlude with a large snake, we had a beautiful evening under the stars and my baby daughter was conceived.

As strange as it may sound, I began vomiting the very next morning. I thought I had overdone the No-Doz. Into the second week of vomiting, I knew I was pregnant and even had a bet with my doctor, who thought it must be a virus. I won my bet; it was morning sickness, and the intensity of it surpassed even that of my first confinement. But life had to go on. To overcome my constant nausea, I tried to keep busy. One afternoon, as I quietly worked one of the racehorses around the paddock alongside the gravel road, the old school bus came trundling along, the red dust billowing in its wake. I was only ever an average rider at the best of times and could handle the thoroughbreds as long as everything was going well, but as the bus rattled down the bumpy road, the horse shied and decided to put on an exhibition. She began bucking across the paddock. Hat and sunglasses went flying in separate directions as my brain scrambled through my mental bucking horse manual. She was having fun! How ridiculous I must have looked, bouncing along like a sack of spuds. To add fuel to this explosive situation, the kids hung out of the bus windows, whooping, yahooing and cheering as if they were at a local rodeo. This spurred the horse on even more. I promised the powers that be that I would give away riding on my own if only I could survive this one last catastrophe. I hung on with more luck than good management and, thankfully, the mare decided that the game was up and came to a halt at the stables. Apart from a few bruises in unmentionable places, there was no real damage done. So when the bus finally pulled to a halt at the gate, I dismounted and took a bow, pretending that I had it all under control. Only the mare and I knew the truth. After that, because of my pregnancy, I decided to send the racehorses into town to complete their training.

Katherine was a cattle town. Built on the Katherine River, its main street boasted the Commercial and the Katherine pubs. Although frequented by rowdy ringers, it was always a great place to grab a cold ale and savour a cool breeze on those preposterously hot days. There were also a post office, railway station, cafes and two general stores and, of course, there was the police station, from where the local officers kept a friendly eye on the visiting ringers and rouseabouts. Over the years, we watched this rugged little town grow from corrugated-iron structures to the modern tourist township that it is today.

Most people knew us then, even though we had always kept our lives private. I was mortified when it seemed that most of the locals had witnessed an event after a rodeo that was to become the talk of the town.

Joe and his offsider, Dave Hanson, had been out bush for weeks, but somehow Joe and I had managed to have a misunderstanding over something that still eludes me.

Joe was sulking and I knew it was serious because he sent me a message to say that he was not coming to town for the local rodeo. You can imagine my surprise to hear later from Dave's wife that he was actually in town during the event, drunk, and had ridden the feature bull. Dave and Jenny had come home to the farm after the rodeo, but Joe had not and was obviously not intending to.

I exploded. I left the children asleep with Jenny and, with gravel flying in my wake, I sped the twelve miles to the rodeo arena to sort out my man.

It was very late and everything was quiet when I arrived at the darkened arena. Cars were still parked about, but it appeared that everyone had gone to the pub except for my wayward and obstinate husband, who lay asleep in his swag on the back of his four-wheel drive's tray-top.

I always had a healthy respect for my man because, on the booze, his temperament could sometimes be likened to that of the scrub bulls he caught. So I swerved the vehicle to a halt, leaving the door open in case I needed to make a quick escape, and I approached with caution.

'Joe,' I called as I moved closer, but there was no answer. 'Joe,' I called again, boiling for a showdown, but still no answer. I was getting totally frustrated. I found an open can of beer on his vehicle, so I proceeded to empty that over him. Still no answer! He was dead drunk.

So, feeling somewhat cockier, I said, 'You can't ignore me, mate. You're not going anywhere without seeing me, my friend.'

And with that, I proceeded to let down his tyres. Knowing his departure was now disabled, I headed back to the farm with my heart beating furiously in my mouth to await the outcome. This was no man to be messing with!

He finally woke in the early hours of the morning and went to drive off before realising that he had a flat tyre.

He changed this with his spare, only to find that he had another, then another two, and he saw red. I can only imagine how his head felt.

I was pretty worried about facing him. I had seen him go off so many times in the past when straightening out his men, but so far he had never lost it with me and I wondered if I had pushed him over the edge. Happily, by the time he knocked on my door at around 5 a.m., he was exhausted and we simply fell into each other's arms laughing.

We kissed and made up, and later we drove to the hotel beer garden, where it seemed the whole town had congregated for lunch. But I was alarmed by the cheers, whistles and cries of 'Here comes the female deflator.'

I was absolutely astounded that anyone else knew what had happened. Apparently, there had been people parked in cars around the arena that night who had quietly witnessed the whole scenario.

Joe left again and I spent my days vomiting, mothering my children, feeding cattle, vomiting, riding fences, cooking, gardening and vomiting, or doing anything constructive that I could find to fill in the hours my man was away. I was ill from daylight to dark. By now Pop's cat had adopted me. Being a female ginger moggy, she was not only rare but also really special. She knew I was pregnant. She was a prolific breeder herself, but in the forty weeks that I was pregnant, she never was. She would go hunting for me daily and I could hear her yowling, coming across the paddock with huge bush rats in her mouth. She would deposit them under my bed, just in case I got hungry later, and would be most upset when I threw them away.

Joe and I were not happy apart. By the time I was five months pregnant, Joe had practically worked himself into the ground. On a rare visit to the doctor, he was put off work for six months. Things were not working out with the farm deal, so we moved into Katherine to live. Accommodation was scarce in town but we were lucky enough to find an old cottage not far from the racetrack and there we awaited the new baby.

During that period we went south again for a break to see my parents and, as usual, Joe went off with a livestock agent to look at horses. It wasn't long before he found Knickerbocker and Wool Exchange.

At the time we purchased these horses we had no idea how well they would perform and it was quite an adventure, but the adventure really started as soon as we headed home.

It was almost Christmas. We had bought a new horse float and headed home along the Stuart Highway through the desert country with these two beautiful thoroughbreds in tow.

On the first night out we pulled up at Pimba, just south of Woomera, to give the horses a break. As we passed the railway workers' cottages, we asked them for access to the railway stockyards to let the horses out. They obliged but insisted that we come back and join their party that was in progress. We politely declined and headed off to unload our tired family and horses and set up camp for the evening. I had picked up a young German shepherd stray that was riding in the horse float, along with the kids' pet guinea pigs and rabbits, and I let it out for a run.

Joe had his hands full settling the two grain-fed thoroughbreds into the yards for the night. I was about to give him a hand when I heard a scream and strange voices from back at the camp, so I hurried to investigate. I found the camp in chaos. Two scruffy, drunken fettlers had followed us down to the yards. They had been throwing stones that the dog had been retrieving. Apparently, becoming excited, the dog had grabbed Paula on the head for some reason. She seemed shaken, but no real damage had been done, which indicated that the dog had probably been playing.

The fettlers insisted that I shoot the dog. Not knowing what else to do, I suggested that they buzz off and mind their own business.

'If ya don't shoot that bloody dog, we'll get a gun and do it for you,' they insisted.

As they staggered off to their camp, I tried to convey the urgency of the situation to Joe, but, distracted by the horses, he didn't pay much attention.

It was almost dusk as I returned to the children and I could see these fellows staggering back as promised, with rifle at the ready. I warned Joe to come and prepare for trouble.

Joe handed me the horses that were reefing and snorting and headed out to confront these gun-wielding, drunken railway fettlers.

'What the hell d'ya think yer doing?' Joe demanded.

'Gonna shoot ya bloody dog, mate,' came the reply.

'Bullshit, nobody shoots my dog.'

'Oh yeah? Then I'll shoot you, ya bastard,' the gunman yelled, as he turned the gun on Joe.

For a moment, everything froze, but then, as cool as a cucumber and like greased lightning, Joe grabbed the barrel of the rifle from the fettler's hands. I watched horrified as he brought the rifle above his head and whipped it down with a sickening thud against the fettler's neck. With another heavy blow, he hit him again with enough force to smash the rifle at the breech and sent them both packing back to their camp.

'We'll be back, ya bastard,' they warned as they limped away, 'and we'll be bringin' the rest of the blokes with us.'

I slept very little that night, with our swags out in the open and with no hope of back-up if we were attacked, but

I was extremely grateful that I had bought Joe a rifle for Christmas, and that I had a man like him to protect us.

We were still tired as the night slowly lightened into a crisp desert morning, but we packed early and, without breakfast, we quietly left Pimba heading north again, but, sadly, not until Joe had shot and buried the unfortunate dog out in the desert.

On our return, we settled again into our home in Katherine. Against doctor's orders, Joe continued bull-catching around the Katherine district and training his horses. Racing was becoming an expensive hobby. When I suggested that he rest like the doctor ordered, he replied, 'Money doesn't grow on trees, woman.' I knew then that, because of his horses, nothing would stop him working.

Joe became obsessed with racing and spent most of his spare time with the horses and I was enjoying family life. I was finally sharing a pregnancy with my man when, out of the blue, his mate Gus Trippe tipped our lives upside down again. Gus offered Joe a job managing Fitzroy Station. Fitzroy was across the Victoria River from Coolibah and we had loved that country, so we gladly accepted and prepared for the next exciting phase in the search for our dream home.

31

Shadows of Wondoan

Finally we arrived at Fitzroy, the station where this story began with Katie and me fishing. Like Coolibah, Fitzroy also sat at the base of that imposing monolith called Wondoan, but on the opposite side of the Victoria River.

I was almost eight months pregnant with Mary-Lyn and we were excited at the prospect of full-time management with a permanent roof over our heads. We arrived at this deserted property, with the first load of our racehorses and belongings, in the late afternoon on Good Friday 1973. Joe then returned to Katherine for the final load of equipment. This was a return journey of some eight hours, and so I was left with the children, alone again, overnight in this unfamiliar and rundown property. It always felt pretty daunting to be left alone in a new place, miles from anywhere with no communication. I never got used to that.

At sundown, I noticed our old mother cat staring intently under an old wooden bookshelf on the back veranda. It was almost dark, so I lit the kerosene lamp and laboriously dropped down to my hands and knees to see what had her so worried. I suspected a snake that would have to be hunted from our new living quarters. It was customary, when you first arrived, to stand your ground and turf out any local residents – but I wasn't prepared to see the shiny fat coils of such a huge king brown. Its circumference was that of a man's arm, and its beady eyes glared defiantly back at me in the flickering lamplight.

I felt faint, but clambered to my feet and ran to search among our many boxes for the bullets for my trusty rifle. By the time I found them and returned to the bookshelf, it was quite dark and both mother cat and the snake were gone.

The cat was an exceptional hunter and I eventually found her tracking the snake further up the veranda into what was to be the children's bedroom. There she was in the lantern light, staring under the chest of drawers. With gun in hand, I slowly prodded and pulled each drawer from the cupboard until I realised that there was no snake in there. Unbeknown to mother cat, there was a large hole in the wall behind the cupboard that the crafty snake used to exit. Relieved, I blocked the hole. It was a win/win situation; the snake had won a reprieve, and we had secured our territory. But poor old mother cat was not convinced. In the days that followed she sat crouched at that chest of drawers awaiting the snake's return. One day, I made the mistake of quietly reaching over to wriggle a rope in front of her as a joke, only to have her leap six feet in sheer terror. She screamed, reverse-rolled in mid-air and, with hair on end and legs and claws extended, slammed onto me and proceeded to slide slowly down my pregnant body. I wore those scratches for days and I know she was mortified.

On its way to the Joseph Bonaparte Gulf, the fabulous Victoria River ran past Coolibah and Fitzroy stations and on to Bradshaw, Auvergne and Bullo River stations. Bullo was owned by the now famous Henderson family. These were just some of the properties along the Victoria that were all surrounded by those magnificent escarpments and valleys. Like Wondoan, some of those hills carried tales of haunting and were held sacred by the Aborigines, never to be traversed. One of these was the Wailing Hill where, my house girl Katie said, if you listened carefully, you could hear the cries of the babies who had been held captive there since the Dreamtime.

We settled in quickly and soon it was late May. With the birth so close, I went back to the cottage in Katherine with the children to await the arrival of our baby. Just when I was thinking I would rather die than continue vomiting, the morning sickness and the pregnancy came to an end. This time, Joe's brother Ray drove me to hospital.

Contrary to the brown eyes I had envisaged, my beautiful, blue-eyed, blonde daughter was born. This birth was a totally different experience from the others. I was surrounded by friends, flowers and well-wishers. There was even a large photo in the local paper announcing her arrival. She was born nine pounds, two ounces, on 22 June, the same day that Knickerbocker won the Broome Cup, so Joe had a double cause for celebration. He wanted to name her Knicky after the horse, but I objected, so he insisted that we call her Mary. For once he was taking an interest in baby business, so I reluctantly agreed to meet him halfway and we called her Mary-Lyn Eileen.

While I was in hospital, the children had stayed with Joe's family at the farm. When it was time to leave, Joe collected us and we left Katherine for good, heading bush again with our growing family and our new governess.

The station governesses deserve a book of their own, but suffice to say they were an interesting lot. Most properties faced the same conditions as we did, all having to weigh up the values of family life and education for our children. The only alternative to sending the children away to school was to teach them ourselves by correspondence. These lessons were sent from Adelaide, but eventually the School of the Air was established in Katherine via the two-way radio. Now computers and telephones make communications and learning so much easier, but in those days we all endured the same continual flow-through of governesses, if we could afford or find them. These girls were not school teachers, but were mostly there to support the boss's wife by ensuring that the lessons were completed and that the children stayed in class instead of disappearing up to the stockyards with the men or down to the river, fishing.

It was rare that these often pretty young girls made life in the bush any easier for the owners' or managers' wives in the long term, but out of desperation to keep our kids at home we took on anyone we could get – within reason. The girls were usually after adventure and romance and, naturally, the young ringers were keen to oblige. On several occasions, we had romantic liaisons develop and, at one time, we even held a beautiful garden wedding when our head stockman married our governess. Sadly, the marriage was doomed to failure, but at least I felt we had given it a good start.

One of the rare exceptional governesses was Bryony, who was marvellous with the kids and fitted well into station life.

All station staff were warned that a prerequisite to employment was a good sense of humour. Bryony needed this, particularly the first time the children tried to teach her to pull up a galloping horse. To be safe, the children figured that the house-yard fence would be a good stopper, and they were almost right. As she galloped at the fence, it did stop the horse; but the kids thought it was hilarious when their governess disappeared headfirst over the fence into the canna lilies by the gate. Bryony, to her credit, staggered out of the bushes laughing. She had earned their respect, which is probably why she was not subjected to the terror of finding huge dead snakes under her bed or any of the other mischievous deeds that the less fortunate governesses had to suffer at the hands of the kids.

Life consisted of hard work, interspersed with fishing, race meetings, rodeos and gymkhanas for the kids. All these pastimes were really only an extension of what we did for a living, but with the competitive and glamour factors thrown in. However, one particular weekend was not so glamorous.

We had guests at the time and were headed down to the rock hole to do some fishing. I was in the lead vehicle, an open bull-catcher with no windscreen, doors or hood. There were three of us in the front and I was seated on the outside nursing Mary-Lyn. I was looking off into the distance at some horses as we pulled up at a paddock gate and I looked down in time to see the front wheel turning onto a bent stick which then flew up and hit me on the forehead. It was so sudden and so hard I could only think that a horse had kicked me, and then the blood started gushing down my face. I was holding my head in a napkin when the children, who were travelling in the vehicle behind, ran up and cried, 'Mummy, Mummy, what's wrong?' With that, Joe replied jokingly, 'Oh, she wouldn't shut up, so I hit her with a big stick.'

After a quick appraisal of the gaping wound on my forehead, Joe decided that since we were miles from the station and nearly 300 miles from town, there was nothing much we could do, so we proceeded with our plans for a picnic down by the river. Fish were caught, everyone else was happy and I got through the day okay. Apart from the constant throbbing and the swelling, the bleeding had stopped, but alarm crept in when I finally arrived home to inspect the damage. My forehead was badly swollen with a gaping wound that could have used a few stitches and there was black and blue swelling around my eye. The next day, we were heading to Darwin for the big race weekend that we had planned for so long. I begged to be allowed to stay home, but to no avail.

Off we went to Darwin to the races and I decided to brazen out my appearance by using make-up to minimise the battered-wife effect. I thought I had handled it well until I heard that someone had asked little Joey what had happened to his mum. He replied, 'Well, Mum wouldn't shut up, so Dad hit her with a big stick!' I was mortified, but Joe thought it was hilarious. He insisted that nobody would have believed us if we told them the truth anyway, but I was aghast that anyone would think that of Joe, who would never lay a hand on me in violence, and that he would have been receiving such bad press.

Joe continued to work and play hard and, because of the size of the property, he was still away a good deal of the time. I missed him on those long, lonely nights. I had learned from a wiser woman than I that if you feed your man at home, he won't eat out, but my problem was getting him home. It was either a feast or a famine in our bedroom.

To support Joe and to keep our family together, I kept extremely busy during the day being the good wife, teacher, mother, counsellor, doctor, accountant, cook, domestic and general dogsbody. I had become the key person in the business and I thrived on it. I began to teach myself to write poetry and to paint to while away the lonely nights. I found that as long as I stayed busy, I was happy.

32

The rainmaker

A group of our Aboriginal staff had come with us to Fitzroy with their families. Normally, they preferred to stay in their own country, but these were a mixed group and were quite happy to follow us wherever we went, going back to their own country only for ceremonies and walkabouts. Most adults in the camp were employed by us at some time, either working in the stock camp, doing menial tasks around the house or as garden staff. We were concerned for their welfare and offered what facilities we had, and in exchange they offered unlimited loyalty and affection. I never felt unsafe when they were in residence.

Aborigines were not legally permitted to drink until 1967, when access to alcohol was granted along with their citizenship rights. It seemed to take quite a few years after that for the bush people to take up drinking, because they were still protected by station management. It was sad to watch the deterioration drinking caused to their health and to their society.

After their regular drinking bouts, our little group would come straggling back to the station to nurse their usual multitude of wounds. There they would sober up and live happily, until the next binge. It was after one such binge that Katie whispered to me, 'Ol Blazer, him got him big cut longa him chest, missus.'

Old Blazer was my full-time gardener. He was about seventy-five years old and had one wife of nineteen and one about ninety. He would rotate these women whenever there was a matrimonial dispute. As a young woman, Blazer's first wife, Jandiwama, had lost her first husband to a stray spear in an inter-family dispute and had been left with two teenage sons. She had then successfully danced for her new husband at a women's corroboree and she and the handsome young buck Blazer had been wed when Jandiwama was in her late forties.

As time went by Blazer became established as a true hunter and dignitary of his tribe. At about forty, he was promised a female child at her birth by distant relations, but this unfortunate child was to die before her teens.

In his late fifties, Blazer was once again offered an infant girl child called April, who then became his second wife at the age of twelve. At fifteen, she bore him a beautiful son whom they called Mack.

Even in her nineties, Jandiwama was still called upon to make up Blazer's swag or his meals if April ever failed in her wifely duties. This was seen as a reprimand or putdown to the younger woman.

Blazer lived happily at the station and loved his job around the garden. While he tried to live a quiet life, his young wife April made that nearly impossible. I always seemed to be rescuing April from some drama or another for him. Blazer never talked much, but we didn't need to, as we seemed to have developed a comfortable psychic connection.

After Katie spoke to me, I found Blazer watering the vegetable garden and I asked him to show me his chest wound. That green, smelly cut, oozing pus, was in fact a gaping shovel-nosed spear wound, some six inches long, and deep enough to expose what looked like bone, cartilage or sinew, deep in his chest. Placed a fraction further left, this spear would have undoubtedly pierced his heart. Like many Aborigines, Blazer had an extraordinarily high pain threshold, and this was one of the many times that he insisted he didn't want a doctor. He was convinced that 'the missus, 'im good nuf doctor', and so this became another of the various wounds that I either dragged, stitched, bandaged or begged back into place for him over the ten years that he was with us.

One particularly dry year late in August, Blazer was on leave and I employed Billy to take his place. Billy was a big man in his late sixties and was quite an entertaining fellow with a mission-educated and religious wife.

The weather was hot and there was no sign of rain, so Joe decided to move the cattle from A paddock to Range paddock, about fifteen miles away, where there was more feed and water. So it was all hands on deck, and anyone, other than the cook, who could ride was mounted to help move these 1200 steers.

The mob was moving out when Joe sent a message that little Joey was missing from the team. I found him in the garden with Billy. They were sitting around a small, smoky fire with one of my kitchen saucepans, in which sat a big lump of my mauve quartz crystal in water, and it was just coming to the boil.

'Joey! You're supposed to be mustering with Dad. What on earth are you two doing?' I asked.

Billy looked up with a cheeky grin and Joey announced proudly, 'Billy is teaching me how to make rain.'

'Oh sure!' I said in disbelief, looking up at the one little fluffy cloud that floated across a clear blue dry-season sky. 'Fat chance of that. There's no rain in sight for weeks. Come on, Joey. On your horse and off you go with the cattle.'

'Oh, but Mum . . .'

'No buts, Joey. Get off with you now before you get into big trouble.'

Billy just gave me a smug smile and sauntered off towards the house. He had found an old pair of thongs lying outside the kitchen and, in exchange for making rain, he suggested with a cheeky twinkle in his eye, 'This thong belonga no one, missus. Might be I give it him job, eh?'

I agreed. I considered an old pair of thongs a fair exchange for rain at the time and I had a chuckle at the prospect of having our own rainmakers on staff.

I thought no more about it that morning as I worked away in the office until around lunchtime. Then, in absolute disbelief, I heard the soft patter of heavy raindrops on the iron roof. This patter soon became heavier and the bedraggled riders began to return, one by one, saturated by the unexpected downpour. We all danced about in the rain that day, celebrating the beautiful drenching of the parched earth.

There is nothing quite like the sound and smell of the first rains drumming on a corrugated-iron roof, but this rain didn't look like stopping. It rained all afternoon and the rain gauge ran over again and again, until by the next day it measured twelve inches. Creeks were rushing and roads washed away. In exasperation, Joe eventually agreed that the culprit was Billy and he ordered Joey to 'tell that old bastard to get that bloody stone out of that bloody water'.

The rain finally stopped around mid-morning the following day and no more rain came until the usual wet-season storms in late October.

When Blazer turned up for work again, I could see that he wasn't happy – in fact, he was heartbroken. April was not with him, so I feared the worst. When I asked where she was he replied, 'April him been wanna go alonga them white fella longa river. I been talk okay, but them white bugger didn't bring him back, missus.' April and their little boy were gone.

We were not sure if April had run away of her own volition, but we at least needed to find that little boy. This was huge country and they could have been anywhere, so I put the wheels in motion through the Department of Aboriginal Affairs. The next day we received a message that April had been found, but she was still in trouble. She had been dumped at the Wave Hill settlement and had walked into the midst of a man-making ceremony. It was taboo for a woman to come within cooee of such a ceremony. She was being held for punishment. Somehow, the department managed to intervene and April was returned with their son to Blazer, a much humbler wife than when she had left.

A couple of the local people, Mida and Morry, also lived quietly on the station. Mida would become pregnant quite regularly, but sadly, just as regularly, she would miscarry. Eventually one of Mida's pregnancies made it to full-term. But about eight months into this pregnancy, when Mida went hunting with the other Aboriginal women, she fell into a creek and her waters broke. Fortunately, the pregnancy continued without further ado.

Soon, the wet season settled in with a vengeance and, as is the way of the Top End, it rained continuously for weeks. We were cut off from town by road, flooded rivers and the washed-out airstrip. On cue, Mida went into labour.

With her waters having broken weeks before in the creek accident, this labour was certainly not going to be easy. When I was eventually called to the camp, I knew that we were in trouble. We could lose both Mida and her baby.

As I approached the camp, the men were sitting a little way off in a quiet huddle playing cards in the dust. The sun was beginning to wind down for the day and the camp-fires were smoking lazily awaiting the evening's activities. Katie led me to the shed where Mida lay on a bare mattress in the dust, propped against one of the other girls for support. Soon the other girl left and Katie took over that role.

Mida was obviously in great pain but she laboured quietly without complaint. She had apparently been in labour for some time, but, after several more hours of massage, manoeuvring, grunting, groaning and prayers, we eased an amazing, tiny, dark pink baby girl into the world. It was so lovely to have her arrive safely that, apparently, I hadn't noticed much else.

The next morning, as soon as I could free myself from my tasks, I hurried down to the camp to see 'my baby', only to find her with Katie. Katie sat on the ground in the soft morning sun, with the new babe lying naked on the blanket in front of her. She was busy covering the infant with a red paste that she had mixed in an old jam tin.

'What are you doing, Katie?' I asked in amazement. 'What's in that tin?'

'Him ant bed, missus,' she replied, as she threw a stick at a camp dog that wandered too close.

Ant bed or termite mound seemed an extremely abrasive sort of application for this tiny new body.

'What in the name of goodness is that for?' I asked.

Katie replied, 'Well, missus, this baby him li'l bit pink one. This one ant bed gonna make him nice shiny black baby.'

Who was I to argue? I never went into the science of Katie's theory, but little Annie turned out to be a lovely, 'nice shiny black baby'.

*

The annual rains continued to swamp the land and the now-lush grasses were ten feet high following the big wet season. Soon this prolific growth would be rank and dry and would be a constant fire hazard, but this natural grazing had to last through to the following wet season at all costs.

With meagre interest and support from the American owners, we continued to run a successful cattle-breeding program on a shoestring, so to speak, catching scrub cattle to supplement the limited finances provided to run the station. During our time there, we had handled births, deaths, marriages, bush christenings and plane crashes. We had many memorable experiences along the way. But the cattle industry was slipping further into recession and it was during those years that the real spirit of the industry started to decline.

With the introduction of the dole, or what the Aborigines called 'sit-down money', Aboriginal stockmen were no longer obliged to work, so they didn't. Stations could not afford to pay suitable white replacement staff, even if they could be found. The best white ringers obtained jobs on road gangs, because they could earn three times as much as stations could afford to offer. The big rodeos went into decline and the cattle towns began to look for the tourist dollars. It was definitely a time to work smarter, so gradually the helicopters and four-wheel-drive vehicles took over where larger stock camps used to go.

It was January 1979, and if you could sell cattle at all, they were worth about fifteen dollars a head, which was a fraction of their usual value. Generally, we kept Fitzroy running with our own money, always with the hollow promise of better things to come from the owners. In all those years on stations, I had never been paid a wage. I doubt whether many wives were. I guess we were considered to be working for our keep. It was usually taken for granted that we would keep the home fires burning for the survival of our husbands' positions, and we did. Fitzroy was no exception.

We decided to leave the station. For all their talk, the owners apparently had no money. At least, they had no intention of honouring their financial commitments to us. They had managed to continually sidestep the issue of more than a year's salary owing to Joe, but he got wind of a clandestine visit to Darwin by the owner, Alan Chase. It was time for action.

Chase was unaware that we had arranged for accountants and solicitors to represent us and work out some settlement of his outstanding debt to us. A meeting was instigated in the VIP lounge at the airport terminal, where we had managed to corner him on his way back to America.

During that meeting, Alan showed total disregard for any personal commitment he owed us in exchange for the years that we had battled for him. His final indifferent comment was, 'You just need to get more stock off to market.'

That's when Joe's patience ran out. He was a reasonably patient man and it took a bit to get him stirred up. But when stirred up he was a force to be reckoned with. I must admit here that, although I never condoned Joe's occasional violent outbursts, they were more than appropriate on certain occasions. I reckoned that this was probably one of those occasions. Still, I was shocked when Joe, as quick as lightning, grabbed this fellow by the throat. It certainly had everyone jumping to attention. Alan seemed to hang from Joe's grasp like a rag doll. His face reddened and his eyes bulged. It all seemed to be happening in slow motion. Suddenly, the door to the VIP lounge opened and a steward announced calmly, 'Excuse me, sir, but your plane is ready for boarding.' With that, the wily American extricated himself from Joe's grasp, brushed himself down and disappeared from the lounge. Everything returned to normal. It was like something out of a Monty Python movie and I have never been sure if the steward had not simply come to a timely rescue.

The conclusion by our representatives was that we had a legal right to the cattle in lieu of the outstanding wages that were owed to us. So, after six years of committed hard labour and personal investment, we found ourselves totally disillusioned and on the move again with four children, Katie, Blazer, April and several other faithful staff, nearly 450 head of mixed unsaleable cattle, Joe's beloved racehorses, three dogs, a cat, no money to speak of and nowhere to go. But, unbeknown to us, we were headed for a future of extraordinary change.

33

Thirteen miles to Grove Hill

We had heard that a small property further north of Katherine was for sale. Although it was getting out of real cattle country, it had suitable paddocks, feed and water, and we could hold our cattle there in anticipation of more prosperous times. Because of the recession, the property was valued at a mere $75,000 but that was much more than we had. We had nothing but overdrafts!

One of the cattle agents was prepared to lend us $50,000 against our stock and it was left to me to approach the new bank manager at our bank to secure the remainder. The bank managers then were usually a part of the whole land package, almost family, and they often joked that they were used to accepting loan applications scratched on the back of tobacco tins from the rugged cattlemen in the past.

Apart from the vehicles, this was my first attempt at any real borrowing and, although we had no collateral, I had prepared what I thought was a fairly positive application. With nothing more than enthusiasm, I met the manager and put our case forward. We had a good relationship with this bank, but this new manager was a doozie. I hadn't even considered a knockback. I was heartbroken when this tunnel-visioned fellow explained that cattle were a thing of the past.

'I can't use livestock for collateral. I need bricks and mortar. Besides, chicken is the way of the future, Mary, you mark my words!'

I thanked him for his time and, with as much dignity as I could muster, I walked out of the bank and stood on the footpath outside and cried tears of frustration.

Then I remembered a story I read about some African-American who had been knocked back in business, but had persevered and succeeded. So I turned on my heel, walked straight back into the bank, barged into the manager's office and told him all the reasons why he was going to lend me the money – and, amazingly, he did!

I think he was just as amazed as I was when we signed up, and it cemented a conviction within me that my mother-in-law was spot on when she had told me, 'Girl, never say die till a dead horse kicks ya!'

We had inspected Woolner Station and it was everything we'd ever wanted. However, it was well out of our price range, so we purchased Prices Springs Station at Grove Hill later that year. We went ahead and signed the contract and the property was ours. I don't remember the month, though I do remember it was on the thirteenth, because, superstitiously, I had the agent backdate the documentation to the twelfth. We were very excited to take over, but spent our first night sleeping in the car at a flooded creek crossing, arriving at Prices Springs on Joe's birthday, 29 January 1979.

Not only was this purchase a solution to our dilemma, this episode started the ball rolling into what eventually became a successful family business. It certainly didn't happen straight away, but little by little, and under our own steam, it did happen.

At that stage, imperial measurements were a thing of the past, but even to this day the Territory pastoral map still shows properties measured in square miles – and at sixty square miles, Prices Springs was the smallest property on the map. It was in what we cattle people called billy-goat country, because the grazing prospects were so poor. But luck was on our side. It was only a matter of months after our takeover that the industry suddenly kicked back to life and livestock markets and cattle prices rose astronomically, just as Joe had anticipated. So our move paid off handsomely. As a general rule of thumb, what goes around comes around and, in that sense, our former employers on Fitzroy had paid much more for our services than if they had paid our wages honestly.

Grove Hill was an old mining town in the Hayes Creek area and the road sign had always caught my attention from the highway because Groves was our name. It was also, curiously, thirteen miles from the Stuart Highway. The homestead, if you could call it that, was a rusty tin shed with drop-down sides for windows and the interior walls only went three-quarters of the way up. It had been built with old corrugated black iron (untreated) remnants left over from the war. There was no ceiling and at night you could lie on the floor and see the stars through the old nail holes in the rusty tin roof. Often, I would open the oven to see a furry quoll that had squeezed its way through the back gas jet opening peering back at me. These yellow-spotted carnivorous native cats would sometimes run over us at night as we lay watching the snowy black and white TV. Young Stephen had a baby kangaroo that he was hand-rearing and that slept under his bed at night. He was horrified to wake one morning to find only its skeletal remains after the quolls had found the unfortunate creature. But all in all, the place was relatively safe.

We parked a large caravan alongside the building for extra bedrooms and proceeded to renovate on a shoestring. Our new home was fun and pretty in an antique sort of way and we loved it, particularly when the big golden shower trees bloomed over the front veranda and the local parrots came to call. Prices Springs was certainly no advancement on Fitzroy living standards, but the station and the surrounding countryside were packed full of history and character. Above all, it was ours.

The men were kept busy either working stock or racing horses, and finances were pretty tight. Our next-door neighbour Alf Collie helped me to do some of the exterior repairs with whatever materials we could find lying about. But he was kept busy with his own problems, so I just kept chipping away by myself, painting and sprucing. Soon the place began to feel loved like a home should. But I had a habit of overdoing things. The structure had walls that went only a bit higher than the window frames. I decided that it would be both artistic and clever to go down to the creek and collect the huge sticks of bamboo. I would cut these into metre lengths and insert them vertically between the tops of the walls and the eaves, to close in the front, at least.

One Saturday morning the men were outside under the big yellow cassia tree, having a beer and discussing their projects and plans for the races in Darwin that afternoon. I found a huge painter's trestle and leaned it against the wall, then asked April to stand at the bottom and hold it while I climbed up and inserted the bamboo. I figured if I fell I could still catch the eaves and swing like Tarzan's Jane. It may have been a good idea in the comic books, but in reality it was not so effective.

I had almost finished the job when April yelped from below, 'Look out, missus!' I was airborne for a few seconds before the trestle and I hit the floor with a resounding thud. I bounced for a while before becoming very still on the kitchen's cold cement. Gasping for breath, I saw April's shocked face as she stood back wringing her hands in fear and disbelief that she had let the ladder slip. The children ran in to see what the commotion was about. 'Mum, Mum, what's wrong?'

All I could do was gulp for air like a fish out of water, so they ran out to get their father. I still laugh when I remember him storming into the kitchen, surveying the scene and bursting out with, 'Bloody hell, woman, haven't I told you not to use that bloody ladder before?' Pausing for a second, he followed that with, 'Do ya wanna coffee?' A coffee was the solution to most problems for Joe, but it wasn't going to fix my predicament that day. Even under the circumstances, I couldn't fail to see the absurdity and humour of Joe's reaction. Because I knew that he knew no better, and I would be wasting my time looking for sympathy, I staggered to my feet and checked for broken bones. Everything seemed to be functioning okay, so we pretended that the accident had never happened – but it wasn't over for me yet.

It was a big day's racing in Darwin and Joe refused to go without me. I was the business end of the partnership and he needed me there. Paula was about fifteen then and she was doing most of the horse training while Joe worked. Our horses, Knight Lover and Seraglio, were a 'sure thing' that day, so, like it or not, I was off to the races with my swollen nose, black eye, cracked ribs and bruises. I defi-nitely looked like I had done a few rounds with Muhammad Ali. The horses won, which helped to ease the pain, and a good time was had by all, including me – and at least we now had a very tropical and effective entrance to our little abode.

Meanwhile, back at the coalface, while we battled the elements, the children battled through their correspondence lessons, continually distracted by the lure of the gold pan and the ongoing excitement of the cattle- and buffalo-mustering. Days of exploring the Margaret River and surrounding abandoned goldfields were idyllic and definitely more appealing to the kids than books and numbers. For history and geology, it was definitely more educational for them. There were many historical graves scattered around the property and one still in reasonably good condition was that of William Knight Hay, who died at Grove Hill on 23 May 1885.

In the 1890s, Grove Hill had been quite a township, with a large population – including 30,000 Chinese – working on the railways and in the gold diggings. The old cemeteries and burial sites around the station commemorate the passing of this exciting era. It was adjacent to Brocks Creek, which was the mail and communications centre for the old telegraph line that served the whole isolated Top End in those bygone days of Captain Bradshaw.

The Chinese had worked hard building the railway and digging in the mines and, while they worked without complaint, it is said that they sent a lot of gold home to China, secreted in the urns that carried the bones of their dead. History tells that they were receiving about a shilling a day for digging. When they suggested that they receive a raise, their employers rejected the request, so in their true humble style, they returned to work. However, they spent the night before cutting down the size of their shovels to ensure that they moved only what they considered equal dirt for equal pay.

But the prosperous and thriving community had dwindled to nothing more than the old Grove Hill pub by the railway siding. The train had eventually stopped running in the 1970s and it was now a sleepy hollow with very little activity, apart from the occasional miner who would appear, seemingly out of nowhere, or perhaps a wayward businessman leaving the highway for a quiet booze-up.

The only permanent residents in the district were old Alf Collie and Margaret Lucy, the daughter of Territory pioneers. Alf lived next door to us in the now defunct pub with his lady friend Margaret, the daughter of the former publican.

Margaret had suffered a chronic attack of meningitis and was in the hospital when Cyclone Tracy hit Darwin. During the turmoil, Margaret had disappeared without a trace, but Alf was tireless in his efforts to track her down. He finally found her in an Adelaide care centre and brought her, incoherent and incapacitated, back to her beloved sanctuary at Grove Hill.

Meningitis had left Margaret totally disabled, mentally and physically, and we often wondered how Alf could tolerate so patiently her constant frustrated screaming sessions, but he doted on her. She was a large woman and, to move her, Alf had developed a style of lifting her where he would hold her around the middle, stand her feet on his, and shuffle her to and from his car. Alf received no financial assistance for Margaret, because his principles would not allow him to sign an application stating that he had a de facto relationship with her. Because he was not otherwise related, he never qualified for government support as a carer, so he managed the best way he could. Each wet season, when those dry creeks ran, Alf used to pan and fossick enough gold to provide adequately for them both for the following dry season. This was indeed a unique love affair that had weathered adversity and the years. In their younger days, Alf had only been the gardener at the pub, was not Catholic and was therefore not considered a suitable marriage partner for the publican's only daughter. Yet Alf was devoted to Margaret, nursing her until her death in the late 1980s.

When he could get away from Margaret's side, Alf would teach us all about the area's history and about the Chinese coins, antiques, machinery and horse gear that we found. He also taught us about mining and how to pan for gold in those rugged creek beds. Alf was clever at anything he turned his hand to, from building furniture to mechanics. He was a shining example of the genuine, generous nature of the true bushman. He was blind in one eye and I cried when I heard that, after Margaret eventually died, he lost the sight in his other eye when a large splinter struck him while he was chopping firewood.

It was Alf who taught me how to divine or dowse for water with wire rods. My curiosity was aroused, but I never dreamed then that it was going to become so integral to my energy studies later in life.

The water supply in the well that we used on our new property was running out, so family and staff had to walk about a mile down to the creek in the evenings to bathe. The Geo Peko mining crew were on the property at the time and they owed us a few favours, so they offered to drop a borehole down for us.

Because the property was notoriously dry, the big question was: *where?* Joe asked me to search with the divining rods for a place near the homestead. Alf had taught me to use simple fencing wire bent at one end. I soon found a spot not far from where the current faulty well was situated. The mining expert disagreed and said that it was definitely not a suitable bore site, but with my heart in my mouth and my faith in old Alf, I asked them to proceed anyway. Then, in absolute fear of failure, I disappeared to busy myself in the kitchen. I simply couldn't watch as the huge and expensive equipment commenced drilling.

Joe kept coming into the kitchen, teasing, 'Ten feet and no water . . . Thirty feet and no water . . . Fifty feet and no water . . . Seventy feet and no water.' By this time, I was feeling quite ill. Then he burst into the kitchen with a joyous, 'Eighty feet and we've struck oil!' And it probably seemed more valuable than oil to us at the time. It turned out to be a 2000-gallon-an-hour bore with sufficient water to supply all our needs. I was naturally quite chuffed, as the first of my many water-divining attempts had been successful and I could only thank the Lord and old Alf next door.

Prices Springs was catacombed with old mining adits (tunnels) and shafts. It was not unusual to be mustering cattle by helicopter, only to see them disappear out of sight down one of these mineshafts that were hidden in the long grass. It was always a concern when we were out bull-catching that vehicles didn't follow the same downward path.

Originally, we had meant the property to be a base for us, our belongings and our stock, so that Joe could continue working on other properties as a livestock contractor, but in fact we had hit a bonanza.

There were already several hundred cattle on the property when we arrived, but there was also a constant flow of water buffalo wandering the land. Joe had never previously considered mustering buffalo, and originally considered them only as pests that insisted on breaking down the fences around our cattle paddocks. But Sid Parker, a leading stock agent from Darwin, was an old friend of Joe's, and he eventually talked Joe into catching a few buffalo bulls for the live export trade to Asia. Dealing with these tougher, intelligent animals with the huge horns was a nerve-racking experience for the boys, but they soon had it mastered and we never looked back. The more buffalo we took out of the place, the more these nomadic animals poured in from the neighbouring areas. This was the start of a huge buffalo-mustering operation such as the Top End had never seen before.

Not everyone was happy with the change in circumstances, unfortunately. Although our Aboriginal staff had been excited about the move to Prices Springs and seemed to settle in okay, this was not river country. After several months, the group that had come with us from Fitzroy were homesick. They were many hours away by road from their own country and they were also unused to, and very uneasy about, the buffalo. So, sadly, we parted with that little group, and began to lose touch with our Aboriginal friends.

Now, without that help, I continued the endless schooling, cooking, bookwork, fighting off miners, gardening, renovating and helping out wherever I could, while Joe kept the buffalo and cattle and the money coming in. Finally we were working for ourselves, taking our own risks on our own account, and loving every minute of it.

We had our own vegetable garden with chooks and pigs and were almost self-sufficient. One Saturday afternoon, I headed out in Joe's open bull-catching vehicle to a neighbour's property to pick up a boar pig to service my sows. It was a hot, dusty, dry-season day and to help I brought along the kids and Dean, a strapping young footballer from the south, who had just started working with us as a yard builder and musterer.

I had just driven through a gate when a mangy dingo suddenly ran across the road in front of us. Dingoes were killers around young stock and we had to shoot them, so I pulled out the .22 repeater rifle that Joe had left sitting between the seats, and, while still driving after it, I neatly put a bullet between its ears. It fell dead to the ground.

This was a one-in-a-million shot, the type you see in the movies, and I was so chuffed that I sat the rifle back down and continued on our way – pretending, as you do, that this was nothing unusual!

On arriving at the pig farm, I stooped over to help drag the big boar, in its cage, up onto the back of the vehicle. Then I stood upright and BANG!

It happened so quickly and with absolutely no warning. Every nerve in my body virtually screamed at me. I felt this strange sensation run from the top of my spine and part my hair as a bullet from the rifle I had so carelessly left unlocked between the seats whizzed skywards. My immediate thought was, 'What a strange place to die!' I looked around in amazement as this scene in this hillbilly pig yard appeared in slow motion, and I thought again, 'What a really strange place to die.'

Slowly, I readjusted my senses and I realised that, incredibly, I was feeling no pain and was actually still alive.

I turned to see my eight-year-old son Stephen standing in complete shock, still with his hand on the rifle that he had moved to give me room.

This was an indelible lesson for us all and we learned that an automatic repeating rifle definitely needed to be treated with much more respect than I had previously shown it. Luckily, unlike the poor dingo, in this instance my life had been spared.

We had many adventures over the two years we were on Prices Springs, but amid the humdrum of daily life the thirteenth again came into play in a big way.

It was late in the season and we were pushing hard to get as many animals to market before the wet season closed down our operations for the year. In those days, you could sell stock for roughly eight months of the year in the Top End before the roads became impassable. We had our pilot, Alan, fly his chopper over from Katherine for a final muster, but his machine kept breaking down. Finally, after several days and a forced landing with Joe on board, Alan conceded defeat and took his machine home for repairs. This gave our team time for their much-needed break in town.

It was the weekend before Monday 13 August, and we watched as the last of the work-weary but happy staff piled into the back of one ute headed into Darwin. We had no inkling of the disasters that would follow.

Paula had been waiting patiently for this work break, hoping that she could attend a special gymkhana near Darwin, so Joe loaded her horse onto the float and delivered her there. He then proceeded on to Marrakai Station on the Adelaide River floodplains, to discuss a mustering contract there.

Paula was an excellent barrel racer and her sure-footed pony never stumbled, but she competed twice that day and both times her reins snapped and her brilliant piebald pony fell. Although their pride was bruised, thankfully neither Paula nor the pony was injured.

Meanwhile, Joe had driven about twenty kilometres and had just pulled up at the Humpty Doo service station bowsers to refuel when fire exploded under the bonnet of our car, causing major damage. This was a dangerous situation to be in when just one spark could have ignited the whole depot, but thankfully Lady Luck was also with Joe and he was eventually able to contain the fire.

To top all that off, when I pulled up at a service station in Darwin on that Monday the thirteenth, I was approached by a detective for information about one of our staff who had been shot dead the night before. This poor fellow had so happily left for town on the back of the ute with the boys. Apparently, he was having a liaison with a married woman in Darwin but late that evening she pulled out a rifle and shot him dead; simply, in her words, because she didn't want to go to the casino with him. All these events had happened during that same weekend in August, so, naturally, our wariness of the thirteenth began to pick up momentum.

34

Mustering Marrakai

The following month, Joe secured the contract on Marrakai, on the black soil floodplains between the Adelaide and Mary rivers, just across country from Grove Hill as the crow flies but over two hours by road. Those were the days before the fifteen-feet-high thorny weed *Mimosa pigra* had taken over the land and the water buffalo still roamed in large numbers. We had packed everything we could fit into the caravan and vehicles, left a caretaker at Prices Springs and headed out to set up camp on the plains at Wild Bore, an old buffalo abattoir. It was a beautiful area and the short plains grass looked like it had been mown, right down to the edge of the lovely waterway thick with huge-leafed red lotus, waterlilies and many varieties of water flowers. Clusters of buffalo wandered through, birds of all descriptions kept the landscape alive with movement and sound, and wide-mouthed crocodiles sunned themselves on the banks.

Joe went back to Prices Springs with the boys to get more equipment and I was left alone with Paula and Mary-Lyn to set up camp in this idyllic setting. We were still waiting on the water trailer to arrive, so we decided to go to the billabong to bathe before nightfall. Our predicament was that we could not get to the water without getting muddy. We also had to keep an eye out for the lurking crocodiles we had seen throughout the day. I decided a little water-hole under a tree would do and, cleverly, I devised a way of floating out on a makeshift raft, a flat polystyrene sheet that I had found nearby. Asking the girls to keep watch, I stripped off, grabbed the soap and pushed out into a shallow area under a mangrove tree. In hindsight, that was probably a perfect place for a crocodile nest.

Before I even had time to get my balance and get wet, I heard a high-pitched scream from behind me. Little Mary-Lyn was bolting like a startled gazelle back to the camp, while Paula sat splitting her sides laughing on the bank.

'Paula, what on earth is happening?' I asked, naked and helpless on the raft in the waterhole.

'Ssssheee's got a leech, sheeee's got a leech on her,' was all Paula could manage through her laughter. Meanwhile, Mary-Lyn's little legs seemed to cover the 300 metres back to the camp in huge strides, to drop salt onto the dreaded creature that had attached itself to her ankle.

Trying to keep control of the situation from my precari-ous position, I admonished Paula for her ill-timed humour and, as I did, I looked down and noticed that the two-metre white board on which I sat was literally crawling with leeches. They were approaching from all directions with voracious intent. I think I made history then as the first woman to ever walk or run on water. Instead of a bath, we decided to spend the evening with a lick and a promise, so to speak.

*

The boys returned the next day and Joe wasted no time at all setting up the camp ready to commence catching buffalo. Almost immediately, he asked me to book the helicopters to muster, but I was concerned because it was so close to the thirteenth of that month.

'Work it out the best way you can, woman, but we need to muster within the week,' was Joe's reply.

I explained to Alan that he needed to avoid the thirteenth, but he was not superstitious. He laughed away my concerns but, to put my mind at ease, promised that he would finish the two-day muster by the evening of the twelfth.

He arrived on the eleventh. The second day of the muster was long but successful and without incident, and he rolled his swag that evening by the campfire to sleep. As the sun rose on the morning of the thirteenth, Alan had breakfast then headed for home over the floodplains. With a sigh of relief, I watched him disappear, thinking, 'Phew! Thank goodness, he's away from here safely.'

But it wasn't long before we received an urgent message over the two-way radio. It was our manager from Prices Springs telling us that, while flying over our property on his way home that morning, Alan's helicopter had developed engine trouble and had crash-landed. He crashed into the same paddock at Grove Hill where he and Joe had force-landed in that disastrous lead-up to the thirteenth the month before.

This time, his chopper was written off completely, but luckily Alan escaped with just a few bruises. After that, he had a healthy respect for the thirteenth, proclaiming that it would be his day in the office henceforth.

Coinciding with our purchase of Prices Springs, there had been a mining boom and the old leases on the property, that had been dormant for decades, now became promising for the mine owners. My life was now all over the place, between fighting the invasion of mining companies that were threatening to take over Prices Springs, schooling the kids, cooking and keeping the camp running smoothly on Marrakai Station.

Joe and I made a good team. While I fought them on the legal front, Joe physically fought off the encroaching hordes of enthusiastic miners who continually invaded our property, leaving gates open, cutting fences and disturbing stock. Legally, we really didn't have a leg to stand on, because we had only grazing rights on the land. But after a couple of years of disputes, our nuisance value was high because gold prices were at a premium. Happily, we were finally bought out by Geo Peko for well over what we had paid for the property, simply because they wanted us out of their way.

During the defence of our rights as pastoral lease owners, I learned a lot about mining and I decided that, if the big companies were going to drive us away, we should also take a cut of the action.

We had a mining friend working with us at the time called Ben Hall. He was tall, wiry and had been a ruggedly handsome man. He was another of the wonderful Territory characters of that era. Ben was a successful cattleman in his day and, at one stage, he and his wife Kath had bought the same store at Mataranka that my parents had once owned. He was a well-educated and capable man with a pilot's licence, but his life was plagued by a chronic hearing problem and excessive tax penalties incurred on the family property following his father's death. One thing led to another and, finally, he hit the booze big time. His marriage dissolved and he became a hermit and a miner, but he was an extremely good geologist and, before long, he was tracking gold through the Grove Hill area that was as fine as talcum powder. This gold was definitely too fine for the old Chinese miners to extract back in the Grove Hill heyday, but Ben had found a way. He was a real fossicker and had a selection over towards the Mary River that he called Rustlers Roost. It was great to hear of his success there in later years.

So Ben took out a few mining leases with us under the stockyards at Prices Springs, where no one had dared to lay claim. Ben agreed with me that this was a rich area, so I figured, 'If you can't beat 'em, you might as well join 'em.' Who knows? Some time in the future we might finally strike it lucky with our leases there.

We were racing fairly constantly by now with Paula doing most of the training on the station while her father attended to the mustering. Paula had actually got her licence to ride, becoming the second female jockey in Australia. She was born to ride and, with her natural ability, was having quite a bit of racing success. We had become members of the Darwin Turf Club. It was fun after chasing stock all week to then get dressed up to the nines and hobnob in the members-only area. That was, until New Year's Day in 1981.

We had enjoyed a successful day's racing, and were celebrating in the members' bar later that night. It was packed, but surprisingly a member had admitted a couple of very rough-looking characters wearing ragged jeans, shirts and thongs, who were breasting the bar and intimidating the barman and members; but they didn't bank on Joe being there. Joey was mingling in the crowd and Paula, who had been riding that day, was sitting quietly minding her own business and talking to another jockey. I had just finished attending to a little boy who had knocked himself out on the pool table when an almighty ruckus broke out. I turned to see Joe challenging the interlopers.

Somebody warned me to tell Joe to back off as these two had just got out of jail the day before, but that didn't bother Joe. Being hard of hearing, he was an excellent lip reader. He had read them talking smut about his daughter, so it was on for one and all. He was handling the two of them quite well, until one of the members pinned Joe's arms behind him. The crims proceeded to use him like a punching bag. I saw red. I couldn't believe that all these members were standing back and allowing this to happen. Suddenly, I remembered Joe telling me about a time that the same thing happened to him in his younger days. He was nearly killed, but he had played possum. Dropping to the floor, he had come up with a bar stool and sorted out his attackers; so the first thing I thought of was 'BAR STOOL'! I didn't know what I was going to do with it. But the young fellow who held Joe also had to hold the stool at bay so Joe released himself in a flash. Then a fully fledged bar brawl broke out. Joey had come to his father's defence with fists flying, and Dennis, our jockey friend, also rushed in fists flailing. It was sorted fairly quickly and the unwelcome visitors were ejected, swearing and cursing. On the way out, they put rocks through some members' windscreens, but the worse thing was that we figured that one of them had a diamond worth $14,000 embedded in his jaw. It belonged on the ring worn by our friend Dennis the jockey and was never seen again.

Everything settled down and nothing was said about the brawl until a week later. Joe and I received a letter from the Turf Club withdrawing our privileges to patronise the social or members' bar at the committee's pleasure. I guess I had behaved in a grossly unladylike fashion and Joe was a bit of a handful, but I never forgave the injustice of it. These two reprobates continued to frequent the members' bar while we were banned! But Joe's response was 'stuff 'em'. It didn't seem to bother him at all, and the lack of privileges made no difference to our continued success in racing – rather, they made it all the more satisfying.

It was on 23 July 1981, my mother's birthday, that we lost my wonderful brother Mark in a vehicle rollover on the Nullarbor Plains. It was so sad to see my parent's heartbreak as we laid their second boy to rest on that cold, bleak and windy day at Port Augusta.

After selling Prices Springs that year we bought a lovely house in Darwin. Meanwhile, we continued contracting on Marrakai Station. As they grew older, educating the children on the stations had become increasingly difficult, so we had decided they should complete their formal education in town. Almost simultaneously, Woolner Station became available again and, happily, with a bit of juggling, we were now able to afford it. So, at last we bought our dream property, and once again we were packing to start a new home together, and planning to stay forever.

35

The back-up driver

Woolner Station was originally named after the district's Wulna Djeramanga people, who occupied the area east of Darwin when that town was founded in 1869. Only 120 kilometres by road from Darwin, it was a magnificent 647-square-kilometre property with the homestead built overlooking Lake Finniss, a huge lake that constantly teemed with birds of all descriptions. There were white egrets, spoonbills, pelicans and the little jacanas that flitted across the lily-pads on their spindly legs. There were the big black and white jabirus, with their huge black beaks, that strode on red, reedy legs in search of prey, and the elegant, high-flying grey brolgas that would put on their wonderful dancing displays or spiral high into the skies above. Black and white geese and brown wood ducks swarmed to the lake and beautiful kingfishers and parrots of all descriptions frequented the woodlands nearby. These were just some of the wonderful assortment of creatures that added their special signature and sound to this land. There were blue-winged jackasses, but not the real laughing kookaburras – which, my father had once pointed out, was possibly because there was not enough in the Territory to laugh about.

The property was bordered by the Adelaide River and Chambers Bay, where marine life was unlimited. If you rose in the helicopter a few hundred feet above the homestead, you could see the coastline, and we enjoyed many exciting trips out to the Escape Cliffs area or Marie Island. Escape Cliffs still contained remnants of an early explorers' settlement which was every bit as exciting as the previous Bradshaw stories.

When we arrived, the homestead was extremely basic and in a shoddy, rundown condition. Cockroaches and white ants overran the place and the water was of poor quality. But the beauty of the property overshadowed all that. We were thrilled with our acquisition. And by now, I was used to renovating!

It was an exciting prospect, with the same set of circumstances as most other properties, except for our proximity to Darwin. We were now resident owners, but didn't enjoy the privileges of 'old money', or the advantages of spending corporate tax dollars, as most white-collar management did. To make this venture work, Joe had to muster enough stock, which I then had to turn into enough money, to keep the wheels of our operation turning. I was anxious, but Joe never doubted our ability to do just that.

About this time, a mate of Joe's had developed the bionic arm bull-catching method. With the aid of a hydraulic winch installed on a speeding vehicle, a metal arm was lowered over a galloping bull's neck. This was much quicker and less stressful than throwing the animals and soon Joe and the boys had this method down almost to an art form. When an animal was spotted, one vehicle would haze the animal, running it straight to a point where the other vehicle's bionic arm could be lowered, trapping the animal. It would then be hauled directly onto a waiting truck. This was used mainly on rogues or in conjunction with the helicopter mustering.

One hot, dry day, late in the season, Joe had a huge helicopter muster planned. That morning, the swarms of geese lifted from the lake in the front of the homestead as the thumping of the helicopter blades heralded the sunrise. It had been another 4 a.m. start for me to prepare breakfast, then I sat, coffee mug in hand, surrounded by breakfast dishes, and watched as the day exploded, coming alive with a bang. The noise was deafening as the three Bell 47 helicopters warmed up. With blades thumping, they flew off in formation over the homestead, headed for a big day's buffalo-mustering over the Paperbark area on the neighbouring Mary River Reserve, about twenty-five kilometres from the homestead. Accompanying the roar of these helicopters was the revving of the four bull-catching vehicles as they prepared to work in unison as back-up mustering machines.

Helicopter mustering was always a big financial risk and it depended on the stealth and know-how of the man in charge to pull off such a risky exercise. On this occasion, the portable steel yard panels were already set up and the boys finished running out the hessian wings that would funnel the running animals into the yards.

The helicopters moved backwards and forwards over the area for hours, chasing the little family groups of buffalo hiding in the thick scrub. The pilots broke only to refuel. The ground crew had finished erecting the wings and pulled up around midday for a meal in the shade. They then sat, talking or dozing while they waited for the buffalo to appear.

I was beginning to spend more time at the homestead, concentrating on the cooking, the office and Mary-Lyn's school work, although that day she was allowed to attend the big muster. At about three o'clock that afternoon, Joe arrived at the homestead unexpectedly to fetch afternoon tea. I could see that he was pensive and concerned that the machines were still away and that we had only a few hours of daylight left. He knew that if the helicopters had not brought the animals across the floodplains before sundown, the whole operation would be a waste.

Although I had been unceremoniously phased out of driving the bull-catchers, Joe nevertheless sidled up to me that afternoon as I prepared the evening meal to ask if I wanted to go out with him and watch the muster, but I was less than enthusiastic.

'Aw, come on, hon, you'll enjoy it. It should be a good one,' he insisted.

I could see he wouldn't take no for an answer, so, as usual, Joe got his way. I conceded, thinking perhaps it would be nice to spend some quality time driving with him, but he promptly added that perhaps I could bring out the extra bull-catching vehicle for the muster.

Aha! I was beginning to smell a rat . . .

'Perhaps you'd even like to drive back-up?' came the guarded suggestion. Driving back-up was usually considered a privilege but I was over it, and by now over any romantic notions of spending special time with my husband.

'Okay, so I'm a back-up driver again,' I sighed exasperated that I had been conned again.

He just grinned, and we returned to the muster in separate vehicles. I delivered the smoko and the crew all enjoyed fresh fruitcake and billy tea while we quietly waited under the trees out of sight. Any loud noise can travel for miles and the littlest noise could spook these wild animals, scattering them in every direction.

The plains were dry and the trunks of the paperbark trees stood out starkly like a white hedge in the distance. I could see Joe was getting more anxious as we caught glimpses of the helicopters, zigzagging over that huge area of swamp. The sun was going down and, although we could see the choppers in the distance, there was still no sign of animals breaking onto the plains.

While we waited, I thought to ask Joe where the yards had been set up. They were usually set deep into the scrub, so that the animals could not see them. Once they were trapped in the hessian wings, the animals could only see to run ahead and would be funnelled into the open yards. The helicopters and bull-catchers would be hot in pursuit and, once the buffalo were all yarded, the men would fly out of the vehicles to slam the gates closed before they could get their bearings and escape.

Joe pointed with his usual flat-handed five-fingered point which meant 'in that general direction'.

Suddenly, before he could finish explaining, there was action. We watched in astonishment as the animals broke out of the paperbarks way off in the distance. As far as we could see, a huge, black, shadowy, moving mass of animals spread quickly over the floodplains. Flocks of magpie geese squawked and rose in waves ahead of them, and the dust rose in their wake. This was going to be the largest mob of buffalo we had ever handled in one go. They came stampeding across the plains, head down and stopping for nothing.

Just as suddenly, with a yell from Joe, everyone was in position and the bull-catchers roared into action.

'Okay, you mob,' Joe ordered, 'follow my lead. Mary, follow us, but stay on the tail of the buffalo.'

The vehicles all slipped into gear and the line of hunters headed out across the flats to back up the helicopters for the last crucial chase up the wings and into the yards. During a run it was the driver's job to work with the pilots and keep the animals running straight into the wings. Any stragglers that broke from the outer perimeters were pushed back into the herd by either the vehicles or the choppers.

When these buffalo came, they came fast. They were running for their lives. Because they were coming towards us so quickly, it was soon impossible for me to get to the tail of the oncoming buffalo. Most of the vehicles by then were positioned behind the mob and were pushing past, while I was still trying to get to the rear. So I gave up. Instead, I began assisting one of the helicopters by chasing the breakaway animals back into my side of the mob.

In the last light, the line of trees where the yards were hidden had become indistinguishable. It looked black and uninviting along the tree line and, by this time, it was anybody's guess where the yards were. Then, suddenly, my headlights lit up the hessian wings.

I froze! I knew I was in big trouble.

Hardly daring to breathe, I sat in my open bull-catcher in the wings in the dark. I was right in the path of the oncoming mob as they speared towards what they thought was the safety of the trees. But, at least, now I knew that the pilots had seen where they were heading.

With the speed of the chase, time did not afford the luxury of fear. At that stage, it wasn't the mob I was afraid of as much as Joe. If I caused the mob to scatter, I figured there would be hell to pay. The preparation and financial cost of this muster had been enormous, not to mention the bragging rights that could be lost with one wrong move at this crucial moment. From overhead, above the thwack of the blades, the roar of the engines and the rumble of the animals, I heard the frustrated yelling of the pilot over his speaker, 'Get out of the wings, you stupid bastard!'

But I was now surrounded by galloping buffalo! The main defence of herd animals is to run after the leader. Wild animals are extremely sensitive to strange noises, smells and movement, so one wrong move and I could frighten the lead buffaloes away from where I now sat, right in their path to the yards. I had little time to think. I decided not to move. Instead, I turned off the engine, switched off the headlights and sat silently in the almost darkness, becoming the least of their obstacles. All I could think of, as my heart thumped in my chest and the rumble of 900 stampeding buffalo rocked my vehicle, was, 'Struth! Am I in trouble now!'

I could just make out their forms as the dust rose thick around me. The solid thud of the hooves seemed endless as the black mass of buffaloes ran with their heads down, thundering past with the other catchers hot on their tails. A strange stillness fell as the last few animals lumbered past and on into the yards, where they were finally secured. And then it was all over.

Joe was extremely busy finalising procedures, and I kept well out of his way so as not to give him an opportunity to go crook at me for being caught in the wings. I hoped he hadn't even noticed in the rush. Then, leaving the men to finish off, I dusted myself down and drove home to finish where I had left off preparing their evening meal.

The boys straggled home about nine that evening, tired and dusty, but elated at their success. They were exhausted, so showers were excused. They washed up and slumped around the table with their beers as I dished up their meals. As expected, my actions had been reported to Joe. Boy, did I cop a razzing at dinner that night, during all the excited regurgitation of the day's events. Often that's the bushman's way of paying a compliment, so I chose to accept it as that. Personally, I argued that it was unfair that I wasn't credited with saving the day by finding the wings in the dark, but the boys would have none of that. Nobody admitted that they had not known where the yards were in the darkness, or that if my lights had not shown up the wings, those buffalo would probably still be running. I felt like a hero, however unintentional, but in my experience in the bush, displays of gratitude were seen as a sign of weakness. You were just expected to perform well. So I excused the lack of appreciation. After all, no one but the chopper pilots could really have seen my predicament in the melee. I don't believe that Joe or the other drivers realise to this day just how close I came to wrecking the biggest run we ever had.

36

Unexpected celebrity

Over the years we had many celebrities visit Woolner, probably because it was such an amazing property and so close to Darwin.

While Joe continued contracting on other properties, we kept in contact via the two-way radio. I looked after Woolner and the kids' education while he was away, and acted as gofer, relaying men, food, messages and spare parts back and forth on the long trips out to his isolated camps, several hours away at Wagait Aboriginal Reserve, or in Arnhem Land.

Well into the season, while Joe was catching feral buffalo on Wagait Reserve, I received a message from him that Kerry Packer, Australia's leading media magnate, wanted to inspect Marrakai Station, the property next door, for some obscure reason. Because I was the only one available who knew the country, Joe wanted me to do a survey with Mr Packer and show him the various waterholes and landmarks that he was interested in. I agreed, and we planned to meet at about nine o'clock the following morning at Wild

Bore, the abandoned meatworks near our old campsite by the Marrakai airstrip.

I left my two daughters at home, and took the only four-wheel-drive vehicle on Woolner, an old knockabout, long wheelbase tray-back that we used for fencing. I tracked through the bush for about forty minutes to our rendez-vous point, then, while I waited, built a fire in readiness for morning tea. I boiled water in the old black stock camp billycan from the tucker box on the vehicle and awaited the arrival of the guests in their Jet Ranger helicopter.

The visitors were running fashionably late. On arrival, they sat around discussing plans and sipping tea from our old chipped enamel mugs. Kerry seemed totally at home on the land and I felt comfortable with him imme-diately. I thought that I had suitably impressed our high-flying visitors as they keenly devoured the fresh rock cakes I had made that morning. Things were going to plan until Kerry asked for milk in his tea. Hmmm. I hadn't thought of that. Usually, nobody had milk in billy tea, but I took a spoonful of milk powder, direct from the tin where it had sat for months in the tucker box, and whisked it into his pannikin for him. Then, much to my embarrassment, we both watched in amazement as the yellow powder floated to the surface in an ugly curdling mess. Talk about making an impression! Kerry was a down-to-earth sort of guy, so with a grin he decided to forgo the tea and just settled for more rock cakes, tucking into them with gusto.

Finally, we were off on our flight with two of his men and me in the back seat and Kerry with the pilot in the front. The plains were dotted with herds of feral buffalo, brumbies and cattle. There were pigs and dingoes and crocodiles that lay sunning themselves, unperturbed, on the banks of many of the waterholes that we flew over.

We flew for some time over Marrakai. Each time we landed to inspect a waterhole Kerry would alight and, like a true gentleman, open the door and help me to the ground, then get back in again, closing the door behind me. It was lovely to be treated like a lady for a change. Suddenly, though, he remembered that he had an appointment in town and, without consulting anyone, he ordered his pilot to head straight into the Darwin airport for a noon deadline. I was flabbergasted!

I needed to get home to my girls, but we flew directly over Woolner, way down on the floodplains. I protested, tongue in cheek, that this was kidnapping. By the looks on the faces of his men, one didn't question the big man, but he replied jokingly, 'How much do you think I will get for you?'

'Don't know,' I answered, but, during a bit of cheeky banter, I insisted that I really needed to be returned to Woolner.

Because of the noise of the chopper, there was little point in talking. Within half an hour, we were disembarking at the Darwin airport. All I had were the clothes I stood up in. Again I protested, only half jokingly this time, about this kidnapping. I don't think he was used to my dry sense of humour, or my protestations. He left me with a bemused look on his face, hurrying off to catch a Learjet that had just landed. Thankfully, as he departed, he instructed his fixed-wing pilot to return me to the airstrip on Marrakai Station.

Within the hour, we flew out of Darwin in another aircraft that was on its way back through to Adelaide, and we landed at the lonely airstrip on Marrakai again later that afternoon. I disembarked and watched until the plane was out of sight, making sure that the young pilot got off the rough airstrip safely. Then, turning to the old tray-back to drive home, I was horrified to see that the vehicle had a flat tyre. Well, it was flat on the bottom, anyway. Luckily, for once there was a spare tyre in the back that was not flat. But there was no wheel brace or jack handle, and I was at least thirty kilometres from home or the nearest neighbour.

Boy, was I in a pickle!

In desperation, I set to the laborious task of raising the jack by twisting it a fraction at a time with a shifting spanner that I had found in the glove box. Then I removed the wheel studs by clumsily tapping them off with a hammer and the spanner. Eventually, after struggling with that wheel for what seemed like hours, I had it changed.

Because it was late, I decided that I would take a shortcut home along a bush track that Paula had told me about several days before, but alas, after a huge downpour the previous night, all fresh wheel tracks had been obliterated. Luck was not on my side and I became completely lost. I would follow one disused track after another for kilometres, only to find they led to old mustering yard sites or to waterholes.

I had inherited my mother's terrible sense of direction and became confused as to where I was. Round and round I went, trying to break through the impenetrable scrub, praying that I would not get bogged and hoping that the wheel was actually on tight enough to get me home.

Here I was, lost in the brilliant gold shadows of twilight in this beautiful bushland setting. The shadows lengthened as the sun slid into the late afternoon and plagues of flood-plain mosquitoes swarmed with a vengeance and attacked like heat-seeking missiles.

I could picture myself being stuck out there with the mosquitoes all night. I prayed that my daughters would not worry and come looking for me in the family sedan, because they would surely get bogged in the process.

Panic was now beginning to rear its ugly head. I decided to turn the vehicle completely around and try to retrace my many tracks back to the meatworks that I had left hours ago. In so doing, I eventually found the long way home.

I had left Woolner at about eight that morning. When I finally staggered home just on dark, my sense of humour had completely evaporated. The girls knew I was late, but were unaware that I had gone missing and no one, including the Packer group, had any idea what I'd been through that day.

Although at the time I could not laugh at the comedy of errors, I quite often laugh now about the day that I was kidnapped by the richest man in Australia.

Our operation was getting bigger and, as time went by, we soon had three mustering helicopters that we operated commercially.

Among the many hats that I had to wear was that of licensee air operator. This was an extremely responsible role, which, initially, I knew nothing about, but in desperation I soon learned. I became the only female air operator in Australia at the time and had it not been for the gentle encouragement of Dave Allen, the Department of Civil Aviation's Examiner of Airmen, I probably would never have had the confidence to persevere with it. I studied the hundreds of pages of air ordinances and regulations required to operate aircraft and to keep the pilots safely within their legal limitations, but any aspirations I had of becoming a pilot were squashed fairly quickly after my one and only attempt at flying. It dawned on me then that the urge to take to the air is something you're born with, or not. Also, I felt that my appalling sense of direction would have led me well astray in the air.

To supplement the upkeep of these expensive machines, we decided to run helicopter tours over the property, so

Paula and I put a tourism program together that was a big hit, for the time that it lasted. The grand opening was on 12 April 1987 and it was a beautiful dry-season day. The Territory's Administrator, Commodore Eric Johnston, officially opened the proceedings and it was attended by the Lord Mayor of Darwin, Alec Fong Lim, along with many other local dignitaries and friends.

Our excellent pilots were not afraid to thrill their passengers with low-level flying, chasing buffalo, brumbies, pigs and crocs, hovering so low that they could almost touch them. They visited baby jabirus in their nests in the tops of trees and surveyed the coastline to watch the swarms of crabs and jellyfish and all types of marine life that swarmed the waterways at that time of the year.

Before Paul Hogan made *Crocodile Dundee*, he and his partner Strop had come to visit Darwin. They were planning to make a movie about a stockman who threw bulls by the tail for a living, and they wanted our boys to show them how to do this. In exchange for the tuition, I planned a promotional flight over the wetlands for Paul, hoping to sell our tours. He was not comfortable about flying, so he tried to dodge it, commenting that he'd seen it all before. Suddenly he was in a rush to depart, but he wasn't getting away from me that easily! Finally, I 'persuaded' him to take the flight and he was thrilled by the experience. However, Strop and Paul decided to do the crocodile movie in preference to the cattle theme and nothing more came out of our meeting.

It was uncanny, though, when I found out years later that 'Charlie', the buffalo they used in the now-famous movie, was one that I had previously rescued as a young calf. Very early one morning, several years earlier, our mechanic's wife and I were off to town when we came across a buffalo calf lying in the middle of the Arnhem

Highway. It had probably fallen from a vehicle loaded with buffalo meat that someone had poached the night before – more than likely they had saved him as a pet. His back hocks showed severe rope burns where they had been tied together, which later served to identify him. At that time, due to the brucellosis and tuberculosis eradication campaign, or BTEC, all calves were supposed to be killed by the contractors. I certainly wasn't going to do it and it was not a problem I needed, so I closed my mind and kept driving in the hope that someone else would put him out of his misery.

I had driven for only five minutes before his plight turned me around and I went back. We hoisted this large, week-old calf into the back seat of my brand-new Ford Fairlane, and I took him as far as a government-run zoo near Darwin. Pulling in, I handed the calf to the first attendant I saw, disappearing before anyone recognised that I was a buffalo stock contractor.

Charlie the buffalo was fortunate enough to be reared by the manager of the zoo. They had him desexed, which caused him and his horns to grow huge. It was not until years later when I was talking to the zoo manager that I realised Charlie had become famous and my good deed had turned out so well. He lived for about twelve years and died a celebrity at the store at Adelaide River.

37

Woolner warriors

On the surface, Woolner was everyone's version of the Garden of Eden, and over the years it seemed that everyone wanted to claim it, but the public may have thought twice if they had to deal with the problems that we inherited with the purchase of that property.

The business was beginning to take shape and we were operating three helicopters from a new hangar that we had built. Finally, Woolner started to feel like our home. After a couple of years, we decided to extend, so we had built a modest, modern, two-storey attachment to the old house and it looked quite swish. But what I thought would be my dream home turned into a nightmare to build. We had only intermittent generated power and limited refrigeration, so getting builders to come out of town was always going to be a problem. Unless they had their eskies or ice boxes filled with cold beer, the job was never going to happen. When they weren't working, our stockmen liked a beer or three, even Kimberley cool (i.e. warm), but for these builders, being an hour's run out of Darwin without cold beer was almost equivalent to perishing in the Simpson Desert. They drank constantly. Nothing much had changed in the Territory in that respect in a hundred years, and I quote the famous poet Banjo Paterson's description of the Top Enders of his day: 'They start drinking square gin immediately after breakfast, and keep it up at intervals till midnight. They don't do anything else to speak of, yet they have a curious delusion that they are a very energetic and reckless set of people. But it's all talk and drink.'

It was now the late 1980s and things hadn't changed since the late 1890s. Obviously, working in the oppressive heat can induce this condition, and perhaps old Banjo himself didn't do much more physically than push a pen. Still, this was our first new home and should have been a pleasurable experience. But every step of the way we struck dramas with the building and, once again, I had to embark on legal battles to stay afloat.

Not only did we have to fight the elements to survive in the industry, but immediately on our arrival, there was an application launched by a company which wanted to mine the Woolner floodplains for shell grit. Soon, Woolner began to make the battles on Prices Springs seem like child's play. We would dispose of one problem and another would take its place. We were beginning to feel like Monty Python's famous Black Knight who, as every limb is hacked off in turn, continued to bounce about, inviting the opposition to 'Have another go, mate!' This naturally got us down – but we were certainly far from out!

Joe and I sat together one hot Saturday afternoon on the bare boards of the yet-to-be-built upper storey of the new house, looking over the lake. After a particularly trying week, Joe was just beginning to relax when, on cue, one of the staff yelled from below, 'Hey, Joe, there's a group of blokes just driven through the main gates. I told 'em to piss off but they said they're goin' through the property to the Mary River Reserve.'

This was the last straw. Joe's face drained of colour. 'I'll show the bastards which way's out,' he growled. 'I'll have their guts for garters!'

My heart sank as he stomped down the stairs and, with several of the boys, roared out of the compound in his bull-catcher in a cloud of dust. I just knew that the results would not be pretty.

Joe ordered the intruders off the property, but they refused to go, so he stood his ground and a fracas ensued that finally had them turning tail and running for cover. Unbeknown to Joe, in their hurry to depart, they rolled their vehicle in the loose bulldust on the first bend outside the property. Luckily, no one was hurt.

Totally put out by this humiliation, the culprits were picked up by a group in a second vehicle that they had waiting, and they headed straight to the newspapers to complain about how unfairly they (as trespassers) had been treated. This was all we needed! Not only did we have to contend with shell-grit miners, pet-meat hunters, conservationists, land claims, range wars, the BTEC, mimosa infestations, pigs, saltwater ingress and pig hunters accusing us of shooting at them from our helicopters, but now we had to defend ourselves publicly against trial by media. Finally, we were legally cleared of any wrongdoing and the furore soon settled to a dull roar.

Eventually, the house was completed almost to our satisfaction and normal life resumed. At last, we had a home with colour television and air-conditioning, at least in the living room. We could now close the doors and windows and keep out the swarms of wood bugs and flying ants that were attracted to the lights at night. Woe betide anybody who happened upon one of these wood bugs in their meal, as they tasted revolting! These plagues of insects were so thick that we used to shovel them off the veranda each morning.

Not everything in life would turn out so well though. To begin with, my marriage was apparently floundering. I have always believed the adage that behind every great man is a woman, so I had allowed myself to become Joe's very silent partner. He had always made it clear that, in this man's world, it was paramount for him to be seen to be running the show, so there was always that invisible barrier between us. Consequently, over time, I began to feel more like Joe's performing wife Mary, more his manager than his wife, and the emotional connection between us had begun to fray.

Then, on 30 November 1986 – my birthday – I received the news that my kid sister Kate had been involved in an awful accident and would probably never walk again. We were such close friends and I was shattered. She was forty, beautiful, very intelligent, and had almost finished raising her two children on her own after her divorce. She was just beginning to socialise and enjoy life again, but now was a quadriplegic, confined to a wheelchair. Even then, Kate could see the humorous side of that awful event. As a single mum she had begrudged herself an eighteen-dollar manicure prior to heading to Naracoorte for a big barn dance, but as she had her eye on a particularly handsome man, she decided to splash out. She relates how, after the rollover on a country road, she hung upside down in the seat belt awaiting rescue and looking at her manicured nails. 'Damn!' she thought. 'I knew that manicure was a waste of money!'

Jokes aside, Kate went through hell after that, rearranging a life that she was not sure she wanted. But, definitely her mother's daughter, she would surmount the huge obstacles put in her way, becoming an inspiration to us all.

My kids were almost adults and, although we enjoyed the challenges together and worked long hours, sometimes seven days a week, we did take time off periodically for fishing, rodeo, horseracing and gymkhanas, so there were plenty of fun times too. In her two years jockeying, Paula won twenty-seven races and usually placed. Fashion and fame never took her fancy, although she did well in the Miss Australia quest. After working with her father's horses for so long, Paula became an excellent racehorse trainer. She was now away, successfully training in Western Australia, and later went on to train Crush for the $240,000 Group One Goodwood Handicap in South Australia. Crush came second in that race in 1990, followed by a win in the same race the next year, when he was ridden by the late Ken Russell.

Mary-Lyn had a great childhood, being closer to town than her siblings, but, like them, it was a constant struggle to keep her studying. She never took to riding horses but her life on Woolner was nevertheless action-packed. Her many friends would come to visit, and they could be found flying through the scrub on her quad bike. She often went fishing with her dad and recalls how he would shoot the bait and then, in case of lurking crocodiles, stand guard with the rifle while she went in to retrieve it, much to my displeasure. One particular day, they got so carried away with their fishing that they missed the tide, so that afternoon was spent pushing and tugging the barramundi boat back across the mud flats together. Our girls were as capable as the men, but they were also brought up to be young ladies. I always insisted that, as there were plenty of 'blokes' in the

Territory, a truly ladylike girl was a rare creature and had to retain her femininity at all costs.

Stephen was working with his dad and driving cattle trucks at fifteen, but I decided that he deserved a better opportunity, so I sent him away to Scots College in Sydney for a polish. I spent a couple of days personally introducing him to Sydney, to give him a crash course on self-preservation, showing him the notorious Kings Cross area. As we walked along the footpath, he was smitten when a tall, statuesque blonde in skimpy shorts and top came mincing towards us on ridiculously high heels. That was until I explained to him that things are not always what they seemed in the big city. When I told him that this 'she' was really a 'he', his face turned white.

Stephen excelled at school sports, but, ironically, after having survived his wild bush life with no injuries, he broke his arm during an altercation with a lad at college. So that spoiled his chances in the rowing and football. Scholastically, his heart was never in it. So I gave up after that year and brought him home to continue working with us. He became an excellent cattleman and helicopter pilot. In his time off work, he continued to follow very successfully in his father's footsteps on the southern rodeo circuit.

Joey was our jack-of-all-trades and could handle most problems presented to him. One of my fondest, funny memories of working with Joey happened after an afternoon mustering with the bionic-armed bull-catchers. It was somewhere out on the floodplains on Marrakai and, just on dark, we had pulled up close to a huge banyan tree to set up camp for the evening. As the team wheeled into the camp, Joe directed them to do their chores. Joey's was to grab some wood and set up a fire before it was dark. We all flew out of the vehicles to go about our various tasks and, while Joe and I unloaded equipment, he turned to Joey, who stood leaning, frozen, against the vehicle where he had landed.

Joe snapped, 'Hurry up, son, get that fire going!'

Joey replied, 'Okay, Dad, but there's a snake crawling over my foot.'

'Oh, okay,' Joe said apologetically, before he turned back to our conversation.

It would have almost been five minutes later when Joe exploded, 'Joey, hurry up and get that bloody fire lit!'

I will never forget the plaintive, shaky reply that wafted back through the evening shadows. 'But, Dad, this snake is still crawling over my foot.'

So then we all froze as the huge, dopey old king brown we had disturbed slowly slithered across Joey's foot in the half-light and headed to safer ground.

Joey was an excellent rodeo clown and bull rider and rode the famous bull 'Chainsaw' for seven of the required eight seconds. He eventually took over our livestock transport operation with me and so the family business thrived.

Both boys were scallywags but toiled like men from a very early age. Their bull-catching with bionic arms and helicopter piloting featured in many TV documentaries and we were justly proud.

Staffing was still a constant concern and often we had to take whoever we could get. We had two or three really good men who stuck with us through thick and thin. After a full day waiting for the helicopters to muster the buffalo, the boys would often be still loading them onto the trucks well into the night. For humane reasons, the animals we mustered had to be kept moving before they had time to think or baulk. The mosquitoes were thick on the flood-plains and conditions were hard, but thankfully our men were tough. They loved the bush, the adventure and my homemade bread, and so they stuck around.

The true bushman is usually a gentleman, but the character of the staff was gradually changing. Prior to Woolner, Joe had always insisted that there was to be no swearing in front of women. But as time went by, that couldn't be upheld because the women cooks we occasionally employed would swear worse than the men, much to my embarrassment. Like my mum had done on that train so long ago, here I was, trying to protect my family from the tide of social corruption, but as we moved closer to civilisation, I was fighting a losing battle. I was literally becoming a voice in the wilderness and it seemed those genteel days were almost gone.

Robert was one of our top men. He was a wild, handsome young man of eighteen when he and his crazy dog joined us six years previously, back at Fitzroy. We were very fond of Robert. He was as close to the boys as a brother and, like our boys, he could turn his hand to practically anything. If he was not catching bulls, he was welding or truck driving or cooking. Whenever Robert was around, the camp was complete.

We found ourselves short-handed at one time on Woolner, so Robert and I headed off to town to pick up stores and to look for new men. I had the bright idea to put an advertisement over the radio for stockmen. We were on the move all day picking up parts and stores, so our message was for any interested parties to meet us at a certain service station on our way out of town – but we were in for a shock!

We arrived at the designated service station to find a crowd resembling a riot, all waiting to be interviewed. We looked at each other in horror and wanted to keep driving, but decided to face the music instead. We explained the work and conditions to each one and the romanticised view that these folk had of the ringer's life was soon shattered. Finally, of the fifty or so applicants we interviewed, we had one willing applicant left who had to go and fetch his swag. It came as no surprise that this fellow never returned, so we arrived home defeated in our search and simply managed with what staff we had.

We worked really hard at Woolner trying to make a go of it. At times, we were turning out a record 3000 buffalo a week for export or to the meatworks.

Sadly, the better we performed, the more obstacles the government put in our way. It never failed to make me sad to see those animals trucked to the abattoir, but I consoled myself that their sacrifice was ensuring the survival of their species, although the government was doing its darnedest to quash that theory in its determination to completely annihilate the herds through BTEC. We were just beginning to make ends meet when we were confronted with the final onslaught of the BTEC program. It spelled the end to the harvesting of this lucrative natural resource of feral animals in the Top End and, of course, our income. In the eight years that we were at Woolner, we watched this program decimate the herds and bring the buffalo industry to its knees with untold thousands of animals left to rot. They could have fed people in Third World countries or at least gone into pet-meat cans.

The pastoralists were told by the government that the GATT, or General Agreement on Tariffs and Trade, with America was at risk. So even though the risk was unsubstantiated, and regardless of the huge cost to our pastoral industry, the bureaucrats completely ignored the other overseas markets available and proceeded to wipe out this natural resource, all in the name of the BTEC.

Bovine tuberculosis was reportedly transferable to humans at a rate of one in 13 million and it was treatable.

My two-year-old nephew contracted it and he was nowhere near buffalo at the time. He grew into an extremely fit and healthy young man. As there were only 19 million people in Australia at the time, I could not see that this was an operation worthy of such huge expense. With Joe's encouragement, I continued to battle for the buffalo. In a manner of speaking, he loaded the gun, while I fired the bullets.

The phone rang at daybreak one morning. It was our softly spoken neighbour Charlie Onn. He sounded very distressed. 'Mary, the department are here with a heap of helicopters and the bastards are shooting all of my stock around the homestead paddocks.'

In the background I could hear the rapid fire of SLR rifles blasting away. It sounded like war and Charlie was desperate. Charlie's place was closer to town and convenient, so I figured that because he was such a gentle soul, they were using him as an example to us all of what could happen if we didn't comply with the BTEC. Charlie didn't live long after that, and I figured it was the stress or the heartbreak that contributed to his passing.

Because I was considered a champion of the cause, I went around Australia pushing for something to be done. I was desperate to make this cruel and senseless slaughter and the subsequent waste of this lucrative industry public. I always hated being in the public eye, but I endured TV and radio interviews that caused me to go weak at the knees. At most times, I had such bad stage fright that I remembered nothing of the interview afterwards. While my interviews with Kerri-Anne Kennerley, the ABC and the various current affairs programs probably made interesting news and footage, my pleas fell on deaf ears and the slaughter continued. Still, the dedicated buffalo association group that had formed back home refused to go down without a fight.

In the meantime, to try to counteract the feral-animal issue, we had a tested domesticated buffalo program in place. Buffalo domesticate quite readily and are docile, intelligent animals that are easy to handle. They are tick resistant and prolific breeders. They are also very matriarchal and will adopt and rear many more than their own calves at one time. Intellectually, they are the bovine equivalent of horses, and are a responsive and affectionate animal by nature. But we were fighting a losing battle to keep enough numbers to support a domesticated market.

Joe and I survived, but only just. The BTEC scheme destroyed a way of life for many property owners and their families. These folk have since left the land and will probably never be back. But guess what? The buffalo are back!

Because Woolner and the adjoining floodplain were so close to Darwin, we not only had the usual stock problems but we also had local pet-meat hunters jumping our boundaries, while wildlife hunters, fishermen and drug farmers continued to trespass, to shoot, encroach on and interfere with our harvesting. So we were continually busy, just with self-preservation. We were constantly harassed by these various groups who thumbed their noses at the law, and the law of the land seemed powerless or unwilling to intervene. Certainly, we were not leaving without a fight. Everything we owned was tied up now in that property.

As the animals became cunning and harder to muster, we used to fire shotguns behind them to frighten them out of hiding. But soon pig hunters were accusing us of shooting at them from the helicopters, even though they had defied our prior warnings for them to stay clear. Eventually, after the media had a field day with the story, it was proven that the allegations in the newspapers were baseless. The headline read: COPTER SHOOTING GRAZIERS CLEARED.

Following that vindication, the newspapers carried a Rambo cartoon, which probably made the public think twice about trespassing, but another of the cartoons shows signage blocking everyone's entry onto Woolner, alias Cottonwood Station. The then Chief Minister, Ian Tuxworth, was depicted standing at the front gate of the station dressed in cowboy gear, along with an Aborigine in tribal clobber who is asking, 'Now who's locking up the land?' This, of course, was suggesting that we had no right to stop people trespassing on Woolner.

We felt like we were never going to be left in peace. I decided to counter these latest innuendos with a cheeky advertisement in the newspaper, offering to sell Woolner to the highest bidder. I was more or less telling the public to put their money where their mouths were.

COTTONWOOD STATION

For Sale – best offer over $3 million

Due to increasing public demand, theft, defamatory and derogatory public statements concerning this family, we have decided to make available the above station. This property, being the culmination of our lives' labour, employs up to 20 persons, consists of staff quarters and accommodation, just completed workshop, various heavy equipment, 70 km of new heavy-duty fencing guaranteed to provoke trespassers, and for the real man on the land, we have available ready to shoot and kill approximately 4000 head of quiet cattle and buffalo, some horses, pigs, about 10,000 geese and ducks and several hundred wallabies. All animals being somewhat protected are guaranteed to stand while you shoot. Also available is a

*huge assortment of defenceless flora and fauna. This should
be a real steal for the enterprising hunting club. For further
information, contact the management of the above station.
Genuine offers only.*

This was meant as a slug against the blood-thirsty hunting
clubs and pet-meat catchers. We had no intention of selling,
but to our surprise we were made an offer we couldn't
refuse – a fraction of its worth today – by the same people
who had bought Prices Springs. So we chose the quieter
life and let go of all the hassles involved in owning such a
sought-after property. After eight exciting and exhausting
years and a flood of tears, it was time to go.

So we left Woolner, moving on to what I thought would
be a simpler way of life. On the day of our departure,
I tried to coax Joe to come on a holiday around Australia
with me. We had never been on a real holiday before. But
he declined. Joe was determined that he was not going to
let go of his grip on the industry that he had helped to
establish. I look back now and realise that his decision then
had a negative impact on our entire future together.

38

Ya gotta have a sense of humour

After living at Woolner, the family was definitely not going to be happy settling into life in suburbia. It was late 1989 and, following the Woolner sale, I had my own bank account for the first time. We still owned the race-horses, and a helicopter and cattle truck to enable the boys to continue contracting, so I bought the Twin Rivers farm at Berry Springs. It was a 130-hectare property, sixty kilometres out of Darwin, that would serve as a racing complex and a base on which to leave our conglomeration of stock and equipment.

Settling into a more populated area was pretty nerve-racking for me. We had been warned that the area was pretty rough, inhabited by bikie gangs and derelicts, so I was decidedly nervous about living there. Ironically, due to the media coverage of our dramas at Woolner, I was told later that the locals were also bracing for the arrival of the Groves, as if we were a mafia family taking over their area. But as time went by we settled in and this all turned out to be idle gossip. The locals proved amicable, the neighbours were great and life in the area prospered because of our business involvement.

Twin Rivers was another hard, lacklustre and underdeveloped property with only basic accommodation, but we saw promise there and planned to develop it. The original farmhouse became the men's accommodation and they swore that, while they watched TV at night, the doors would creak open. They would shut them, only to hear them creak open again. The general consensus was that it was the ghost of Tommy, the original owner, who had died there several years earlier, but we all learned to live with him in residence. We loved his property, so we figured that at least he would remain a happy ghost.

The boys were now making a living by fencing Twin Rivers, contract catching and livestock-hauling for other properties. We employed truck drivers, ringers and farmers and some worked in all of these fields. Any staff members who got a job with us had to be good at what they did and they had to know stock, but the main prerequisite to employment was set in stone: 'Ya gotta have a sense of humour!'

This humour came into play when Joe came across some marijuana seedlings hidden on the farm. Some of the young fellows had intended to grow them. Joe found the culprits and made them eat every last seedling. Talk about eating the profits! It was hard to tell whether they really found it that humorous, but they never made that mistake again on Twin Rivers.

Joe and I left the boys and some of the staff living at the farm while we settled tentatively into our modern suburban home in Darwin. I ran the office from there, enabling Mary-Lyn to go to high school. Paula had come home and was training our horses, while Joe spent his days either with the horses or sitting in front of the TV set. The TV could have been blank for all the notice he took of it.

He was sulking like an old brumby stallion that had been trapped, but certainly never tamed. I could almost see his mind cranking over with thoughts of escaping, back to the freedom of the bush and out of this inhospitable concrete jungle. He was not a happy man!

Joe was sixty-one and I hoped that a break away from the constant stress of running a property would do him good, but city living was choking the life out of him. He had never really confided in me – intimacy not being one of his finer points – and I could feel him gradually pulling away. The stress that we had endured over the years was beginning to affect our relationship. Not surprisingly, although I begged him not to, it wasn't long before he purchased a large, defunct peanut and sesame property on the Daly River called Ruby Downs.

I hated the idea of us going back into that area after having experienced how barren and dry Prices Springs had been, but I gradually realised that I wasn't part of the equation.

We had enjoyed the ultimate symbiotic relationship as J. & M. Groves for twenty-six years and I was shocked when my accountant, Richard, strongly advised me not to go back into business with Joe after we sold Woolner. I argued with him that we were totally compatible and that our exceptional partnership was the basis of our success, but he was a wise friend who had obviously seen that compatibility fraying well before I had.

Sadly, it became obvious that Richard was right. It appeared that because of all the inadvertent public attention I had generated defending our rights and the buffalo cause, Joe thought he was losing control of me. The pupil was outgrowing the teacher, so to speak. He wanted a place of his own, but he still required me to run the business. So I invested in steers for his export operations and, once again, I became involved behind the scenes, supporting him just as I had always done. But this time, after deciding to sell the Darwin home, it would be from the base at Twin Rivers. Once again, against Richard's advice and my own better judgement, I became the key person not only for Ruby Downs, but also the trucking, helicopter and racing operations that the three eldest had branched into.

Contrary to my expectations, Ruby Downs turned out to be a beautiful property. It was bordered by the Daly River, which meant good fishing – always an attraction for Joe. It had deep, red, loamy soil on which the government had tried to establish crop farming and had, yet again, failed. Always the strategist and forward thinker, Joe saw unique possibilities and once again jumped onto the back of a boom, this time in export steers. This soon became a lucrative alternative to his feral-animal harvesting.

Although Ruby Downs bordered the Daly River, the Department of Natural Resources insisted that it was a dry property. They had tried on various occasions to sink bores without success. There was certainly not enough water when Joe arrived to supply the numbers of stock that he intended to run to make his export operation feasible. So he called me in as a water diviner. He wanted water near the homestead stockyards if possible, so I pulled out my trusty wire rods. Initially, I could track only a very weak supply, but we went ahead anyway and sank a 1500-litre-an-hour bore. It wasn't much, but it was enough to supply the cattle yards at least, while the original bore watered the house. While the drilling rig was on the property, Joe asked me to dowse the main paddock for him. This paddock had good grass, but it was well away from the homestead water, so this grazing was being wasted.

It was a stinking hot Saturday and the undergrowth was thick as I ploughed through two-metre-high spear grass, following my rods. The energy in the rods showed weak veins of water running to one strong point, so I marked that spot with an X where I wanted the drillers to bore and returned to Berry Springs.

The following Monday morning I received an unexpected visit from John the driller. He was wondering if I would reconsider the drilling position. The Department of Natural Resources had insisted that there was no water to be found on that side of the property and John was worried about the expense of drilling a dud. Believe me, so was I!

'No,' I told him, 'we need to drill right where I have marked.'

'Oh! So you're a water diviner?' John asked, and added, 'So am I, but I never tell anyone.' I presume he was wary of being ridiculed.

So John went off to Ruby Downs to drill the new bore. It wasn't long before I received a call from Joe to ask if they could move the marker a few metres, because a large tree was interfering with the rig.

'No.' I was adamant. 'The tree goes, the cross stays.'

So the drilling proceeded and they struck water again. It was nearly as exciting as striking oil in that area. The driller almost lost his drill in the process, having hit an underground river. It gushed at a handsome 40,000 litres an hour and this was call for celebrations!

During the following years, although I was invited to Ruby occasionally, Joe kept in constant contact by phone. While I continued to run the office, farm, finances and family, it was also my job to ensure a steady flow of staff and live-in housekeepers and cooks, women to cook and take over where I had left off. I was kept too busy to consider my alternatives and the cracks were beginning to show. Just as the indomitable Territory termites patch their mounds, I would just keep patching the problems, but I was fooling everyone but myself.

Life went on as usual with the comings and goings from the station. Ruby was 200 kilometres away from Twin Rivers and Joe would venture into town only for emergencies, the races, or to pick up stores if I was too busy to run them out for him. Although I had learned that it is not a perfect world, I expected things to balance out eventually. Our first happy days together had turned into months, years and then decades, but that happy home we had dreamed of so long ago looked further away than ever. I could see Joe was absorbed in his own life and happy with the setup; he never suggested that I move to Ruby to live with him. He was king of his own castle and now it seemed that we both probably preferred it that way.

Our son Stephen was working with Joe on the station. He was a quiet achiever and Joe's right-hand man. He could turn his hand from running contract mustering operations to cooking to driving trucks and flying helicopters.

Steve was just beginning to get his mustering hours up in our Bell 47 helicopter. Early one morning, Joe had just bade him farewell when, minutes later, there was an almighty crash down in the paddock. Being hard of hearing, Joe didn't know that our chopper had gone down until, white and shaken, Stephen appeared back at the kitchen door. Due to some malfunction, the helicopter had not elevated properly. It had clipped a tree, exploding on impact, and was now a smouldering wreck. The $200,000 working machine was a write-off but, thankfully, our son was still in one piece.

When I asked him how he had got out of the machine alive, Stephen said, 'Mum, all you can do at a time like that is stick your head between your legs and kiss your arse goodbye!'

Miraculously, he had been able to flee the wreckage unharmed.

By now, Joey and I were operating six big prime movers, each with triple-deck cattle trailers, and our livestock transport business was flourishing. We had an excellent name for service, but it was hard on both the drivers and me as we were on call twenty-four hours a day, seven days a week. It was not unusual to be summoned in the wee hours to make a late-night run with spare parts to breakdowns as far as 600 kilometres away. Naturally, livestock can't be pulled up on the road for too long, so even though the drivers were sleep-deprived, the humane delivery of stock was always a priority.

There weren't many people in the Top End who didn't know Joey and the trucks, so we were surprised to hear that someone had been impersonating him for several years.

Because Joey was in the public eye frequently, this character knew quite a lot about him. Over several years, we had calls from hospitals demanding payment of unpaid accounts. From all over Australia, people started hammering Joey for money that they thought he owed them. I even received a call from a car dealer in Brisbane to let me know that the twelve new, fully outfitted bull-catchers that we had ordered were almost ready for delivery. What a disappointment this dealer was in for on finding out that he had zealously wined and dined a conman.

Joey eventually trapped the impostor in the Berrimah pub one day. He was wearing one of our company shirts displaying our logo. Joey meted out his own justice and took photos of the fellow holding a sign, disclaiming any connection to Joey. Happily, there has never been a claim since. It was quite hilarious to see this grubby little bearded fellow who had managed to pull off this charade over such a long time. As colourful characters go, he was an extreme case, even by Territory standards.

During my ten years at Twin Rivers, I had tried to turn my hand to many agricultural ventures to make my farm viable. I tried hay, free-range chickens, redclaw and mango farming, none of which succeeded. It only served to prove Joe's point – to make money one should always stick to what one knows best. The only things that worked for me were the improved pastures and my herd of Brahman breeders. We were heavily into rodeo at this time and the indoor bull rides were now happening at a local Berrimah pub. Most of my stock turn-off went to replenish Joe's stock on Ruby Downs, but I selected some great bucking bulls for these local rodeos, and did they love to buck! Some of them even made it big time in the rodeo scene down south and lived a life of pampered luxury.

The racehorses were a big diversion for Joe and Paula while Joey was building high-powered machines for mud buggy-racing and Stephen remained keen on rodeo.

Paula had decided to wed her special man, Don, and her beautiful wedding at the farm was followed not long after by Stephen's wedding to Kim, so soon I was experiencing the wonder of grandchildren coming along.

Mary-Lyn was also very talented and could turn her hand to almost anything we needed doing. She was blessed with a wonderful singing voice, but she was also the maverick. She and I were so much alike that it was as if history was repeating itself. The more I tried to encourage her to follow a particular path, the more she dug her heels in and did the opposite. Her dream was to try her luck in what she considered to be a normal way of life in the big city. Much to my alarm, at fifteen, she decided to leave Twin Rivers to flat with her girlfriend and work in Darwin. I could feel the sands of time shifting again as my last baby walked away. It was even worse than when I had lined up the little school shoes in Katherine all those years ago because, this time, I could have no more babies.

39

Pushing the boundaries

By September 1992, I had begun to push my own boundaries. For the first time in my life, I wanted to take a trip
overseas. I tried to talk Joe into coming with me, but he
refused. So I told Mum I was thinking about going alone.
I thought she would insist that a woman's place is by her
man but, to my surprise, she said, 'Love, never die wishing
you'd done something.'

'But, Mum, are you well enough? You won't kick the
bucket or anything while I'm away will you?' I replied, half
jokingly.

'Nah, darling. Of course I'll be here when you get back,'
she said, laughing.

So, with my mother's encouragement, I applied for my
first passport and travelled alone for forty days through
Britain, Europe and America.

Joe was certainly unhappy that I actually went without
him, but it was an amazing experience that I would not
have missed. My mother's roots were Irish and I feel
strongly that my trip was, unknowingly, a pilgrimage back

to Ireland for her. I felt an attachment to Ireland that can only be described as spiritual and experienced at first hand an awareness of what the Aborigines describe as their attachment to the Dreamtime.

The rest of my trip was informative and exciting, but I could well have come home immediately after my Irish experience had I not pre-booked for America and Europe. As it was, two days after I arrived home I was summoned to Adelaide, because my mother was dying.

I flew to Adelaide immediately, and although I tried to handle things bravely, I found myself sobbing the address to the taxi driver who picked me up.

When I walked into the hospital ward, Mum was surrounded by family. She looked directly at me with her beautiful blue Irish eyes and said, 'See, love? I told you I'd be here when you got back.' But she soon lapsed into semi-consciousness.

Mum was ready to go and she would fashion her passing her way. There would be no crying and no flowers in her room. Several days later, she couldn't work out why 'they' wouldn't take her, insisting that the priest come back and perform the last rites again to ensure it was done properly, but still she continued to lapse in and out of consciousness. When she was little, because of her asthma, her doctor had warned her mother that she would never make old bones. Now that she was old bones, she wondered what it would take to put her down. It took Mum thirteen days to finally pass and, in that period, she passed on to each of us the incredible wisdom that only a person in her position could know. Then, on 29 October 1992, that wonderful woman finally took up her ghost and left us.

When I rang home, Joey answered the phone.

'Hello, love, I'm just ringing to let you know that Grandma passed last night.'

'Mum, you're not going to believe this,' he replied. 'Last night, I dreamed that Grandma, with two nurses helping her, got out of the left side of the bed and sat in a big leather recliner in the corner of the room.'

I was dumbfounded, because that is exactly what had happened. As Joey went on to describe his dream in more specific detail, I realised that Mum had said goodbye to my family in Darwin on her way through. After such an amazing life, it didn't surprise me that my mother's passing would be so memorable.

My father had lost his life's companion and, alone now, except for his church, he passed away quietly in the winter four years later.

Joe finally resigned himself to my travelling and bought me two tickets for a Pacific cruise for Christmas that year. As usual, he refused to come, so I took my sister, Frances. At the time she was on chemotherapy for lymphoma. Like my mother, she was another amazing person, truly an outback queen who, after rearing five fine sons into the pastoral industry, would run rings around me and my achievements. Although she was on chemo on board the ship, we had a wonderful time together. Sadly, after a brave thirteen-year struggle, my beautiful sister would ultimately succumb to that awful disease.

I was still running the whole operation when I was nominated by a friend and became a finalist in the ABC's Rural Woman of the Year awards. I was extremely busy and totally unprepared. I had no idea what it was all about but, because it was paid for, I went along for the adventure and met some fabulous women.

I smile when I think of the day I rushed into a Fannie Bay boutique to try to find something appropriate to wear to those functions. I was searching through a rack of dresses when I heard the sales assistant say, 'Good afternoon. Can I help you?'

'Yes please,' came the reply. 'I'm looking for something to wear to the judging of the Rural Woman awards.'

My ears pricked up.

'What did you have in mind?'

'I dunno, but it will have to be good, cause I'm up against that Mary Groves.'

I was astonished. I didn't see that I offered a challenge to anybody in the field of fashion. Not knowing what to do, I stayed quiet. When I finally popped my head up, the woman was still at the counter. I hadn't met her before, but the sales assistant knew me, and the woman wore that 'God, I hope she didn't hear me!' look on her face.

Pretending that I hadn't heard, I left empty-handed so as not to embarrass her, and didn't meet her again until I boarded the plane to fly to Alice for the final judging. When I checked in, I was allocated a seat in row thirteen and my heart sank. When we finally boarded, I found myself sitting beside Lynnette Walker, the woman from the frock shop. We introduced ourselves and, in the course of conversation, discovered that we were both born on the same day. We were so similar that she even had a tiny mole like mine on the end of her nose. We could well have been sisters. She was a mango farmer and I was a pastoralist. Obviously the number thirteen hadn't dogged her like it did me, because she went on to become the Territory winner of the award that year. But a great time was had by all.

40

The Cannonball Run

With the businesses and my social life in full swing, life was galloping past and I was not giving myself much time to think. I concentrated all my efforts on doing only what the day required.

I met Allan Moffat at a function where he was promoting the inaugural Cannonball Run. There were no speed limits in the Territory then and this would be a car race/rally from Darwin to Uluru and back. It was more of a time trial than a race, but each day there would be the magic mile where contestants would put pedal to the metal to score points. It involved a journey of some 4000 kilometres and, because I loved driving, particularly in my new sports car, the thought of it made my heart race. Allan's encouragement only fuelled my intent and, before long, to my amazement, we were fitted out and ready to leave. There were several other women along, but my girlfriend Jill Vidotto and I were the only competing all-female team in that race and we were quietly serious about winning. My Toyota Supra had a computer chip installed to improve its performance and I signed up some sponsors. We christened our vehicle 'Thelma and Louise'. The local TV station actually ran that movie on the eve of the race, which made it all the more glamorous.

During the lead-up to the race, Joey came to me one morning and announced, to my surprise, 'Mum, I'd rather you didn't go in this race.'

'Why is that, son?' I asked, smiling, half expecting him to think that I would embarrass myself.

'Because I had a dream that there was a big smash involving a red and a white car, and more than one person was killed.'

How prophetic this dream turned out to be! At the time, I could only hug my son and assure him that I was an experienced driver and I would be coming home safely. If I knew then how intuitive he was, I may well have changed my mind.

Marshall Perron was the Chief Minister then and he promoted the Cannonball as a lucrative boost to the economy. It was run just before the election and, although it became part of a political bunfight, it was nevertheless a fabulous event, and the mood in the Territory was euphoric. We all had a ball. People came from everywhere for this gala event. Station people sat along the highway with tables, chairs and bottles of champagne to wave as we drove by.

Jill and I were running a very healthy eighteenth place in the race when we left Alice Springs that crisp, sunny morning, but my heart sank to see an ambulance overtaking us as we left town and I said a little prayer. It was quite a while before we came across it again, at an awful scene that claimed the lives of two Japanese Ferrari drivers and two marshals. Total chaos followed. We were not hardened race drivers and we lost interest in competing, slowly wending our way into Uluru where we awaited further instructions.

After a couple of days waiting for the media scrum to clear, we were permitted to cruise back to Darwin at eighty kilometres an hour, like naughty children, obviously to avoid political point-scoring by the Opposition. That was until one of the drivers wailed over the two-way that he had just been passed by an old lady in a VW Beetle towing a caravan. I think that was when the organisers felt sorry for us and allowed us to pick up speed, but with communication breakdowns the finish was really a non-event.

While all that was going on, the business still operated. The livestock export industry was fickle at the best of times and, to supplement income, Joe had a good crack at growing hay to supply the export market and feed his stock. He took great pride in his production of hay and improved pastures, but, as a cattleman, he made an average farmer. He often lamented that we never found Ruby Downs while we still had youth on our side! Inevitably, after years of hard labour and rodeo riding, Joe's back was starting to give him major problems, signalling the inevitable end to his working life. It was time to cash in, but that was easier said than done, because now the markets had slumped.

I had felt the end of the line looming and I wanted to sell all the businesses when the economy was on a high, but the boys were happy. They needed my support, so I hung in there. We eventually sold Ruby Downs to the McBean family, who had been our neighbours and friends all those years ago on Fitzroy Station.

The sale of Ruby was a momentous event, because it heralded the end of an era for us. Joe had opted out of the trucking operation when we left Woolner, but I was shattered when he broke the news that he no longer wanted to be part of our J. & M. Groves business venture. Instead, he wanted to work with Stephen in a separate helicopter operation. I shouldn't have been surprised, I suppose. We now had very little in common.

Joe was from a different era of tough men, who were taught that softness is a sign of weakness. His image was paramount, but under that tough exterior I knew that he still loved me and I still cared for him. I am told the Greeks believe that there are forty-three different ways to love, so I guess we slotted in there somewhere. It was obvious to me that true love never dies, no matter how many dry gullies you drag it down, but, kept in the shade, it won't flourish either. It seemed that ours was dying under an impenetrable wall of pig-headedness. Although I was a totally supportive wife and continued to idolise Joe, the children were the main reason that I had persevered with this lonely relationship. This was a perfect opportunity now to opt out completely, but, to me, the J. & M. Groves partnership had meant everything for all those years. It was a unique partnership in every sense. Even though I had sensed this coming for years, still the selfishness of it all gutted me and I felt hurt and betrayed.

It felt strange stepping out of my comfort zone, the umbrella of J. & M. Groves, but at least I had a life of my own. I was now able to enjoy normal social interaction. I began to see a lot more of the friends I had neglected for so many years. I tarted up for lunches and went to the races and thoroughly enjoyed the company of these ladies who had led lives not unlike my own and whose children had grown up in similar circumstances. But, while it was a relief to be totally responsible for my own decisions, I must admit I have always missed the security of that big shoulder to rest my head on from time to time.

I started to paint again and I would lose myself for hours in a huge, acrylic mural on the wall at the farm. I also began to study alternative therapies. It appeared that I had a natural ability to work with energy and I studied certain therapies that would serve me in good stead in the years to come. It became obvious that my former experiences and my studies of natural energies were leading me towards a future purpose in life.

The more I studied, the more I realised that there were alternatives to my rigid way of life, and I began to drift away from the old ways that Joe so doggedly hung on to. The more I did to distract myself from the inevitable separation, the more I realised that life is like the galaxy, it is in constant flux, continually moving and changing. Nothing stays the same. And so I allowed myself to move and change too.

Realising that there was a life outside Twin Rivers, I let Joey take over the farm and trucking operations completely and I moved into a unit in Darwin overlooking the Arafura Sea.

41

Back in the Dreamtime

August 1997 and two of my cousins, Ellen and Marian, were visiting me from the south. It had been quite a few years since I had ventured back into the old country myself and, for some reason, I felt an urgent need to return there. I invited my cousins to come with me to visit my sister Frances and to explore the vast area that lay between Darwin and Broome, where she lived.

After a hectic weekend enjoying the Darwin Cup, among the thousands who thronged to Darwin at that time of year, we headed south-west in Joe's four-wheel drive, carrying the barest essentials in camping equipment. My guests were completely oblivious to the epic journey they were embarking upon. The cousins, both a little older and more sophisticated than me, ensured that the emergency supplies of gin and tonic, lemon wedges, ice and biscuits were packed, along with the crystal glasses.

We headed out at first light. That first day we saw the townships of Pine Creek, Katherine, Timber Creek and Kununurra flying past. We were attempting to devour as many of the miles in as short a time as possible to make our rendezvous with my sister.

We had fifteen kilometres left of the 1200 we planned to travel that first day into Halls Creek, and we were almost out of diesel. I was petrified of wrecking Joe's new motor, so we waited in vain by the side of the road for help to come. Rather than miss an opportunity, the girls laid out the lace cloth on the bonnet and we saluted our first beautiful mauve and pink Kimberley sunset with our gin and tonics. We flagged down a truckie, who didn't seem enthusiastic about sending help, and as there was no traffic coming by we decided then to crawl along at snail's pace, arriving in town with not a smidgin of fuel to spare.

After having slept that night and the next in small motels, we travelled a further 690 kilometres through craggy hills and grotesque banyan trees, to arrive at Fran's place in time for lunch. That next sunset found us sipping cocktails in the balmy evening breeze at the famous Cable Beach Resort on the coast at Broome.

We spent a delightful four days with Frances and her sons in that most unusual area with its unique, tropical township. We saw pearl farms and shopped for pearls. Then we were surprised by a horse and buggy ride along my first nude beach, where we sat watching a string of camel riders, silhouetted by a wonderful sunset, while we wined and dined at the end of another perfect day. It was wonderful to spend some quality time with Frances and, as she was still battling lymphoma and was not well, it was very sad indeed to take our leave the following day.

We had planned to venture home again at a much slower pace to allow us to absorb the true beauty of the Kimberley country, and we spent our first night in a modern resort at Fitzroy Crossing. The resort seemed quite out of place among the surrounding corrugated-iron-clad dwellings, which looked most uncomfortable to me these days. I was spoiled with my creature comforts in Darwin.

By 6 a.m. the following day, we were on the road again to drive the 500 kilometres to Turkey Creek. From there we took a scenic helicopter tour in a Jet Ranger over the Bungle Bungle National Park. It was a typically hot Kimberley day and the brilliant blue sky, with the occasional fluffy cloud, made that harsh, mysteriously bulging, rocky landscape stand out.

Continuing on after lunch, we headed through the Kimberley Ranges, passing huge termite mounds and distinctive rocky outcrops, then on through Kununurra with its amazing Ord River irrigation scheme. From there we were soon following the beautiful Victoria River to arrive at my old stamping grounds at Timber Creek.

The further we travelled into my old country, the more Stetsons and riding boots we saw, which, more than anything, brought memories flooding back from the past. It was certainly a nostalgic experience and I was moved to search out old Blazer and the Aboriginal families who had worked and lived with us in that area almost twenty years before.

The good old days were gone and nothing seemed the same at Timber Creek. We should have seen that coming when the novelty and magic of microwave cooking and frozen food came to town all those years ago!

The township now boasted streets, a medical centre and a couple of stores. The old pub and store that my sister Frances had run back then was the heart of the tiny township in its heyday. It had always seemed so alive and important then, but now it stood waiting on the sidelines to die.

Twenty years previously, the Aborigines in the area generally had little English. I was amazed to see now an incredible difference in the communication skills of these same people, some of whom I vaguely remembered as my house girls.

A smart-looking Aboriginal stockman carried groceries from the store to an equally smart four-wheel drive. As he loaded them I recognised that it was Jerry. Jerry had worked for us as a ringer and had certainly come up in the world. He was happy to see me again.

I proceeded to make inquiries around the area about different Aboriginal families and was disappointed to learn that several of our Aboriginal friends had passed away or moved on to other areas and that contact had been lost. But I was amazed to hear that old Blazer was still alive and was probably now in Darwin or at Mataranka.

We refuelled and left Timber Creek. The highway wound through the Fitzroy Station property that we had managed back then, and the memories came flooding back. The mystery and magnificence of those escarpments still enthralled me and soon that beautiful monolith called Wondoan came into view.

Wondoan always felt like home to me and so it should, as we dwelled at its base for almost ten years on either Coolibah or Fitzroy stations. The sun was setting and casting long mauve shadows and beautiful golden rays through the escarpments along the river road.

After travelling nearly 1000 kilometres from Fitzroy Crossing, we were beginning to feel the strain of far too much excitement for one day, so we decided it was time to pull up and make camp. I had promised the cousins a camping trip and there seemed no better time than now. As darkness fell we selected an area in a dry part of the riverbed and we commenced to make camp in the sand of the Victoria River.

It was a hot and horrible dusk and a ceiling of unseasonable clouds had rolled in so low that you could almost touch them. It was a real threat that we could get washed out of the riverbed or, worse still, be irretrievably bogged in Joe's new vehicle. As it was, we had needed the four-wheel drive to get into our position, so our chances of getting out during heavy rain were dubious indeed. After our long day, we were really too tired to move again, but I was reminded of days gone by, and my gut feeling was that we would probably survive this ordeal. We decided to call it a day and, tired and hungry, we went to bed.

Our camping equipment may have been made of corrugated iron for all the comfort it offered in that sandy riverbed, and mosquitoes buzzed incessantly. We would just start to doze in the quiet of the night when a crocodile would bark further downstream and my terrified cousins would leap up in terror.

Somewhere off in the distance a dingo howled to its mate and there was an eerie feeling in the air. I must admit that, even for someone who had camped out a good deal of my life, secretly I was not feeling all that comfortable. Then, deciding to leave our fate in the hands of the Almighty, I finally drifted off into a sweaty and fitful sleep. I woke again at 4 a.m. to find that the sky had cleared and we were being treated to the most breathtaking and spectacular panorama one could imagine.

Excited, I woke Marian and Ellen, which was not an easy task, and we quietly stargazed, spellbound by that bejewelled sky. We wished on the many shooting stars on their final journey across the heavens and watched the satellites until the novelty wore off and the girls pulled the blankets back over their heads to catch up on lost sleep. The morning air had taken on a smell and freshness that was invigorating and I finally lit the campfire that I had promised the girls, but they refused to be roused again.

I sat until daylight gazing into the flames, thinking of the many times I had done this before, remembering the folk I had known back then and just how wild and wonderful my life in the bush had been. Those memories stirred all kinds of different emotions as I sat there alone in the early dawn shadows.

So that they wouldn't miss the sunrise, I roused the girls again and we scratched up a meagre breakfast of toast and potatoes cooked on the coals, followed by a cup of black billy tea. Inspired by the natural beauty of the area, and undaunted by the primitive conditions and the empty stomachs, we spent the next few hours with paints and pastels, trying to capture the beauty of that exquisite morning in the riverbed amid the escarpments.

Although our camping experience had started out being so ordinary, this little section of our trip turned into one of our most memorable.

We left before lunch and were soon on the road back through Katherine to my original hometown of Mataranka and the famous hot springs. To my dismay, nothing looked the same. The town had grown and I felt like just another tourist.

In the 1960s the hot springs had been a little natural spring in the Roper River system which catered for just enough Territory locals to justify it as a business enterprise. It was now under cement, and looked more like a Roman bath than a natural thermal spring. Movement was restricted in the pool and the fun factor was all commercial. It was catering for as many bodies on that day as would have been the year's quota in days gone by, all looked after with bars, bands and fast food.

We still had a fun time there and left the hot springs next morning, heading north towards Katherine. Along the way, I enquired among the blacks at the Mataranka pub for any information regarding Blazer and I was told that I might find him at the Katherine hospital.

The next leg of our journey to Katherine Gorge for the boat cruise took us past the hospital, and I had every intention of popping in to catch up with old Blazer until the moment I pulled up at the hospital gates. A strange and intense feeling of foreboding came over me. I told my cousins that by now, after twenty years, Blazer would not remember me and was probably bedridden and without his faculties. I certainly didn't want to see him like that. But the girls would hear none of it and they insisted that I complete my mission.

I turned into the hospital car park and parked about 150 metres away from a veranda in the front of the building where half a dozen old men lounged, yarning in the morning sun. As I drove into the compound, I felt a steel gaze fixed upon me and was unnerved by its intensity. Surely this elder with the snow-white beard and hair wasn't Blazer? And surely he could not see me from that distance, or recognise me after all these years?

I headed for the veranda where the old man sat prodding a bowl of cereal. I asked if anybody knew of Blazer and the old fellow did not lift his head.

'He's probably inside in bed,' I was told.

Inside, a nurse told me that he was on the veranda eating breakfast, and that he would be thrilled to see me, as he never had visitors. Apparently no one seemed to know or care that he existed.

As I approached the old man again with the nurse it was obvious that it was Blazer, as I had suspected, but he dropped his head even lower and became intent on his cereal. Much to our bewilderment, he refused to acknowledge either the nurse or myself.

'Come on, Blazer, you've got a visitor. What's the matter, old man?' the nurse asked, assuring me that he was not deaf or senile, he still had all of his marbles, and he had never acted like this before.

Finally, I put a photo of his old boss, Joe, with his first grandchild on the table in front of him and left him in peace.

As I made my way back to the car, I felt he still somehow had a steel grip on my mind. It was a feeling I had never experienced before. A great sadness washed over me, along with an intense realisation that he needed to go back to his old country before he died. By the time I returned to the car and the cousins, I had decided to put it all behind me, shake off this weird experience, and proceed to the gorge to lunch with friends and enjoy the cruise. This would be easier said than done, though!

The cruise proceeded in the normal manner but, almost immediately, I was engulfed again by intense sadness and thoughts of old Blazer. I began scheming on how best to return him to wherever his birth country was. I conjured up plans of taking him for a day trip from hospital in our helicopter and landing him for just a few hours in his own country. At the same time, I knew full well the possible consequences and that it was inadvisable to meddle in blackfella business.

We were cruising deep into the gorge with its towering walls and wherever I looked I saw images of Blazer. He was standing on one leg with the other foot balanced on his knee, leaning on two spears. He seemed much younger than I had ever known him and his hair was held back in a bun, tight against his head, as he gazed arrogantly into the distance. Then I looked further down the gorge and there he was, lapping water from a rock ledge. His back glistened in the sunlight and his distinctive tribal scars stood out like black brands against the rich, chocolate-coloured skin of his chest and shoulders as he raised himself to cast a gentle, smiling glance in my direction. The tears started to well in my eyes and run down my cheeks. I thanked God that I had worn sunglasses as there could be absolutely no explaining the cause of my emotion to any enquirer. How could I explain when I was at a total loss to understand this phenomenon myself?

It was a typical crisp, clear, dry-season day and only an occasional wispy cloud floated across the sky. The colours in the gorge were vibrant blues and greens, with the crystal flecks on the water reflecting the rich reds, browns and yellows in the cliff faces and rock formations along the water's edge. But all the time the richness of Blazer's colour stood out stark against all the others.

After quite a while, our boat landed in an area where the Aboriginal art adorned the cliff faces. Blazer's energy was so strong there that I became totally confused and had to bolt away from the group to sob behind a boulder against the ravine wall. I had never been one for public displays of emotion and I managed to conceal it well. Although I was still shaken as we boarded the boat again, the visions seemed to fade on the return voyage down the river.

My mind was still scheming on how best to return Blazer to his own country, wherever that might be. After twenty years I had forgotten his registered details, but planned to make immediate enquiries through the Department of Aboriginal Affairs. Then, like a clap of thunder, I remembered that the gorge *was* his country, and this had actually been where he was born.

With a heavy heart, I left the Katherine district and returned to my family in Darwin. On recounting the story to my son, he was surprised that I didn't already know the reason for Blazer's lonely isolation.

Mack, April and Blazer's son, had been a friend of Joey's at Fitzroy all those years ago. He had told Joey that April was off on another of her drunken escapades with some derelict white man when Blazer finally cracked and held her head under water until she drowned. In his own time, this would have been an appropriate penalty for the continued dalliances of his younger wife, and the tribe would have handled the consequences. Naturally, I was not in a position to judge his actions one way or the other, but I did realise assimilation and white intervention had played a big hand in this outcome.

I discussed with my family my desire to return Blazer to his country for just a few hours, but I had to finally agree with Joe that we should not interfere. That Joe was so adamant was a relief really, because I knew in my own heart that if I had taken him back, he probably would have refused to return to the hospital, and I was not in a position to take on that responsibility.

For months I worried about having let Blazer down in his last request, when finally I met a man well-versed in the study of metaphysics and spirituality. He consoled me with his assurance that, far from letting him down, Blazer had actually returned in spirit through my eyes and mind via the boat cruise through the gorge. I like to think that this is correct. I remember vividly how I was driven, almost against my will, to find him in the first place. It taught me such a huge lesson about telepathy and spirit. I know in my heart that this was blackfella magic, and I am so happy to know that, physically or psychically, Blazer had managed to return to the gorge that one last time through my eyes. Either way, I sincerely believe that neither he nor I will ever forget our trip together back to his country in the Katherine Gorge.

42

The full circle

It was a hot, balmy afternoon in Darwin and Ellen and Marian had just left to return south after our exciting trip to Broome. I sat alone, reminiscing, on the balcony of my third-floor luxury apartment with my gaze fixed on a ship far out to sea.

'Why on earth am I not happy here?' I wondered.

A lone mosquito buzzed irritatingly and I slapped at it as it landed on my shoulder, the shock jolting me into reality, bringing back memories of the swarms of the horrid creatures that we had endured on the floodplains while catching buffalo.

Where had my life gone? My journey from Melbourne had taken me almost forty years thus far. It had been a hard but truly satisfying life. It had taken me through many harsh and inhospitable situations and introduced me to the most generous and unusual characters that one could hope to meet. But now all that was over.

What was my purpose now? I was obviously no longer who I had been, so who was I? Was I really a Territorian or perhaps just a lost Melburnian? As a white, fifty-four-year-old bush woman, where did I fit in?

My gaze reverted to the horizon, this time in awe as the changing kaleidoscope of colours of a northern sunset splashed across the banks of cloud that heralded another oppressive, monsoonal build-up. As bolts of sporadic lightning illuminated the huge cumulus clouds to the east, I prayed for the rain that would break that debilitating heat. I jumped when a large green frog nearby raucously croaked its support as it edged behind a pot plant.

My trip to Broome had allowed me to review the past and the experience with Blazer in the Katherine Gorge particularly had reawakened my fascination with spirituality. I found the study of spirituality exciting and yet unnerving but, although it was totally alien to my lifestyle, my teachers had begun to appear as if by magic. Apart from that and a bit of golf, I was going nowhere. I had sat stagnating in that unit in Darwin for six months, watching the tides come in and go out, until it finally dawned on me that I had completed a full circle, from the city to the bush and back again. It was suddenly obvious to me that my life's cycle had actually reached high tide. Now that tide was turning. It was on the way out and I could swim with it or against it.

A black and white Torres Strait pigeon rustled in the palm fronds against the balcony as it fossicked among the red berries. I watched it for a while and wondered if it too was alone. It's ironic how lonely a big city can be! How many years had I been alone in the bush, but seldom felt lonely?

As the sun began to slip away, I watched the evening shadows lengthening through the park across the road. My mind wandered again to that happy, innocent little girl I'd been so long ago. Overcome by the euphoria of spring, I had lain on my back in my mother's garden, mesmerised by a poppy contrasting against a sky that went on forever. How far did that sky go? I had wondered all those years ago. I recalled thinking that same thing thirty-five years and 3800 kilometres later, when I lay beside a lily-covered billabong on the floodplains at Marrakai. Squawking white corellas hung in the trees nearby as I gazed up in childlike awe at the exquisite blue petals of a huge waterlily that I held aloft, its soft colours melting into an endless sky. It occurred to me now that the sky hadn't gone anywhere. Here it was before me again, lit with the exquisite mauves, oranges, pinks and yellows, brilliant colours that were slowly fading like so many of my memories.

There was a flurry of activity as the pigeon was joined by its mate and I stepped onto the balcony to catch the breeze. To the left, the glittering yellow lights of the city began to illuminate the skyline ahead of the storm. What a beautiful and sophisticated place Darwin had become after its destruction by Cyclone Tracy twenty-three years before. This flourishing cosmopolitan city had been devastated and yet now it seemed as if that disaster had never happened. 'How resilient humanity is,' I thought. 'We fall down and we get up again.' But how could I rebuild? It occurred to me that I was stagnating – but I did have a choice. To survive, I simply had to keep moving!

The pigeons startled again and with a flurry of black and white feathers they scampered off for their evening roost in the park and I drifted off to sleep.

I awoke several hours later with a mixture of sea spray and heavy raindrops on my face and I skittered inside as the wind began to whip the palms and the skies began to open. Bolts of sporadic lightning now lit the horizon where that beautiful sunset had been. Tendrils of crackling energy spread across the backdrop of the city that lay at its mercy, followed by the gut-rumbling rolls of thunder. The palms and the trees in the park twisted and swayed in a dance of surrender and the night became cool as the rain poured off the roof.

In the months that followed, my metamorphosis began to take place. It was not easy, but I made the decision and prepared to leave the Territory. Still the business partner, I had reached my use-by date, but I was desperate to retain my role as mother. In my eyes Joe and I had raised our children and completed our business and marriage contracts successfully, but we were both miserable. Although I had planned to stay with him forever, it was now time, for both our sakes, to finally cut the cord and let it all go.

So I took the plunge, said goodbye to my treasured family, closed down my interests in the Territory and headed alone into the unknown.

I continued to expand my horizons with many different adventures. I settled in Queensland early in 1999 and opened a boutique stress retreat in the Gold Coast hinterland overlooking the Pacific Ocean. Nobody was confronting the stress issue then, and I knew from my own experiences that such a retreat was sorely needed. The business worked well.

As a ten-year-old I had painted a picture for my mother of a house on a hill overlooking the sea. I said then that I would marry a Queensland station owner. And so it all came to pass, although not in the sequence I had anticipated. Obviously, I had no idea then how these things would come to fruition, but gradually they happened in an extraordinary sequence of events, over which it seems I had no control.

When I finally returned to Melbourne, I had found our old weatherboard home still standing at the army barracks on Sturt Street. Like me, it looked strangely lost, dwarfed in that huge city among the high-rises. Much flashier trams pulled up near that corner block across the road. I used to daydream there in makeshift cubby houses that I built among the tall grass. Like that child, I can still daydream. I am still excited, although much wiser and warier as the final half of my life unfolds.

As I close this book, I am blessed with a close-knit family and fifteen wonderful grandchildren. Both of my sons still live on stations in the Territory with their families, while my daughters and Joe have settled nearby in Queensland. My new life is full of wonderful people and new adventures. But now that I have completed the full circle from the city to the bush and back again, I have learned from my experiences to seek only the wealth that lies within, trusting the universe to provide the rest.

I am often asked if I would change my life in the outback.

Never!

Would I do it all again?

Not in this lifetime!

For updates on Mary's remarkable life go to:

www.anoutbacklife.com